The Best
AMERICAN
SPORTS
WRITING
1999

The Best AMERICAN SPORTS WRITING 1999

EDITED AND WITH AN INTRODUCTION BY
Richard Ford

Glenn Stout, *Series Editor*

HOUGHTON MIFFLIN COMPANY

BOSTON • NEW YORK 1999

ISSN 1056-8034
ISBN 0-395-93056-1

Printed in the United States of America

QUM 10 9 8 7 6 5 4 3 2 1

Contents

Foreword

FOR MUCH OF the past year, the task of serving as series editor of *The Best American Sports Writing* has been relentless. It has never been any kind of strictly seasonal undertaking anyway, in which, after a period of repose, I oil my gear, buy my license, then, at the appointed time, rise before dawn and stake out my mailbox in anticipation of an annual migration of newspapers and periodicals on the southern flyway. Around here, it's open season all the time. For as I work on the details of this volume, I am still helping to promote the previous edition, *The Best American Sports Writing 1998*, and am already reading material for next year's, *The Best American Sports Writing 2000*.

Matters were a bit more complicated this year. In the midst of my perennial search-and-reprint reconnaissance, I also had to consider the centennial, to look to the past to read and accumulate candidates for a companion volume, *The Best American Sports Writing of the Century*. In this I had to learn to eschew my usual quarry for those which compared favorably against a more elusive and ethereal trophy target, one with sufficient spread and points to merit hanging on a hundred-year wall.

I'm not complaining. I like tromping through the woods knee-deep in words. But it struck me, as I followed these wordy old trails of sports writing back, just how much the animal and the surrounding terrain have evolved.

Sports writing was once the near-exclusive province of the newspaper, and in the newspaper, of columnists. Features, at least those we would recognize today, were just about nonexistent. The bulk of a newspaper's sports page was simply raw reporting. The columnist had the remainder of the field and could pick and choose his subject at something approaching leisure, without worrying too much whether his daily work would be rendered obsolete by press time or worth remembering a week or two later. Telling the story of what just happened, of which he (or, regrettably far less often, she) was usually the only observer, was the writer's main responsibility. Telling it well was an occasional and sometimes accidental luxury.

Of course, there were and are still giants that managed to do both regularly, and for examples I refer the reader to both this and the centennial volume. But as I read through every early collection of sports writing I could find, I was struck by how so much writing that was once so celebrated seems so commonplace today. We may want to believe the past was a much better place, and maybe it was, but in terms of sports writing, I found that not to be true. Anyone who thinks this is so is experiencing fishermen's memory, which over time turns the small fry into the record catch.

Over the last half of the century, in the wake of television, sports writing has migrated from the sole province of the sports page to a variety of other locations. There is something almost deterministic about this, for cities that once had several competing newspapers now usually support only one. Yet interest in sports writing, despite competition from the electronic media, hasn't diminished. Newspaper writers continue to produce lasting work, while some in the magazine industry have taken advantage of the contraction of voices in the newspaper to provide a growing forum for all varieties of sports writing to flourish.

That's not to say I don't find stresses in the population. I do. Over the past several years a number of newspapers, such as the *Dallas Morning News* and the *Miami Herald,* have suspended the publication of their Sunday magazines, sources I valued for both the quality and variety of sports writing they presented. Reading of their demise was akin to discovering a strip mall carved out of the woods behind my house. It makes my job harder, and I wonder where the writers who so delighted me in those pages will find an outlet. For the sports page seems increasingly determined to ape either the inelegant informational overload of the Internet or the disposable glibness of sports talk radio rather than develop a constituency for its own forms. Sadly, I now find a lot of magazines doing the same.

The irony is that while the multitude of voices is ever more endangered, "sports" is an ever-increasing part of our cultural landscape, of which I hope this series provides some proof. When I came of age in the mid-1970s, there was a spirited debate over whether sports had value at all. Much of the serious writing about sports then consisted of attacks on its institutions, questions about the increasing focus on money, doubts concerning the win-at-all-costs attitude, and other such issues. For several years I abandoned sports altogether, stopped playing, reading about it, even watching it on television, as I wrestled with some of these questions and spent most of my time either in the library or leaning on my elbow talking.

Today that debate appears quaint and long decided. Sports has won and makes a lot of money — or is it that sports makes a lot a money and has thereby won? — which seems to be the justification for all.

Fortunately there are still cracks in that parking lot. The best part of my job is that after the guest editor has made his selections, I am occasionally able to penetrate the office barricades of voice mail and fax machines to actually speak to the authors.

They often have their own story to tell. Over the years, I have been delighted to discover that on occasion we have selected a writer's first published work, or a work that inspired rejection letters from coast to coast because it didn't fit a convenient marketing niche, or a piece that the author has had to battle with editors over, sometimes to the point of quitting or being fired. Several years ago, one writer responded to the news that her story had been selected for this series by laughing hysterically. It was her last week on staff. She'd just been canned, and one of the reasons for this involved the story we had just selected. Her editor had despised it and, if I remember correctly, had even cited it in her dismissal. The publication she worked for, I'm happy to say, doesn't exist anymore.

As this series enters its ninth season, I am starting to get an idea of what *The Best American Sports Writing* has come to mean to its core constituency: writers.

The sports writing series matters, even when it infuriates or disappoints. Those who've been around the block appreciate the series because it gives a little more life to stories that otherwise simply sit between covers in a library forever. But for younger writers, it means something else. This year I had a contributor tell me that he started reading this series in high school, which made me feel old and young at the same time. I remember when a writing life seemed so remote that to imagine myself included in such a book was a delusion so embarrassing I never dared voice it. Now I hear writers say things like that to me. One writer this year was so surprised and skeptical of my call he was certain he'd been hoodwinked. He called me back to make certain I wasn't part of some elaborate practical joke.

Best of all is the knowledge that for at least one writer I spoke to this year, reading this series long ago made him want to be a writer. That's important, for so much of what one reads risks the opposite conclusion. In our culture, sports needs the continuing replenishment provided by those who think and feel and write about it just as much as it needs the next generation of athletes. That some find their way to writing through this series makes the extended season it requires worth the effort, a realization I hope is shared by the reader.

Each year, I read every issue of more than three hundred sports and general interest magazines for writing that might merit inclusion in *The Best American Sports Writing*. I also look at the Sunday magazines of about forty newspapers and read as many papers as I can. To make sure I don't miss anything, I ask the sports editors of some three hundred newspapers for submissions. I also send requests to the editors of more than three hundred magazines, asking for complimentary subscriptions and submissions of stories. I ask for both because I don't want to depend solely on some editor to do the selecting for me, but neither do I think my eye is faultless. Still, without fail, we seem to select a story that the editor of a publication didn't deem worthy of submitting, and the reverse is often true, too: I read a story submitted to me that makes me ask, How'd I miss that?

I encourage writers, readers, and other interested parties to send me stories they've written or read in the past year that they would like to see in these pages. Writers should be particularly aggressive (although not to the point of sending me your entire yearly output). Timidity isn't a virtue here.

Each year, I submit the best seventy-five stories or so to the guest editor, who makes the final selection. This year, Richard Ford's carefully considered selections have resulted in a volume that we are both proud to be a part of.

To be considered for inclusion in *The Best American Sports Writing 2000,* each nonfiction story must have been published in 1999 in either the United States or Canada and must be column length or longer. Reprints or book excerpts are not eligible, although pieces adapted from books that appear in serial form before publication will be considered. Due to the tyranny of deadlines, I must receive all submissions by February 1, 2000.

All submissions must include the author's name, date of publication, and the publication's name and address. Photocopies, tearsheets, and clean copies are acceptable. Reductions to 8½ x 11 inches are best. Submissions from on-line publications must be made in hard-copy form. Submissions cannot be returned or acknowledged, and I don't feel it is appropriate for me to comment on or critique any individual submissions. Publications that want to be absolutely certain their contributions are considered should provide a complimentary subscription to the address listed below. Those that already do so should make sure to extend the subscription annually.

Please send subscriptions or submissions to this exact address:

> Glenn Stout
> Series Editor
> The Best American Sports Writing
> P.O. Box 381
> Uxbridge, MA 01569

I may also be contacted by e-mail at ChinMusic@compuserve.com. However, no submissions of material will be accepted electronically. There is no way for me to make certain any such submissions were really published, so please respect this request.

Copies of previous editions of this book can be ordered through most bookstores and on-line dealers. Earlier volumes may be available from out-of-print booksellers listed in the Yellow Pages.

My thanks go out to my new editor, Eamon Dolan, and to Emily Little and Larry Cooper, all of whom helped shepherd this volume home. Thanks also to guest editor Richard Ford, my wife Siobhan, and my daughter Saorla, who has indicated that sometime after she learns to read she just might consider learning to write as well. But my unending gratitude is reserved for those most rare of all animals, the writers who call out to me each and every day.

GLENN STOUT

Introduction

MOST SPORTS WRITING operates at a disadvantage — the disadvantage being that it's about sports. No matter how the culture tries to amplify it, sports (especially the spectator kind) is simply not a very serious human pursuit. Oh, yes, people make handsome livings at it — playing it, owning it, promoting it, litigating it, televising it, remembering it, even writing about it. People occasionally even *die* from it or have their lives markedly changed *because* of it (bungee jumping with a poorly measured cord, stroking out at a hockey game, hitting your horse at OTB). Sports, as well, enters our lives vertically in all sorts of other influential ways: lavishly consuming our dollars and our precious time; infiltrating and corrupting our language and with it our ways of representing, even assessing, what *is* important ("They're playing for all the marbles over there in Kosovo"; "It's fourth and long in that Russian economy"). And sports routinely promotes into our attention real people who have no real reason to be there except that they're very tall, or very fat, or very bad-tempered, or very rich or like tattoos. These same people are then promoted (often by sports writers) as interesting models for our human behavior and conduct, so that we often go away confused about what's good and what's bad.

There are other kinds of sports, of course, the kinds we perform ourselves rather than simply observe at distances or on TV. And because we *choose* to do these, because we act them, sometimes gain pleasurable skills from them, draw close to experience through them, they can begin to seem less *un*serious. They can even take over our lives in ways we or our loved ones don't like (golf addiction, tennis addiction, canasta addiction). But they can also give us relief from noxious duties, distract us from our bad decisions or dreams, contribute to our fantasies, harden our muscles, keep us in mind of our youths, etc., etc. Positive things — as far as they go.

Each may have its downsides, but nothing's really wrong with these sporting realms. Nobody seriously wants them to quit existing. Part of their satisfying unimportance includes their having almost no victims, offering as little as possible to worry about, being morally uncomplicated — indeed, in their having almost no innate importance whatsoever, except what observers and participants decide to dream up for them. They're free, in the sense of gratuitous. And in a world that seems not always free of what sports are innocent of (moral consequence), this makes them *seem* good, sometimes even important.

What each of these realms lacks, and what might (in another world) promote either to a plain of genuine importance, is some feature of moral necessity, some "I can do no other" quality of human motive — that spiritual standard by which we routinely appraise action and character and deem each lasting because the events and changes they occasion are so inescapable and important that we employ them to help us understand who we are: if we're good or if we're bad, rather than just good *at* or bad *at* something.

Oh, I know. The lives of important brain surgeons and army generals and cult novelists have been lengthened, their thoughts clarified, their decisions made more certain because they fished for trout on the Rangeley Lakes or played varsity squash at Princeton or exceeded at curling up in Manitoba. Whizzer White became a Supreme Court standout only after (and impliedly because of) his All-American football days at Colorado. The scholar-athlete, that deeply serious unserious soul, holds a place of almost Apollonian esteem among American hero figures as the perfection of the sporting ethic made consequential *outside* of sport: *the lessons of the gridiron served young Jonkel well in his march to the statehouse in Bismarck* . . . Ja, ja, ja.

Only they didn't *have* to play sports in the way, say, Hamlet *has* to kill his uncle. They merely wanted to. And indeed, each of these characters could've done something else — or better yet,

done nothing but sit home reading books — and everything
would've worked out fine. The really impressive part is that sports
didn't cripple their progress more than it did. Auden wrote that
poetry makes nothing happen, by which he meant that poetry
causes many important things — we just can't see them. But sports
really does cause very little of lasting value to happen in the world,
except by accident. And this is the fundamental element of sports'
character that sports writing has to wrestle with and overcome in
order to make itself interesting.

Twenty-five years ago, I used to listen to a sports call-in show in
L. A. wherein a guy who billed himself simply as "Superfan," and
whom I envisioned as a congenial cross between Harry Von Zell
and Walter Winchell, nightly dispensed vital sports info, inter-
viewed colorful celebrity sports guests, mediated fan disputes, is-
sued insider wisdom on local teams — in essence did all he could
using the AM band to make himself a vicar for citizen needs and
to assure us that there was a benevolent good, and his name was
sport.

   And he was great. My wife and I, without a TV, used to eat our
dinner, get finished with whatever piddling duties we had, and
then park ourselves on the couch in our little beach house and
utterly immerse ourselves, sometimes for two hours a night, in
whatever Superfan had on his mind: Dodger news (Marichal was
making a comeback with a new club; it fizzled), Laker championship prospects (they won with Wilt and Zeke), Ram quarterback
indecision (pretty much the same as now). Like the song says, "I'll
never know what made it so exciting." Maybe it was just the Tech-
nicolor sports universe cracking open to give me a virtual peek.
But it *was* exciting, and the two of us grew completely involved in
the little life of the show — in the caricatured personalities of the
callers, "Beano from Encino," "Frankie from Oxnard," "Just Newt
from the Valley"; in the ironbound dedication of everyone involved
to the unquestioned rightness of our dedication to and use of our
time for sports. And in Superfan himself, his chummy, voluble
willingness to have faith that dark sports clouds would always give
way to bright sports sunshine, all the while staying careful not to
be a shameless homer.

   What I remember most vividly, though, about those evenings
lasting into dreamy summer nights was Superfan's boilerplate sign-

off, there at the end of each night's séance with the voices of
sport's invisible devotees. "Just remember," he'd say, and a certain
breathy solemnity would open in his meaty voice as he was packing
up before heading out onto the swarming 405, "just remember,
folks, that in the crowded department store of life, sports is, after
all, *just* the toy department." Fade to theme.

In the intervening years, I've tried to take counsel from that bit
of complex intelligence, not only because it meant to assure me
that there *are* important things in the world and we need to keep
our priorities straight about them (Superfan never said what they
were), but that it's also important, if not exactly equally so, that
we not take *everything* so seriously; that in the toy department there
are genuine attractions worthy of our dedicated notice, and part
of what's good about sports is precisely its optional, inessential
character, into which we may choose to thrust ourselves a little, or
almost wholly. This wisdom has always reminded me of the old
stand-up comic's rule that if nothing's funny, nothing's serious. In
the world according to Superfan, if everything's serious, maybe
nothing is.

Good sports writing — the best sports writing — always comprehends and often engages this fundamental truth about practically
everyone's involvement with sports, be they couch-bound or iron-
man contestant: that sports is an unserious subject we are willing
to seem to take seriously because doing so can make us happy.
From this tension between the pseudo-serious and the fanciful,
sports writing is often able to generate drama that animates and
fosters good writing. In a highly abbreviated form, this tension is
what makes the famous anecdote about Joe DiMaggio and his
then-wife so vivid and memorably affecting: two larger-than-life
characters, who *were* models for conduct the world over, disagree-
ing sweetly but unswervingly over nothing more serious than
who'd heard the most cheering. It's probably the greatest two-line
sports story of all time.

A. J. Liebling was as good as there ever was at advertising sport's
basic triviality at the same instant that he made it a sweet virtue by
harnessing it to his great wit and writerly felicity, occasionally even
affording himself a try at "truth" normally reserved for serious
literature. "Jackson was fluttering like a winged bird," Liebling
wrote, describing the large but overmatched heavyweight Tommy
"Hurricane" Jackson in his 1954 match against the Cuban Nino

Valdez, "making a difficult though harmless target. And Valdez," Liebling continued, "conscious of the three-knockdown rule, was following him about, eager to bring him down, even for a half a second, before the round ended. Valdez has had many fights, has always finished strong and was in good condition, but he seemed at this point to be heaving. Perhaps it was merely emotion, for he could not have anticipated a chance to knock off work so early."

Any one of us would be happy to have written any one of these sentences as our on-the-record response to seeing two men beat each other up in public. It's privilege enough just to read them. The "winged bird"; the little second-thought parenthetical "even for a half a second," expressing, or more likely inventing, Valdez's patient boxological opportunism; and certainly we prize the provisional aside, placed so carefully at the paragraph's end, reminding us that we are, by the way, reading about feeling human beings here. Beating each other up is just their job, albeit an unusual one.

W. C. Heinz, novelist, war correspondent, and great *New York Sun* reporter, was another writer who mastered the artful balance of humors sports writing observes when it's done excellently. Recalling his youth and his apprenticeship to the sports reporter's vocation, Heinz wrote in the late 1970s:

> "That was how bad I had it in high school, when I was too frail for football and afraid of a baseball thrown near the head and had been a reluctant starter and worse finisher in street fights. Once, when we were both eight years old, they put the shoemaker's son and me together in the high school playground with gloves on, and he punched me around for three one-minute rounds.
>
> "You know," I said, a long time after that, to Sugar Ray Robinson, the greatest fighter I ever saw. "You and I fought the same guy. When we were little kids he punched my head in a playground fight."
>
> "Who was that?" Robinson said.
>
> "Vic Toisi," I said.
>
> "Vic Toisi," Robinson said. "Did I fight him?"
>
> "Yes," I said. "You fought him in the Eastern Parkway, and knocked him out in the first round."
>
> "Is that so?" Robinson said.

End of anecdote.

Boxing, of course, might be a special case, enticing good writing and the best writers with its built-in moral dramas of men in action and its dangerous aura of near-death creating the feel of honest-to-God necessity. Yet here is Heinz again, this time on American football — cartoonish, dubious, cumbersome — although in this instance Heinz's focus is on one of its cult figures from the 1940s, the New York Giants' coach Steve Owen.

> On this morning, it was cold, but the air was clear and the sun was shining. The Giants were running through passing plays in deep right field near the outfield wall with the signs painted on the dark green, advertising razor blades and hot dogs and ice cream. Steve Owen was standing with his hands in his hip pockets, talking to several of us and watching Arnie Herber throw the ball.
>
> Herber threw a pass to an end named Hubert Barker. It was deep and Barker ran for it, but when he was about to run into a wall where the sign advertised Gem blades, he slowed and the pass went over his outstretched hands.
>
> "What are you scared of, Barker," Owen said, shouting at him. "What are you scared of?"
>
> "He's scared of the five o'clock shadow," Bert Gumpert, who wrote sports for the Bronx *Home News,* said.

End of anecdote — the good clincher line given to a colleague, no doubt just the way it happened. Though the story itself, its immaculate timing, the atmospheric outfield details, the positioning of the great but stern Owen as straight man to the small-time beat reporter for the local rag — all that is pure Heinz.

Locked into these two lovely, simple-seeming passages are the elements of fine sports writing: an actual sporting act is described; no strained attempt is made to rig up events as emblematic of anything, or as metaphor for life; some sense of sport's often drably repetitive, one-dimensional nature is not shirked; a possibility of absurdity lurks alongside the possibility of athletic excellence; all is rendered in the form of good sentences — words well chosen, apt details observed, the reader's attention husbanded, and his intelligence respected by the writer's willingness to acknowledge the obvious while putting together what hadn't been joined before for the purpose of saying something new.

These virtues are, of course, the virtues of most good writing, writing that *would* serve as the axe for the frozen sea within us. Sports writing, however, because it is about a game we or others choose to play and could as easily not choose, is best when it restrains itself from claiming too much, best when it sees itself as a little life within a larger, more important one.

Plenty of writers fail to exercise this restraint, and the result is often bad writing — none of it to be found in this volume, of course. Such faulty writing typically fails to realize, for instance, that human beings are not interesting *just because* they're athletes; or that behind-the-scenes business shenanigans are not more interesting just because the rich guys happen to own ball clubs or are players dressed in oversize "business" suits no one but they would ever think of wearing. Or else it fails to recognize that sports has really little to do with producing satisfactory role models and probably never has; or that as a useful metaphor for life, sports generally draws upon an inadequate vocabulary and almost always makes life seem simpler, less livable, less interesting than it really is — more like a game. In my view, life beats sports every time.

Best is a difficult concept. But a collection of at least quite good American sport writing seems appropriate for our culture. And not just because we are a sports-besotted country, and writing is an art losing ground to other media, and therefore sports writing could use some bucking up. But rather because we have a long history of wonderful sports writing in America, writing that fully comprehends its station and makes the most of it, and in so doing enriches our national spirit by relieving some of that spirit's natural tensions. There's just something in the American sensibility that values joining the often primal yet contrived acts of sport to the intensities and suave logics of well-made prose. It seems to free us in the way conceptual art frees us. Plus reading sports may be the only reading for pleasure most Americans ever do.

Finally, as much as I love the purely essayistic writing of Liebling and Heinz and Red Smith and John Lardner, and their modern-day inheritors, Roger Angell, Tom Boswell, Tom McGuane, Roger Kahn, Jim Murray, George Vescey, and Mark Kram, I cannot overlook the fact that American sports writing is good in a variety of writerly ways: essays, yes, but also news stories, profiles, news features, and more. And so I've selected the sports stories that follow with what I think of as a spirit of acceptance. My rules have been very few: no pro wrestling, since only the spectators don't know the outcome there, and no stories that fail to describe an actual sporting act. Sports writing, after all, gets boring when it strays from sports acts themselves; when it goes into the counting rooms and doesn't return, or into the jail cell or the rehab unit or the divorce court and leaves actual sports behind; when, equipped with its powers of observation, of sensibility, analysis and pure description, it fails to tell us anew how some difficult feat is performed, how something exhilarating might feel, or how a beautiful act appears to a trained observer, and what difference any of it makes or doesn't.

The appeal of sports writing, then, is exactly what I began this essay seeming to complain about — that it's about sports. There is much pleasure to take in the little life that's there, in human endeavors that lie aside of the great and weighty issues of life, and which can be turned felicitous and absorbing and even memorable by someone who can write — can be made to seem almost if not quite necessary. Indeed, if we can take the time for this pleasure, turn our notice for a moment away from the necessary, we can relish and possibly even understand more of life.

RICHARD FORD

The Best
AMERICAN
SPORTS
WRITING
1999

SHIRLEY POVICH

Recent Baseball Feats
Require Footnotes

FROM THE WASHINGTON POST

DURING MY RECENT and enforced sabbatical, called for by the rewarded pursuit of better health, three things happened in baseball that evoked some ruminations plus the inevitable compulsive comment.

These happenings were the home run binge of Mark McGwire that catapulted him beyond Babe Ruth's record pace and aroused the chants of "The king is dead, long live the king," David Wells's perfectly pitched game for the Yankees, and the startling strategy of Arizona Diamondbacks Manager Buck Showalter, who, with two out and the bases full, opted to intentionally walk Barry Bonds, which forced in a run and cut the Arizona lead to 8–7.

Let us treat first McGwire, the St. Louis Cardinals' big-muscle Adonis, who seems to specialize in three-homer games and has won the belief of the *Washington Post*'s Tom Boswell that McGwire is the game's new image as a royal nonesuch of home run hitters, not excluding even the fabled Babe Ruth.

Nobody writes baseball better or as well as Boswell, a student and unmatched chronicler-philosopher of that game. Not to quibble, Boswell puts it bluntly: "Was Babe Ruth really a better home run hitter than this guy? In the past four years the correct answer has been clear. No."

Whoa there. Give McGwire the last four years, and he may be cast to hit more homers in a single season than Ruth did, but don't confuse him with the guy who inspired such sobriquets as Sultan of Swat and the King of Clout and made the name Bambino the recognized property of only one man in the entire world.

McGwire weighs 245 pounds, stands six foot five, and bulked up by strength coaches and Nautilus weightlifts, plus the new diet of "nutrition shakes" popular in the clubhouses, may well hit the ball farther than the 215-pound Ruth, although there are stubborn nonbelievers. As Walter Johnson once said, when asked to compare the Babe's swats with those hammer blows of Lou Gehrig and Jimmie Foxx and Hank Greenberg: "Lemme say this, those balls Ruth hit got smaller quicker than anybody else's."

To judge McGwire a better home run hitter than Ruth at a moment when McGwire is exactly three hundred homers short of the Babe's career output is, well, a stretch.

It is not in the mind-set of nice-guy McGwire to challenge the Babe's place as the number-one idol and most famed personality in the game. Too many truths forbid it. Before he started hitting home runs, did McGwire pitch three consecutive World Series shutouts? The Babe did. Does McGwire in the batter's box command the high excitement Ruth did with his head cocked back, a scowl on his face, his toes turned in, and his bat poised for that pirouetting swing that engaged all parts of his body? And if the Babe did whiff, it was with such gigantic gusto that the fans could still chortle.

One of McGwire's specialties has been the exciting three-homer game he's been producing as a special treat for his fans. But halt, Ruth was no stranger to the three-homer afternoon. Take, for example, the high drama of the last big-league game he ever played, in Pittsburgh in 1935. His farewell salute to himself was three home runs into the seats. And remember, Babe was doing this when he was forty years old. It was the little things that set him a long way apart from the others in the game. 'Twas said of the Babe, "Put a camera on him and he performs."

The gem of the 1998 baseball season thus far is Wells's perfect game against the Minnesota Twins. There can be no demeaning the perfect game. It is far more rare than the no-hit game, which can sometimes be a happening against all logic. No-hitters pop up at the strangest times.

Walter Johnson got his no-hitter in 1920, in the second-worst season of a twenty-one-year career, when he won only eight games.

A contrast was the feat of another Washington Senator, Bobby Burke, who all of a sudden pitched a no-hitter against Boston at Griffith Stadium in 1934. In his entire career, Burke never won eight games in a season, and I recall once characterizing him as "Bobby Burke, who had a nine-year tryout with the Senators." But the most startling no-hitter of all was that by Bobo Holloman of the St. Louis Browns, who brought it off in his first major league start. He was gone to the minors before the season ended, winning only two of his next nine decisions.

It is correct to say that Wells joins the fabled Don Larsen in perfect-game glory. But at the risk of carping, let us recall that Larsen's feat occurred during a World Series against a pennant-winning National League club, the Dodgers, who with Duke Snider, Gil Hodges, Carl Furillo, Jackie Robinson, Roy Campanella and Pee Wee Reese were second best in the NL in runs scored, second in home runs with Snider's forty-three leading the league, and second in doubles. Hardly to be confused with Wells's passive victims, the Twins. Minnesota ranked thirteenth in hitting in their fourteen-team league, and opted that day to bench their top hitter, Todd Walker, because of left-handed pitching. It was very inviting for Wells, and he performed.

This is not to rap David Wells, a helluva pitcher and one of the enchanting personalities of the game, with his I-do-it-my-way attitude. His passion for baseball was known when he paid $20,000 for a Babe Ruth cap and wore it on the mound for two innings before the intrusive umpires made him replace it with Yankees headgear. They couldn't give Wells the number-3 uniform that was retired in honor of Ruth, so he compromised by demanding number 33.

If anybody were to reawaken the fans to the glory of baseball by pitching the perfect game, the scene could have no more appropriate protagonist than David Wells, individualist.

Baseball circles were abuzz last week when Showalter flung his new strategy into the teeth of the San Francisco Giants by signaling an intentional walk to the dangerous Bonds with two out, the bases full, and Arizona with a two-run lead. It worked, Arizona got the last out on Brent Mayne's liner to right field, and Showalter basked in his self-created heroic vale.

Wait, though, and let's play Can You Top This? I think we can. My hero and longtime friend in the cause was the late Paul Richards, former catcher, later big-league manager, and one of the acknowledged dreams of the game.

One night, after dinner with Richards after a Griffith Stadium game, I said, "Paul, in the last fifty years there hasn't been a new play in baseball."

And he said, "One, and I pulled it." He said this was in the minor leagues, and Richards was managing Atlanta, which had a two-run lead in the bottom of the ninth at Birmingham. And Richards said, "Now up comes the only Birmingham hitter who could ruin us.

"We worked it to 3–2 on this guy and now he was fouling off pitch after pitch. I was catching and I called time. Went out to the pitcher and called in the second baseman and shortstop to explain what I wanted.

"I told our pitcher to take a long windup and walk the guy on his next pitch, but give it to me high and outside where I could wing it down to second base. What I had seen was that hotdog base runner on first base running wild on all those foul balls, always ending up between second and third before he had to go back.

"I got the pitch I wanted, the run forced in, but that hot dog on first base was caught between second and third when I threw to the shortstop, who tagged him out. The rule worked for us. He was only entitled to one base on a walk, and he was fair game for any more than that and sure enough we nailed him. Game over on an intentional walk. How do you like that?" The question is referred to Buck Showalter.

GUY LAWSON

Hockey Nights

FROM HARPER'S MAGAZINE

IN SEPTEMBER the streets of Flin Flon, Manitoba, are deserted at twilight. The town has no bookshop, no record store, no movie theater, no pool hall. Main Street is a three-block strip of banks, video shops, and Bargain! outlets. The 825-foot smokestack of the Hudson Bay Mining and Smelting Company rises from one end of the street, and the Precambrian shield stretches out from the other. In the Royal Hotel, gamblers forlornly drop quarters into the video slot machines. Farther up the street at the Flin Flon Hotel, the front door has been broken in a fight, and inside strangers are met by suspicious glances from miners wearing baseball caps with slogans like YA WANNA GO? and T-shirts that read, with the letters increasingly blurry, DRINK, DRANK, DRUNK. Susie, who works behind the counter at the Donut King, says a major shipment of LSD has arrived in town and half the students at the local high school, Hapnot Collegiate, have been stoned out of their minds for weeks.

Described by *Canada: The Rough Guide* as an "ugly blotch on a barren rocky landscape," Flin Flon, population 7,500, straddles the border between Manitoba and Saskatchewan, ninety miles north of its nearest neighbor, The Pas, five hundred miles up from Winnipeg, and a thirteen-hour drive due north of Minot, North Dakota. In this part of the world, Flin Flon is literally the end of the line: the two-lane highway that connects it to the rest of North America circles the perimeter of town and then, as if shocked to its senses, rejoins itself and hightails it back south.

But Flin Flon is also the heartland of Canada's national game. In a country where every settlement of consequence has a hockey arena and a representative team made up of players twenty years old and younger, the Saskatchewan Junior Hockey League is one of the grandest, oldest competitions. And Flin Flon is one of the grandest, oldest hockey towns. I had played hockey in towns like Flin Flon — in a league one level below the juniors — before I went to college. Many of my teammates had gone on to play junior hockey; some became professionals.

One hot day in August, seventeen years after I'd left western Canada, I flew north, arriving from Toronto in a twin-prop plane, to spend the first month of the new season with Flin Flon's junior hockey team. Hockey, as I remembered it from my own teams, was an untold story. It was also the path I had chosen not to take.

At the airport, I was greeted by the Flin Flon Junior Bombers' coach and general manager. Razor (like everyone else in hockey, he goes by a nickname) was in his early forties, solidly built, with a deep, raspy voice and the confident, slightly pigeon-toed stride of a former athlete. He had grown up in Flin Flon and had been a defenseman for the Bombers. He had gone on to play a long career in minor league professional hockey as well as some games — "a cup of coffee here, a cup of coffee there" — with the Boston Bruins in the National Hockey League. As we drove into town, Razor told me that the previous year, his first full season as coach, the Bombers had finished with the second-worst record in the SJHL's northern division. This year, he said, was going to be different. He had big tough forwards, speed, and two of the best goalies in the league.

A blast of cold air hit me as I walked out of the 90-degree heat and into the Whitney Forum's simulated winter for the first time. Meeks, a veteran Bomber left-winger, was alone on the ice practicing his signature trick: tilt the puck on its side with the stick, sweep it up, then nonchalantly cradle it on the blade. Lean and large and slope-shouldered, he was one of the toughest players in the league. As he left the ice, I heard him say to Hildy, the team trainer, "Tell Razor I'm not fighting this year. This is my last year of hockey, and I'm not missing any games." He was twenty years old. He had sat out a third of last season because he had broken his hand twice in fights. His thumb was still out of place, the joint distended and gnarled.

In the Bombers' dressing room, Meeks's sticks were piled next to his locker stall, the shafts wrapped in white tape and covered with messages to himself written in black Magic Marker. One note read MEGHAN, the name of his girlfriend; another said HOCKEY GOD; and a third, WHAT TO DO? While he took off his shoulder pads and loosened his skates, other players, hometown kids like Meeks or early arrivals from out of town returning from last season's team, drifted in. Boys with peach fuzz and pimples — Rodge, Quinny, Woody, Airsy, Skulls, Dodger — they seemed to transform into men as they pulled on their pads and laced up their skates. I went to the stands to watch them play.

The Forum is a squat, dark, tin-roofed building on the shores of what used to be Lake Flin Flon but is now a drained and arid wasteland of tailings from HBM&S's smelter. Dozens of tasseled maroon-and-white championship banners hang from the rafters. Photographs of nearly every Flin Flon Bomber team since the 1920s look down from the walls. And there is a pasty-faced portrait of Queen Elizabeth in her tiara at the rink's north end.

With no coaches and no fans, nobody but me around, the rink echoed with hoots and laughter. Scrub hockey, like school-yard basketball, is a free-form improvisation on the structures and cadences of the real game. Passes were made between legs and behind backs. The puck dipsy-doodled and dangled, preternaturally joined to the stick, the hand, the arm, the whole body, as players deked left, then right, and buried a shot in the top corner of the net. In those moments, the Forum seemed an uncomplicated place where the game was played purely for its own sake: *Le hockey pour le hockey.*

The Bombers, like virtually every team in the SJHL, are owned by the community; the team's president and board of directors are elected officials, like the mayor and the town council; and the team is financed by bingo nights, raffles, and local business sponsorship. HBM&S once gave the Bombers jobs at the mine — with light duties, time off to practice, and full pay even when the team was on the road, an arrangement that was a powerful recruiting tool for prairie farm boys — but these days there are no jobs at HBM&S and there's little part-time work in town. Some of the players do odd jobs to earn spending money. Like junior-hockey players across Canada, most Bombers move away from home by the time they're sixteen. Long road trips, practices, and team meetings leave little time for anything but hockey. For decades, players were expected either to quit school or slack their way through it; now the Junior A leagues advertise hockey as the path to a college scholarship in the United States.

The Bombers' training camp began the morning after my arrival. Eighty-four teenagers turned up for tryouts at the Forum, most driven from prairie towns across western Canada by their fathers. Razor, dressed in a Bombers' track suit, maroon with slashes of white and black, positioned himself at center ice. His seventy-three-year-old father, Wild Bill, stood in the broadcast booth above, scouting the players. When Razor blew his whistle, the hopefuls skated at full speed; when Razor blew the whistle again, they slowed to a coast. At the scrimmages that weekend, Flin Flonners drinking coffee from Styrofoam cups wandered in and out of the arena, their ebb and flow marking the beginning and end of shifts at HBM&S. Like contestants in a beauty pageant, the players had only a fleeting chance to catch the eye of Razor and his coaching staff; unlike beauty contestants, these hopefuls were allowed full body contact and fights. Three, six, eleven — I lost count. The fights seemed to come out of nowhere, with nothing that could sanely be described as provocation but, for all that, with a certain unity of form: the stare-off, the twitching of a gloved hand, and the unmistakable message "Ya wanna go?" Then, striptease-like, the stick was dropped, gloves fell, elbow pads were thrown aside, helmets were taken off — a bravura gesture shunning any effete protection — and two players circled each other, fists cocked.

On Saturday morning, Sides arrived in Flin Flon from Moose Jaw. He was seventeen, skinny, shy; he wore a Christian Athlete Hockey Camps windbreaker. Razor and Wild Bill were excited that Sides, a late cut by the Warriors of the elite Western Hockey League, was in town. Rodge and Meeks, twenty-year-old veterans and leaders on the team, had heard about Sides too, and decided to put the rookie arriviste to the test. Sides had played only a couple of shifts in an intrasquad match before Meeks was yammering at him, challenging him to a fight. Looking both terrified and afraid to look terrified, Sides skated away from Meeks. "Leave him alone," Razor called down from the press box. "Keep in touch with yourself."

"Meeks isn't the right guy. He's too good a fighter," Razor said to me. "We'll send someone else, and if the kid answers the bell and stands up for himself, he'll be accepted by the team. If he doesn't, we'll go from there." Sides scored three goals that session. The next afternoon he fought Ferlie, a man-child six inches shorter than Sides but an absurdly eager and able fighter. Skate to skate, lefts and rights were thrown in flurries. Sides's head bounced off the Plexiglas as he and Ferlie wrestled each other to the ice. The players on the benches stood and slapped their sticks against the boards in applause. Sides and Ferlie checked their lips for blood, shook hands, exchanged a grin.

Northern Exposure — an Exciting Kickoff Tournament of Junior A Hockey started the following Friday when the Bombers played the North Battleford North Stars. A few hundred miners stood along the guardrails, among them Meeks's father in a T-shirt that said TOUGH SIMBA and featured a lion cub chewing on a piece of steel. The Forum's southwest corner was dotted with students from Hapnot Collegiate, the boys near the top and the girls closer to the ice. Security guards in Dadson Funeral Home jackets circled the arena. The Bombers skated out to cheers; the crowd stood, baseball caps off; a taped version of "O Canada" played; then, with sudden ferocity, Flin Flon's preseason hockey began. Players swarmed off the bench, bodies slammed into boards, the puck flew from end to end. Less than two minutes into the game, the North Stars scored on Dodger, the Bombers' first-string goalie, in a scramble in front of the net. Thirty seconds later, Ferlie was sent off for roughing. Less than ten seconds after that, a teenage girl in the stands was hit in the face by an errant puck; she casually threw the puck back on the ice. Four minutes and ten seconds into the opening period, Dodger let in a second goal, a wrist shot from the top of the slot. During the playoffs the previous season, Dodger had made sixty-two saves in an overtime loss in Watrous, a feat his teammates spoke of with hushed awe, but today Dodger couldn't stop a thing. Two minutes and fifty-three seconds later Meeks got a penalty for slashing. Fourteen seconds later Rodge scored for Flin Flon. Air horns sounded and Bachman-Turner Overdrive's "Takin' Care of Business" blared over the speakers. And on it went: sticks whacked across legs, gloves rubbed into faces after the whistle, the game a relentless, Hobbesian cartoon of taliation and retaliation, misconduct, inciting misconduct, and gross misconduct. Rodge, the most gifted player on the Bombers, stopped on the way to the dressing room at the end of the first period to sign autographs for children calling out his name. "It's a *Gong Show* out there," he said to me. "It's always the same in exhibition season."

Between periods, I followed a crowd to the bar in the curling club next door to the arena. A dozen men were sitting at a table drinking rye whiskey. What did they think of their team this year? I asked. "Pussies," they said. What did they think of Razor? "Pussy." A former Bomber, sluffing drunk, reminisced about his glory days — when Flin Flon, he boasted, was the toughest town anywhere. Picking up on the theme, a burly man who called himself Big Eyes and whose son had captained the Bombers a few years earlier, told a story about an all-you-can-eat-and-drink charity fund-raiser a few years back at which a brawl broke out. Big Eyes couldn't remember why or how the fight started; he did remember, he said with a glint in his eye, that the raffle tickets he was supposed to sell the next morning were covered in blood.

I stepped outside for a breath of fresh air. Aurora borealis was out in the northern sky. A few feet away a little boy pushed another little boy onto the gravel in the parking lot. "Faggot," he said. The other little boy got to his feet and shoved back: "Faggot."

In the gazebo in front of Razor's cottage near Amisk Lake a few miles out of Flin Flon, the swarming mosquitoes and no-see-ums kept out by the screen, a red cooler stocked with beer, steaks ready for the barbecue, Razor and Wild Bill and the assistant coaches held a long debate, complete with diagrams, about the dressing room: Who should sit where? Who had earned a prime spot? Who needed to be sent a message? There was also the matter of the tampering dispute with the Opaskwayak Cree Nation Blizzard of The Pas, who, Razor said, had had a Bomber player practice with their team. In compensation, Razor angrily had demanded $30,000 and the big defenseman or two he needed to round out his roster; the Blizzard were offering a forward they had imported from Sweden. The merits of a player from Thunder Bay on the verge of making the team were also discussed: he had the quickness to wrong-foot the defense, but he had a long mane of coiffed blond hair and wore an earring off the ice.

Razor wanted the Bombers to attack. On offense, in the grand banal tradition of Canadian hockey, the Bombers would "dump and chase": shoot the puck into the opposition's end, skate like hell after it, then crash bodies and hope to create a scoring chance. On defense they would "build a house": each player would be a pillar, spreading to the four corners of the defense zone, supporting one another, and moving the foundations of the house as one. Razor's team would forgo the flourishes of brilliance, the graceful swoop across the blue line, the geometrically improbable pass, the inspired end-to-end rush. They would play the man, not the puck. They would play what Razor called "ugly hockey." "You've got to play with balls, big balls," Razor had told the Bombers in the dressing room between periods in one of the Northern Exposure games. "Look at yourself in the mirror before you go back on the ice. Look in the mirror and ask yourself if you've got balls."

The Bomber players were very good, but two or three ingredients short of the strange brew that makes a professional athlete. Rodge lacked all-consuming desire. Woody was too thin, Quinny too plump, Reags too small. Meeks and Dodger were not dexterous enough in handling the puck. When I skated with them at morning practices, though, instead of seeing what they weren't, I saw what they were. They were fast and skilled and courageous: Rodge, with a low center of gravity, calm and anticipating the play; Woody grinning as he flew smoothly past a stumbling defenseman; Quinny letting go a slap shot and boom, a split second later, there's the satisfying report from the wooden boards; Dodger flicking a glove hand out to stop a wrist shot; Meeks trundling down the wing like a locomotive, upright, his legs spread wide, his face blank with pure joy.

Scrimmaging with the Bombers, the pace and sway of the game came back to me. Watching out for me — "Heads up, Scoop," "Man on, Scoop" — the Bombers hurled one another into the boards with abandon, the arena sounding with the explosive thud of compressed plastic colliding with compressed plastic. The speed of the game reduces the rink to the size of a basketball court. Things that are impossible to do on your feet — go twenty miles an hour, glide, turn on a dime — become possible. The body and mind are acutely aware of physical detail and, at the same time, are separated from the earth.

After Northern Exposure, Razor held the year's first team meeting in the Bombers' dressing room. Two dozen pairs of high-top sneakers were piled on the mats beside Beastie's Blades, the skate-sharpening concession next to the dressing room; Razor had recarpeted during the off-season, and no one except Hildy was allowed in without taking off his shoes. This season Razor had also put the team logo — the letter *B* exploding into fragments, a design donated by the company that had supplied HBM&S with its dynamite in the 1930s — on the floor under a two-foot-square piece of Plexiglas, as the Boston Bruins had done with their logo when Razor played for them. The dressing room was a dank cavern at the southeast corner of the arena, rich with the smells of decades of stale sweat. Its ceiling was marked with the autographs of Bombers of seasons past.

In front of their newly assigned stalls, Rodge rubbed Lester's ear with the blade of his stick and Reags rested his hand on Meeks's back. Dodger sat in a corner with his head in his hands. In their final game of the Northern Exposure tournament against the Dauphin Kings, with the Bombers trailing 4–1 in the first period, Ferlie had started a line brawl; in an orgiastic outbreak of violence, all the players on the ice had begun to fight at the same time. Now Razor addressed the topic of fighting. Because of the SJHL's penalty of compulsory ejection from the rest of the game for fighting, Razor said, other teams would send mediocre players out to try and goad Flin Flon's best players into scraps. "I know things are going to happen out on the ice. It's the nature of the game," Razor said as he paced the room. "But Rodge, Lester, Schultzie, the goal scorers, you can't fight unless you take an equally talented player with you. If we lose one of our best, we need them to lose one of their best."

"You told Ferlie to fight against Dauphin," Rodge said.

"No," Razor explained, "I didn't tell Ferlie to fight. We were getting beaten and I said, 'If you want to start something, now would be a good time.'"

The Bombers all laughed.

Razor turned to Meeks. "Meeks, I don't want you to fight. The other team plays two inches taller when they don't have to worry about you. We need the intimidation factor of you out there banging and crashing." Razor said he wanted to change Meeks's role. He wanted Meeks to be a grinder, not an enforcer. He wanted Meeks to skate up and down his wing, using his size to open up space on the ice.

At the barbecue in Razor's gazebo, Meeks had been a topic of concern. The coaches were worried that Meeks was under too much pressure at home. Meeks's father and brother wanted Meeks to ask for a trade; at practice one morning, Meeks's father had told me he didn't think the Bombers had a chance this season because they had too many rookies on the team. Maybe, one of the coaches had suggested, Meeks should move out of his family's house ten miles out of town and billet with another family in Flin Flon. "I want to give the kid the world," Razor said. "He deserves it. If I ask him to do anything, he'll do it. He's vulnerable, though."

The rhythms of the hockey season set in quickly: practice at eight in the morning so that the players still in high school could get to class on time, lunch at Subway, long empty afternoons, fund-raising appearances to sell Share of the Wealth and Pic-A-Pot cards to chain-smoking bingo players. Paul Royter, a hypnotist, came to town for a three-night stand at the R. H. Channing Auditorium, and half a dozen Bombers went up onstage to fall under Royter's spell, which, it turned out, meant lip-synching to Madonna and Garth Brooks. The legal drinking age in Manitoba is eighteen, and most of the players on the team were old enough to go to bars, but Razor had banned the Bombers from Flin Flon's beverage rooms, a rule he waived only once so that some of the boys could go to a matinee performance by Miss Nude Winnipeg. Nineteen of twenty-three Bombers were not from Flin Flon, and Razor told me that resentful locals would try to beat up the Bombers if they went into a bar.

On the second Saturday in September, Razor lifted the Bombers' eleven o'clock curfew to let the team watch the final game of the World Cup between Canada and the United States. Late that afternoon, carrying the twelve-pack of pilsner I had been advised to bring along, I went to Ev's place. Ev was one of the locals playing for Flin Flon, and his parents had taken in Bombers from out of town as billets for years. This season Rodge and Dodger were staying in Ev's parents' basement. With hockey posters and the autographs of the Bombers who had passed through their doors written on the basement walls, Ev's place was a fantasyland for a teenager living away from home: pool table, beer fridge, a couple of mattresses on the floor beside the furnace, a hot tub on the patio.

At twilight, Bornie, Reags, and I piled into a car and drove past houses, searching for the party. We found that Funk, who had played for Flin Flon a few years ago, was having a shake at his house. Rodge and Woody were sitting on the floor of the den playing a drinking game with Holly, Melanie, and Deanna, the girls who arrived fashionably late for the hockey games and sat slightly apart from the rest of the Hapnot section — the girls whom the players, and the town, called Pucks or Bikes.

"You want to play, Scoop?" Rodge asked me.

I looked down at a salad bowl filled with beer.

"No, no thanks," I said.

We got back into Bornie's car and went to Hildy's billet a few blocks away. More than half the Bombers were there, some sipping Coke, most with a twelve-pack of Molson Canadian or Labatt Blue between their legs. It had been front-page news that in the semifinal match between Russia and America, played in Ottawa, the Canadian crowd had cheered for the Russians and booed the Americans. Now Canada was playing the United States.

"All the guys who treat women with respect are here," Meeks said as the game started.

"Who's going to get on the phone and find the chicks?" Schultzie asked.

"Skulls knows where they are," Ev said.

"I do not," Skulls said.

"Don't hold out on us," Schultzie said.

"I don't know where they are," Skulls said. "I swear on hockey."

The game between Canada and America was played at an astonishing pace. Both teams were dumping and chasing, cycling the puck against the boards, relying as much on muscle and force as on skill. The majority of players in the NHL are Canadian, but because franchises in Quebec and Winnipeg have relocated to major-market cities in the United States in recent years and because the economics of hockey are changing and growing vastly more expensive and lucrative, it is a common complaint that the game is being Americanized. Still, three of the players on the Canadian team had played in the Saskatchewan Junior Hockey League, and some of the Americans had played junior hockey in western Canada as their apprenticeship for the NHL. The SJHL influence on the style of play was obvious. This World Cup game was, in its way, ugly hockey.

"Gretzky sucks," Skulls said in the middle of the second period. "He's a pussy."

"You're full of shit," Quinny said. "He's the greatest player of all time."

"He's a floater," Skulls said. "He doesn't go into the corners. He's not a team player."

Lester turned to Dodger. "That Swede Razor might get from The Pas is gay, eh."

In the next second Canada scored to take a 2–1 lead. We leapt to our feet and let out a huge cheer. Chief, a big defenseman from Patuanak, a Native community in the far north of Saskatchewan, stayed sitting.

"I want the Americans to win," Chief said. "They're playing the same way as Canadians and they're playing better."

"Yankee lover," Bornie said.

In the third period the Americans scored to tie the game and then scored again to take the lead. Canada came back with increased desperation. The faces of the Team Canada players were drawn, anxious: Canada's destiny and national pride were at stake. But the Americans withstood the onslaught. In the dying seconds, a pass came to Wayne Gretzky in front of an open net. Gretzky, so many times the hero, missed the puck as it flitted off the ice and went over his stick. Canada had lost.

"I wouldn't mind losing to the Russians," Reags said on the ride back to my apartment. "But not the fucking Americans — always bragging all the time, so cocky. It's not fair. It's our game."

> "Fishy fishy in the lake,
> Come and bite my piece of bait . . .
> Fishy fishy in the brook,
> Come and bite my juicy hook."

Meeks repeated his good-luck mantra as we trolled for pickerel on the southern shore of Amisk Lake. It was the morning after the Canada-U.S. game, and Razor had organized a team fishing trip. Meeks and I were in a small boat, the outboard motor chugging, a cool breeze creasing the black water. At a Bombers meeting a few days earlier, Razor had announced that Lester would be the captain; Rodge, Airsy, and Woody, the assistant captains. Meeks had hung his head in disappointment. Razor told me he didn't want to put too much strain on Meeks. "I'm still a leader on this team,"

Meeks said to me. During the exhibition season, he had often played doubled up in pain, his face contorted into a grimace. He had, he told me, ulcerative colitis, an extremely painful stomach disease brought on by stress, and he had forgotten to take his medication. He had moved out of his family's home and was living in town now with Reags's family.

I asked Meeks what it was like growing up in Flin Flon. "It was different," he said. "There were a lot of rock fights. Guys'd get hit in the head all the time. Once you got hit, everyone would come running and start apologizing. It was a good time."

When Meeks was thirteen, his father and brother had taught him how to fight in the garage after school. "I'd put the hockey helmet on, and they'd show me how to pull the jersey over a guy's head, to keep your head up, when to switch hands." Listening to Meeks, I couldn't help but remember when I was thirteen. My father had made it a rule that if I fought in a hockey game he would not allow me to keep playing. The first time he missed a game, I fought. After the game, the father of the player I fought tried to attack me. The fathers of my teammates had to escort me from the arena. It was terrifying.

A few of the Bombers had told me about the present that Meeks's older brother — a giant of a man and an ex-Bomber, with 30 points and 390 penalty minutes in one season — had given Meeks for his eighteenth birthday: a beating. "Yeah, he did, Scoop," Meeks said sheepishly. "My brother would say, 'I can't wait until you turn eighteen, because I'm going to lay a licking on you.' The day of my birthday he saw me and started coming after me. I grabbed a hockey stick and started swinging, nailing him in the back, just cracking him. It didn't even faze him. Next thing you know, my jersey's over my head and he's beating the crap out of me. My mom and one of my brother's friends hopped in and broke her up."

"Why did your brother do that?" I asked.

Meeks shrugged. "I turned eighteen."

He expertly teased his line. "I just want to turn into a professional fisherman," he said. "Stay out on the water and think about life."

Most days Dodger wandered the parking lots and streets of Flin Flon in search of empty pop cans, nonrefundable in Manitoba but worth a nickel across the border in Saskatchewan. Because his billet at Ev's place was at the other end of town, Dodger had taken to storing his jumbo plastic bags filled with crushed cans in the front yard of the apartment I had rented for the month. During training camp I had met Dodger's father, an anxious, eager-to-please man. "He's hard on himself," Dodger's father said of his son. "I tell him to relax, let life take its part."

Dodger, like many goalies, was probably the most skilled athlete on the team, agile and fast and alert. He was in his fourth season in the SJHL but had played poorly in the exhibition games and practices. He had let in soft goals and had even pulled himself from a game against the Nipawin Hawks after they had scored six times by the beginning of the second period. He had seemed to disappear into his equipment, his face hidden behind his mask, and the slow, ponderous way he had of moving off the ice had been replaced by nervous twitching. It is a hockey cliché that goalies, who stand alone in their net, are the game's eccentrics, and Dodger, who would sit quietly staring at the floor in team meetings and didn't much go for "the rah-rah and all that," was allowed that latitude. Still, Don, one of Razor's assistant coaches, was angry that Dodger wasn't taking the games seriously enough. "He's going around saying it's only exhibition season. I don't like that. That kid's got to be focused from day one."

But there was a reason for Dodger's lack of focus. "I've got a real story for you, Scoop," he said to me one morning after practice. "It's got nothing to do with hockey, though." Dodger's real story, the one that had been playing on his mind constantly, and which he told me in pieces over a few days when I passed the time helping him look for pop cans, began the Easter weekend of 1995, when Dodger was back home in Regina, Saskatchewan. He and Al, his best friend and an old hockey buddy, had been on a jag, hitting bars, going to parties, the same sort of things I did when I was around his age and living in the same city. On Sunday night, after drinking beer and Southern Comfort in the parking lot beside a hockey arena, Dodger was too ill to carry on. Al borrowed Dodger's fleece hockey jacket, took Dodger's bottle of Southern Comfort, and went downtown with another friend, Steve, to pick up a hooker. Unable to coax a prostitute into the car, Al hid in the trunk until they found a woman willing to get in with Steve. She was a Saulteau woman from the Sakinay Reserve named Pamela Jean George.

"I was watching the news the next night with another friend," Dodger said, "and a story came on about the murder of Pamela Jean George, and my friend said, 'Can you keep a secret?' I go, 'Sure.' He goes, 'They killed her.'" Al and Steve, white boys from the well-to-do south end of the city, both athletes, popular, good-looking, had, according to Dodger's friend, taken Pamela Jean George to the outskirts of town, where she had given them oral sex. Al and Steve then took her out of the car, brutally beat her, and left her for dead, facedown in a ditch. Al split for British Columbia the next day without saying goodbye to Dodger. Steve stuck around. One week passed. Another week. Dodger was constantly sick to his stomach. He thought it was only a matter of time before they would be caught. He didn't know about Betty Osborne, a Cree girl from The Pas, who was pulled off the street and killed by local white boys in 1971. In Betty Osborne's case, the open secret of who had done it was kept for nearly sixteen years until, at last, in 1987, three men were charged and one was convicted of second-degree murder.

Finally, with no news of the investigation and the growing prospect that Al and Steve would never be caught, Dodger felt that he was going to crack. At a friend's wedding reception, he told someone who he knew would tell the police. A couple of days later, while Dodger was watching an NHL playoff game, the police called him. "The cops wouldn't have had a fucking clue," Dodger said to me. "They were looking for pimps, prostitutes, lower-class people." Dodger was, he told me, scheduled to testify against Al and Steve in a few weeks, and he was finding it difficult to concentrate on hockey.

"I'll tell you what I'm really bitter about: people hinting that it's all my fault. The guy who told me about it in the first place came up to me at a party and said, 'I know this may sound harsh, but I'm going to have a tough time feeling sorry for you because I know it got out at the wedding reception.' And I was like, 'Who the fuck are you to talk to me? Show a little nuts.' This guy tries to play the role, like it's been really tough for him. I heard girls were calling him and saying, 'I feel so sorry for you, losing your friends. If you need someone to talk to I'm always here.' If girls called me I'd say, 'Fuck you. Don't feel sorry for me, feel sorry for Pamela Jean George.'"

Ever since I had arrived in Flin Flon and had heard about the Pucks and Bikes, I had wanted to meet them. Ev, one of the Bombers who was still going to Hapnot Collegiate, persuaded the girls to meet and talk with me at twilight at the Donut King.

"I don't understand why anyone would write about Flin Flon," Susie said to me from behind the counter as I waited for the Pucks and Bikes. Because I had no telephone in my apartment, the Donut King had become a kind of makeshift office, and for weeks, with increasing bemusement, Susie had watched me shouting over the howling northern wind into the pay phone in the lobby. "There's nothing to write about," she said, smiling. I asked Susie if she ever went to Bombers games. "I went this year to see if any of them were cute," she said. "They might look okay, but once you get up close they have zits or their teeth are crooked. I guess I went to see them lose, because they suck and I want to see them get killed."

"Would you date a Bomber?" I asked. "I'm not allowed to," she said. "My sister says, 'As if I'm going to let you walk around town and have people say, "There's your Bike sister."'"

Just then the Bikes pulled up in a blue Mustang and I took my leave of Susie. The car smelled of perfume and tobacco and chewing gum. We drove out to the town dump, where we sat and watched fifteen or so brown and black bears pick through the garbage and stare at the car's headlights. Holly, who had had a long plume of blond hair when I had seen her at the Bombers games and who now had a pixie haircut — the plume had been hair extensions, it turned out — was the femme fatale of Flin Flon: du Maurier cigarette, bare midriff. She told me that when she was dating Rodge last season her ex-boyfriend, a local she had dumped in favor of Rodge, had jumped up on the Plexiglas at the end of a game and screamed at Rodge, "I'm going to kill you!" This year, though, Holly said she wasn't interested in any of the players. "I don't have a crush. I wish I did. I'm guy crazy like hell, but I'm not even attracted to any of them."

Deanna, who was driving the car and had a pierced eyebrow, purple hair, and an inner-city hipster's Adidas sweat top on, allowed she had a crush on one of the Bombers. Melanie, quiet in the back seat with cherry-colored lipstick and a sweater around her waist, told me she had one real crush and another crush she was faking so that an awkward, shy Bomber wouldn't feel left out.

"The players say we're Pucks," Holly said, "but they're the ones who phone us. We don't even give them the time of day and they're asking, 'What're you doing tonight? You want to come over?' Without us they wouldn't have any friends in Flin Flon."

The spectacle of the bears began to wear thin. The girls suggested we drive to the sandpit on the other side of what used to be Lake Flin Flon and watch the nightly pouring of the slag at the HBM&S smelter. The slag pouring was a disappointment: a thin line of lava red barely visible against pitch black, steam rising and joining the sulfur dioxide chugging out of the company smokestack. Afterward, over strawberry milkshakes at the A&W, the girls told me about teen culture in Flin Flon: cruising around looking for house parties, driving to hangouts in the forest outside town — the Hoop, the Curve, the Toss Off — lighting a fire and drinking beer until the police chased them. Deanna said, "Flin Flon was in *The Guinness Book of World Records* for the most beer bought per capita in a weekend, or something like that."

"I hate rye," Holly announced. "I get into fights when I drink rye." She told me about the Boxing Day social last year. "This girl pissed me off, so me and a friend tag-teamed her. My friend slapped her and I threw my drink on her and she started blabbing at me so I grabbed her and kicked her in the head and ripped all her hair out. She was bald when I was done." The girl had to go to the hospital to have her broken nose set, Holly said, now speaking in quiet tones because she had noticed the girl's aunt a few tables down from us. "And then she went to the cop shop and filed charges, even though she was four years older than me."

Melanie and Deanna exchanged a furtive glance. They had never been in a fight; Holly had never lost a fight.

Saturday night was hockey night in Flin Flon. Game-day notices in the store windows along Main Street advertised that evening's match against the Humboldt Broncos. The night before, in the opening game of the regular season, the Bombers had defeated Humboldt 2–1. Beastie, who drove the tractor that cleans the ice at the Forum, toked on an Old Port cigarillo. "Pretty tame last night," he said. On the ice, the Stittco Flames were practicing before the main event. A dozen girls, including Razor's eleven-year-old daughter, who had recently given herself the nickname Maloots, skated lengths of the ice and worked on passing and shooting the puck. At the end of the session one of the girls dropped her gloves as if she wanted to fight and then, in full hockey uniform, turned and did a graceful lutz.

It had been payday at the company the day before, and seven hundred fans, nearly a tenth of Flin Flon's population, came to watch the game. In the Bombers' dressing room, the players sat and listened to Razor, their foreheads beaded with sweat from the pre-game skate. The new jerseys had arrived, and the pants and gloves the Bombers had bought secondhand from the Peterborough Petes of the elite Ontario Hockey League, the only other team in Canada with maroon-and-white colors, had been passed out. Norm Johnston, the coach of the Broncos, had coached in Flin Flon in the early 1990s, and his teams had a reputation for fighting and intimidation. Razor, in his game attire of shirt and tie, black sports coat, and tan cowboy boots, paced the room and told the Bombers that Johnston would try to set the tone of play but that they should not allow themselves to be provoked. What did Razor want to see from his players? He wrote the homilies on his Coach's Mate as Bombers called them out rapid-fire:

> HARD WORK
> INTENSITY
> INTELLIGENCE
> UGLINESS

"How about the Whitney Forum?" Razor asked. The Bombers began to chatter: "C'mon boys!" "It's our barn!" "Fucking rights!"

"We're going to own the building," Razor said. "We're going to rock the Whitney fucking Forum! We're going to take the fucking roof off!"

Two and a half minutes into the first period, Rodge and Schultzie had scored, and twice "Takin' Care of Business" had played on the loudspeakers. Razor's ugly hockey had the Broncos disoriented and backing off by half a step. I sat with Meghan and her friends in the Hapnot section as they tried, with little success, to start a wave. Meghan was a senior, a mousy blonde, petite and pretty in a woolly-sweater, Sandra Dee kind of way. She was the daughter of an HBM&S geologist; Meeks was the son of a union man. Most after-noons I would see Meghan and Meeks walking down Main Street holding hands. In the stands, she told me she had never seen Meeks fight. "I didn't come to the games last year, before we started dating. I tell him not to fight, because he's not like that. He's really gentle. He should write on his stick: LOVER NOT A FIGHTER."

By the second period, the Bombers were leading 4–1 and completely outplaying the Broncos, but the Flin Flon fans had turned on their own team. Johnston, as Razor had predicted, had seen to it that the Broncos were slashing and shoving and trying to pick fights. And the Bombers weren't fighting back. Humboldt would get penalties, Razor had told the Bombers, and Flin Flon could take advantage of power plays. "Homo!" Flin Flonners screamed at the Bombers. "Pussy!" Woody, the Bombers' best defenseman, fell to the ice and covered his head as a Humboldt player tried to pummel him. A minute later, Turkey, another Bomber defenseman, did the same thing, but the referee, who had lost control of the game by now, gave Turkey a penalty anyway. Ev was sticked in the stomach by a Bronco but didn't retaliate.

"You're a fucking woman!" Meeks's older brother shouted at Ev from the railing. In a scrum in front of the Bombers' net, Meeks was punched in the head, but he, too, followed Razor's instructions and didn't fight. It didn't matter, though: both Meeks and the Bronco got kicked out of the game. Meeks was jeered as he skated off.

A chubby twenty-one-year-old sitting near me, dressed in a leather jacket with the Canadian flag on the sleeve and unwilling to give his name in case the players read this article, explained why he was hurling abuse at Flin Flon: "It's embarrassing to the fans, to the team, the town. You look at all the banners hanging from the rafters, all the tough guys who have played here. The Bombers should have the balls to drop their gloves."

In the dressing room between the second and third period, the faces of the Bombers' coaching staff were pale: Flin Flon was easily winning the game, but they were also, absurdly, losing. The Whitney Forum, territory, pride, tradition, manliness were being attacked. The game was, as Razor had told the Bombers repeatedly, war; it was, in the Clausewitzian sense, the continuation of hockey by other means.

At the start of the third period, after a quick shower, Meeks came and sat with Meghan and me. "I talked to my dad and my brother," he said. "My brother told me to fight. Fuck him." Meeks and Meghan held hands as we watched twenty minutes of mega-violence. When number twenty-two for the Broncos skated to center ice and dropped his gloves, challenging someone, anyone, to a fight, Bornie took him on. There was a loud cheer. Lester fought at the drop of the puck. Airsy beat up a Humboldt player and winked to the Hapnot section as he was led to the dressing room for the compulsory penalty. Schultzie ran his fingers through his perox-ided hair before he swapped blows with a Bronco. "People are getting scared to play now," Meeks said. At the final siren, with both benches nearly empty because of all the players ejected from the game, a Bronco was still chasing Skulls around the ice.

The Bombers' dressing room was a riot of whoops and hollers. Flin Flon had won the game. Flin Flon had won the fights. "That's the way a weekend of hockey should be in Flin Flon!" Razor bel-lowed.

In the midst of the celebration the head of the local Royal Cana-dian Mounted Police knocked on the door and brought a little redheaded boy with a broken arm in to meet the Bombers. "All right guys, watch the swearing," Razor said. The tiny Flin Flonner went around and shook the players' hands.

Six days later, in the middle of a five-night, four-game road trip, the Bombers' bus barreled south through the narrow rutted back roads of Saskatchewan toward the prairie town of Weyburn. Razor and Wild Bill and Blackie, the radio announcer who broadcast the games back to Flin Flon, sat at the front of the bus, Razor thumbing through the copy of *Men Are from Mars, Women Are from Venus* that his wife had asked him to pick up while he was on the road. Behind them, the twenty-three Bombers were splayed in their seats. The dress code most of the boys follow for official team functions — shirt and tie, Bombers jacket or suit jacket, baseball cap — eased as ties were loosened and gangly limbs stretched across the aisle. It was quiet on the bus; after losing to the Yorkton Terriers in the first game of the trip, Razor had told the team that he wanted them to visualize that night's upcoming game against the Red Wings. Razor had also told Dodger that he would be the starting goalie for the first time in the regular season. There had been a mistrial in Al and Steve's case, and Dodger's testimony had been postponed in-definitely; Razor hoped that, with the pressure off, Dodger would begin to play up to his abilities. A few rows behind Dodger, Meeks leaned his head against the window. He was growing his whiskers in a wild, slanted way, with seemingly random slashes of the razor running across his face. He had had a terrible dream the night before. He couldn't remember what it was, but it was terrible. And his medication wasn't working, so his stomach was giving him awful pain.

In the back row of the bus, where I had been assigned a seat, I sat with a few of the players and watched the harvest prairie roll by. "I think it's brutal if people say you can't play hockey and be a Christian," Bornie said to me. "I just watch my mouth, try not to swear, and do my job. If you have to fight, you fight."

"It's not up to Christians to judge others for swearing," said Schrades, the other Bomber goalie. "We don't judge them for not swearing."

"They can do whatever the fuck they want," Ev said.

"You'll go to hell," Sides said to Ev. "That's the truth."

"Judgment Day is so hypocritical," Ev said. "Christians are supposed to be forgiving, and then they say anyone who doesn't believe can't come into heaven even if they're a good person."

"It's hard not to sin out on the ice," Airsy said.

"I'll probably go to heaven," Schultzie said.

When we arrived in Weyburn and walked into the Colosseum I had a shock of recognition. The last time I had been in the Colosseum was in the late 1970s, just before I "got a letter" offering me a tryout with the Regina Silver Foxes, a now defunct franchise in the Saskatchewan Junior Hockey League. Everything about the Colosseum had seemed huge then, the stands and ice surface and the red-and-white banners hanging from the rafters. I didn't want to take road trips and miss school, I had a bad knee, I wanted to drink beer and chase after girls. That's what I told my teammates, Boner and Dirt and Cement. I had lost touch with them long ago, but I knew they had all gone on to play professional hockey. The real reason I quit playing, though, what I didn't tell my friends, was that at the time, I had grown to hate hockey. It was in rinks like the Colosseum that I realized I had become, as they would say in Flin Flon, a pussy.

By game time, the Colosseum was nearly full. Many of the people in the stands were parents of Flin Flon players from farms and towns in southern Saskatchewan. Weyburn had won the league championship two of the last three years and had a team stacked with imports from Quebec and northern California and Latvia. When the Bombers skated out to a chorus of boos, Meeks, following his pregame ritual, went straight to the bench and took off his helmet and gloves and lowered his head and prayed. In minutes the Red Wings were all over the Bombers. Dodger's play, unlike his nervous, uneven play in the exhibition season, was sensational — diving, sprawling, kicking shots away with his leg pads. On a clean breakaway for Weyburn, Dodger made an acrobatic save. A few seconds later he gloved a slap shot from the point. I stood and whooped. The Bombers began to come back, Rodge swooping past the Weyburn blue line with the puck and taking a wrist shot from ten feet out. Frustrated, the momentum now with Flin Flon, the Red Wings started to hack at the Bombers. With only seconds left in the first period, number seventeen for Weyburn hit Woody in the face with his stick.

In the second period, the score still o–o, Seventeen skated past Sides and whipped his feet out from underneath him. Called for a penalty, Seventeen shot the puck at the linesman. It was, I thought, a familiar script: ripples become waves and rise rhythmically, climax-like, toward the fight. But then, suddenly and unpredictably, the Red Wings scored three quick goals on Dodger. "Sieve! Sieve!" the crowd taunted Dodger. Meeks skated out to take a shift. The puck was dropped, and Skulls, who was playing center, went into the corner after it. Seventeen followed Skulls and slammed him into the boards. Skulls's helmet came off, and Seventeen, seemingly twice Skulls's size, kept shoving, ramming Skulls's face into the Plexiglas. Across the rink, Meeks had dropped his gloves. He skated toward Seventeen, throwing off his helmet and tossing his elbow pads aside.

Meeks had explained his fighting technique to me back in Flin Flon: "I can't punch the other guy first," he said. "That's why I've got a lot of stitches. The other guy always gets the first punch and then I get mad." Meeks took the first punch from Seventeen square in the jaw. Meeks's head jerked back. He grabbed Seventeen by the collar and threw a long, looping, overhand right. He pulled Seventeen's jersey over his head. Another shot, a right jab, an uppercut; switched hands, a combination of lefts. A strange sound came from the audience, a mounting, feverish cry: Seventeen was crumpling, arms flailing, as the linesmen stepped in and separated the two. Meeks waved to his teammates as he was led off the ice by the officials to the screams of the Weyburn fans. The Bombers scored four minutes later. Between periods in the dressing room Razor shook Meeks's hand. "Great job."

Two days later we crossed the border into the United States, heading for Minot, North Dakota, and an encounter with the Top Guns, the only American franchise in the Saskatchewan Junior Hockey League. The flat of the prairies became the dun-colored hills and valleys of the North Dakota Badlands, the face of each rise marked by massive stones arranged to spell "Class of 19 —" for each year of the past five decades.

Ev, who had never been to the United States before, chanted every thirty seconds, "This is the furthest south I've ever been. This is the furthest south I've ever been."

"I don't like it here," Rodge said. "It's too far from home."

"People aren't as nice in the States," Bornie said.

"Look at that shitty little American town," Lester said as we drove through a roadside village. "It sucks cock compared to a little Canadian town." Lester and a couple of the Bombers began to hum the Guess Who song "American Woman."

When we arrived at the All Seasons Arena, Liberace's version of "Blue Tango" was echoing through the building as the Magic Blades, Minot's nationally ranked precision skating team, worked on their routine. The rink was in the middle of the fairground, a modern complex, new and brightly lit, with no banners hanging from the rafters and no memorabilia on display. Joey, a Minot player from southern Manitoba and a friend of Meeks and Woody and Ferlie, joked with the Bombers before the game. "They play the American anthem," Joey said, "and we have to stand there and listen, and we're, like, we couldn't give a shit."

For local high school hockey games, one of the Magic Blades told me, the place was packed with more than 3,000 fans, the crowd led by cheerleaders with pompoms and fight songs, but only 452 turned up to watch the Bombers and the Top Guns.

"Let's get ready to rumble!" the announcer yelled over the loudspeaker as the Top Guns and Bombers skated out for the game.

In the stands, eating french fries covered with ketchup and vine-gar, Meeks told me about the Weyburn game and his fight. He showed me his hands. The knuckles were badly swollen and cut. "Seventeen stuck Woody in the face in the first period," he said. "I wasn't on the ice then, but the whole game he was slashing and punching people, going after Sides and Skulls. Between periods, Razor came into the room and said to wait until the third period and someone's going to take care of Seventeen. He looked at me but he didn't say anything. I knew my role. I'd be the one taking care of it."

Meeks couldn't play and wasn't sure when he would be able to play again.

"I called Meghan and told her I broke my hand," he said. "She said, 'You did not.' I said I did, I had to fight. She said I shouldn't fight. She said that I always have a choice."

There was a long silence. On the first day of the road trip, less than an hour out of Flin Flon, Meeks had asked me how to write a love poem. Should it rhyme? he asked. What should a love poem say? For almost a week he had scribbled notes in the blue spiral notebook that he used to write to Meghan. For now, though, Meeks had given up on writing poetry; he could barely bend his fingers, and he thought his thumb was dislocated again.

After the game, driving through the fairground, it was quiet on the Bombers' bus. The Bombers had played four games on the road and had lost four very close games. Cokes and the chocolate chip cookies Sides's mother had baked for the team were passed around. Ahead there was a thirteen-hour ride north through the ancient rock of the Precambrian shield, through swales of mus-keg, endless stands of jack pine and spruce and trembling aspen, the bus swerving occasionally to miss caribou and wolves that had strayed onto the road.

The next day, before I left Flin Flon, I went to skate with the Bombers one last time. At the Forum, Beastie told me about Blackie's broadcast of Meeks's fight in Weyburn. "Blackie pretty near creamed his jeans," Beastie said. "He's describing the bout, all the shots Meeks is getting in, and he's yelling, 'There's a good old hometown Bomber beating!'"

In the dressing room, Reags came and sat beside me. He was

upset that I was leaving with the Bombers on a losing skid. I should stay until Friday, he said, when they were sure to defeat the Melville Millionaires. I pulled on my jock pad, shin pads, shoulder pads, elbow pads, jersey; wrapped tape around pads and fastened Velcro tags — a sequence I had repeated since I was scarcely old enough for kindergarten. I tightened the laces of my skates and stood and walked out of the Bombers' dressing room, past a sign with one of those sports clichés on it — IT'S MORE THAN A GAME — and glided onto a clean sheet of ice, the smack of pucks against the boards echoing around the empty stands.

After I left town, Flin Flon would suffer another losing streak, and after a dispute with the team's board of directors over trading Schultzie for a defenseman, Razor would be fired. Dodger would testify against Al and Steve in the murder trial. The killers, relying for their defense on their intoxication and diminished responsibility, would be convicted of manslaughter and given sentences of six and a half years each, with parole possible in only three and a half years. Dodger would be traded to a team in another junior league. The Bombers' new coach would ask Meeks to fight all the time; Meeks would lose confidence and would have a screaming argument with the coach. Two games before the end of the season, he would get kicked off the team. He would not be allowed in the team photograph. The Bombers would finish last in their division.

On my last day in Flin Flon, after practice, Dodger stopped by my place to pick up the enormous plastic bags filled with crushed pop cans that he had collected in the past month. As he gathered his cans from the yard, Dodger showed me the letter he had drafted to send to Harvard, Brown, Cornell, and a bunch of other American schools, to inquire about playing for them next season. It was still September, but it had snowed in Flin Flon and the cold of the coming winter was in the air. Shifts were changing at the company, and Main Street was lined with pickup trucks. Dodger zipped up his fleece Bombers jacket. Maybe he would try to play professionally in Europe, he said. He was in his final year of eligibility for junior hockey, but he wanted to keep playing.

Endgame

FROM THE NEW YORKER

THE WORLD CUP soccer tournament got off to a strange, promising start with a pageant that closed down Paris — a seventeenth-century-style allegorical masque, with music and dance and speech, which featured four sixty-five-foot-high inflatable giants who walked across the city from four Parisian monuments (the Opera, the Eiffel Tower, the Arc de Triomphe, and the Pont Neuf) to the Place de la Concorde. The giants were steel-framed latex-covered figures — dolls, really — with forklift trucks for feet, and hydraulic hinged arms and hips and shoulders, and even moving eyelids. They turned their heads, and shifted their gaze, and raised their arms in wonder as they slowly shuffled along the Paris streets. Each one was a different color and represented a racial type. There was Romeo, the European; Pablo, the Amerindian; Ho, the Asian; and Moussa, the African (he had purple skin). It took four hours for them to get from their starting points to the Place, where they bowed to each other, and the whole spectacle was broadcast live on television, while Juliette Binoche breathed over the loudspeakers on the streets and to the audience at home. ("The giants confront each other, but do they see a stranger or themselves?" etc.) The theme of the masque seemed to be the Self and the Other: the giants, never having seen each other before — or anything else, apparently — wake in the middle of Paris to find their Selfness in the Others. Apart from that, the commentators on French television were hard put to find something to say as the big guys inched their way along the boulevards toward this revelation, and at one point were reduced to noting that the technology that had pro-

duced the hydraulic giants had military applications, leaving you
with the comforting knowledge that if NATO is ever in need of a
crack synchronized team of huge, slow-moving inflatable dolls, the
French will be the ones to call. (One sees them cornering a particularly sluggish war criminal in a Montenegrin mountain hideaway
with a very large door.)

The vague internationalist symbolism — not to speak of the
snail-like pace — seemed the right allegory for the tournament.
The Coupe du Monde, which includes thirty-two nations, began on
Wednesday, June 10, and would continue through Sunday, July 12.
I set myself the task of watching it all, wanting to figure out what
exactly it is that the world loves in a game that so many American
sports fans will sit through only under compulsion.

I understand why people play it. When I was a teenager, I lived in
London for a while, and I spent most of my time playing soccer, or
at least the middle-class Kensington Gardens version of it. I even
learned how to talk the game. It was the opposite of trash-talking —
tidy-talking, I suppose you'd have to call it. If you did something
good it was brilliant; something less than brilliant was useless; if all
of you were useless together you were rubbish; and if a person did
something brilliant that nonetheless became useless everyone
cried, "Oh, unlucky!" By the end of my time in London, I wasn't
brilliant at the game, but I wasn't useless, either. I suppose this
was all faithful to the game's English-school-playing-field origins.
"Thoughtful ball," a commentator on the BBC would say about a
good pass. In the papers, you'll read things like "The signs of
decline in the still-clever but jaded Teddy Sheringham sadly became too patent to ignore." "For all his apparent world-weariness,
Beckham is still young." "[Anderton] has been stubborn to the
point almost of self-destruction, however, and it cannot happen
again this week." This isn't sports writing. It's end-of-term reports.

As I began watching the Cup games, though, I had a hard time
making a case for soccer as spectacle. I found myself torn between a
cosmopolitan desire to love a game the world loves and an American suspicion that they wouldn't love it if they had a choice. The
trouble wasn't the low scores, although the ribbon of late sports
news often sounded like one of those condensed, hopeless, rising-
and-falling monologues about marriage in Beckett: "Nil-nil. One-
one. Two-one. One-one. One-nil. Nil-nil." The trouble was what the

scores represent. The game has achieved a kind of tactical stasis. Things start off briskly and then fritter away into desultory shin-kicking, like a *Wall Street Journal* editorial. In soccer, the defense has too big an edge to keep the contest interesting, like basketball before the coming of the twenty-four-second clock, or the Western Front before the invention of the tank.

All sports take turns being dominated by their defense or their offense, and fully evolved defensive tactics will in the end beat offensive ones, because it is always easier to break a sequence than to build one up. Eventually, the defensive edge will be so enormous that, to stay in business as a spectacle, a sport has to change its rules, openly or surreptitiously. The big recent change in basketball, for instance, which took place somewhere between the Julius Erving and Michael Jordan eras, was a silent modification of the rule against traveling, so that now, it seems, a player can take about as many steps as he needs — a fact that only Rabbit Angstrom has officially noted. American football changes its rules every few years to allow quarterbacks to survive and prosper. Even baseball has tinkered with the mound and the depth of the fences. Soccer play-ers, though, have come to accept the scarcity economy — all those nil-nil draws — and just live with it, like Eskimos. The defense has such an advantage that the national sides don't need their offensive stars. In this Cup, two of the most inspired forwards in Europe — David Ginola, of France and Tottenham Hotspur, and Paul Gas-coigne, of England and whatever pub is open — didn't even make their national teams.

Since a defensive system keeps players from getting a decent chance to score, the idea is to get an indecent one: to draw a foul so that the referee awards a penalty, which is essentially a free goal. This creates an enormous disproportion between the foul and the reward. In the first game that Italy played, against Chile, for in-stance, the great Roberto Baggio saved the Italians' pancetta by smoking the ball onto the hand of a surprised Chilean defender, who couldn't pull back in time. "Hand ball" was ruled, which, near the goal, meant an automatic penalty and a nearly automatic goal. The other, most customary method of getting a penalty is to walk into the "area" with the ball, get breathed on hard, and then imme-diately collapse, like a man shot by a sniper, arms and legs splayed out, while you twist in agony and beg for morphine, and your teammates smite their foreheads at the tragic waste of a young life. The referee buys this more often than you might think. Afterward, the postgame did-he-fall-or-was-he-pushed argument can go on for hours.

European defenders of the game tend to put on haughty, half-amused looks when the sport is criticized, and assume that the problem lies with the American doing the criticizing, who is assumed to love action for its own sake. When you point out that ice hockey, the greatest of all games, shares with soccer the basic idea of putting something into a net behind a goalkeeper and has the added bonus of actually doing it, they giggle: "Oh, dear. In ice hockey you can't see the ball, or whatever you call it. You can't follow it. Besides, they fight all the time." It does no good when you try to explain that you can always see the puck, and anyway, better to fight like heroes than to spend all your time on the sidelines bickering about who touched the ball last before it went out of bounds, the way soccer players do, even though — as a Tom Stoppard character once pointed out — there is absolutely no doubt on the part of those two players about who touched the ball last.

European soccer apologists tend to overanalyze the triumphs of their heroes. In Brazil's game against Scotland, Ronaldo, the Brazilians' star, took the ball, faked right, and then spun around to his left, leaving a defender fooled while he rushed forward into the gap. Then he let go a weak shot and it was over. A nice move — but exactly the same move that Emmitt Smith makes three times a game with three steroid-enraged three-hundred-pound linemen draped on his back (and then Emmitt goes in to score) or that Mario Lemieux made three or four times a period after receiving radiation therapy for Hodgkin's lymphoma and having three Saskatchewan farm boys whacking at his ankles with huge clubs (and then Mario would go in to score). In the papers, though, that moment became a golden event. Rob Hughes, the estimable soccer writer for the *International Herald Tribune,* treated the three seconds of actual activity as though it were the whole of the Peloponnesian War, or a seduction by Casanova. "Receiving the ball from Cafu on the right, Ronaldo lured Colin Hendry, Scotland's biggest and most worldly defender, to him. 'Come closer, Big Colin, come to me,' the Brazilian seemed to say. And Hendry bought the invitation. Tighter and tighter he came until, suddenly, Ronaldo swiveled 180 degrees. . . ."

Soccer writers seemed as starved for entertainment as art critics — anything vaguely enjoyable gets promoted to the level of genius. In the old days, at the Kitchen, it was the rule that three recognizable notes sung in succession by Laurie Anderson heralded a new, generous lyricism. Ronaldo's magic was like a performance artist's lyricism: it existed but was apparent only against a background of numbing boredom.

In the first ten days, I watched, by my count, sixteen games, including odd, hallucinatory match-ups out of some fractured game of Risk: Denmark against Saudi Arabia (1–0), Croatia against Japan (1–0), Nigeria against Bulgaria (1–0). There were a few players who stood out from the general run of bowlegged men in shorts. There were Englishmen (I root for England, from residual Kensington Gardens chauvinism): the pained, gifted O. J. Simpson look-alike Paul Ince; a speedy, tiny boy with a shiny morning face named Michael Owen, only eighteen and just off the Liverpool bench. The French players were dogged, unelectric, powerful, and, as many people pointed out, mostly not ethnically French, with lots of "exotic" names: Zidane, Djorkaeff, Karembeu. Though their countrymen long for the dash and élan of David Ginola and the vanished Eric Cantona, they see the functionary logic of this harder-working side. There were the Argentines and the Germans, who never seem quite as glamorous as, say, the Brazilians and the Dutch, but who have a brutal purposefulness. Between them they have won four of the last six cups. And there were moments of wonder, when a previously unknown — and probably soon to be unknown again — ballplayer would shock himself and his teammates with a single stunning moment. A young Cameroonian named Pierre Njanka, with no major league experience, made his way through the entire Austrian team, his eyes wide as he ducked and swerved, stumbling forward, out of control, hardly believing what he was accomplishing, and then scored. He may spend the rest of his life defined by that run.

But such moments were mostly drowned in tedium and then by something worse. By the time the English players arrived on the scene, on Monday, June 15, everything was already ruined. Hooli-

gans had invaded Marseilles, where England was opening against
Tunisia, and not merely got drunk and beat up shopkeepers but
overran a beach where Tunisian families were picnicking (there is a
big Tunisian community in the south of France) and beat up kids
and moms there. Everyone had known that they were coming. One
source said that the authorities had done their best to keep out the
hardboiled Category C hooligans, but some of them had managed
to sneak in — a rare case of England having a deep bench.

Though headlines about English hooligans sweep the world, they
don't do justice to the terror involved. "Lager louts" and "hooligans" sound vaguely quaint, but these guys are cruel, violent, and
twisted by inarticulate hatred in a way that terrifies the French and
makes them wild partisans of the Scottish team. The persistence
of English hooliganism — the Englishness of hooliganism — can
maybe be explained by the possibility that at some half-conscious
level a lot of English people are proud of their thugs and approve of
their behavior. This approval consists of a toxic combination of
sentimental left-wing anti-Thatcherism (a kind of *Trainspotting*
pride that at least the thugs aren't businessmen) coupled with a
romantic right-wing chauvinism (it's an English tradition to go to
the Continent and hit foreigners). In the Marseilles attacks, most of
the thugs turned out not to be poor kids, or unemployed kids —
they couldn't have afforded the passage over. The thugs were, apparently, mostly postal workers (what is it about mail?), and they
were not going to be damaged in the eyes of their mates for having
gone over to France to beat people up, or for being sent back from
France for having beat people up.

Despite the reports of violence from provincial fronts, Paris itself
has been relatively blasé about the Cup. The streets are peaceful,
the mood calm, the atmosphere pastoral. The Boulevard Saint-Ger-
main has never been so quiet. The morning after the giants' march,
for instance, with Scotland and Brazil about to begin at the Stade
de France, the only evidence I saw of anything unusual was the
appearance of two Scotsmen in kilts waiting for a taxi on the Rue du
Bac. Expecting to hear a war cry ("Ay, we'll leave them samba-
dancin' laddies guid and bloody"), I tentatively wished them good
luck. "We'll need it!" one said feelingly, and the other chimed in,
"It's simply a privilege to be playing Brazil." They turned out to be
lawyers from Hong Kong — Scottish lawyers from Hong Kong, but
lawyers. They talked about the Brazilian esprit, and then got in

their cab and, in perfect French, ordered the driver to go to the Stade de France.

I saw Italy beat Cameroon, 3–0, from the back of a bar in Venice. Watching soccer in Italy, you have the feeling that you have wandered into a family drama more complex and intense than you can understand. Each player — Vieri, Di Biagio — was greeted with a combination of hoots, cheers, and tears so personal and heartfelt that it was almost embarrassing for an outsider to witness. With Italy into the eighth-finals (eighth-finals!), the papers, from left to right, were bursting with pride. "ITALIA PADRONE!" read one headline. "Italy Rules." The curious thing was that Italy played one of the dullest defensive games of all — the famous "blue chain." But this didn't seem to bother anyone. Whatever they were watching for, it wasn't for fun.

Just afterward, I spoke on the phone to an English friend, a big World Cupper.

"How are you getting on with the Cup?" he asked.

"It's a bit — well, don't you think it's a bit lacking in entertainment?" I said weakly.

There was a pause. "Why would you expect it to be entertaining?" he asked, reprovingly.

Perhaps that was a clue. I came back to Paris resolved *not* to be entertained. I watched a double-overtime confrontation between an overmatched Paraguay and an overpressed France. The Paraguayans, who looked worn out from stress, essentially surrendered the idea of scoring and kept dropping back — kicking the ball out, heading it out, willing it out, again and again. It was obvious that their desperate, gallant strategy was to force a nil-nil draw, over 120 minutes, and then "go to penalties," the shoot-out at goal where anything can happen and anyone can win. The nil-nil draw wasn't a "result" they would settle for; it was everything they dreamed of achieving. When the game finally ended, as Laurent Blanc (a traditionally French-sounding name) stumbled a ball into the Paraguayan net, what was most memorable was the subdued triumph. The French celebrated, but they did not exult; the Paraguayans cried — really cried — but they did not despair. They did not seem ruined or emptied out, as American losers do. They seemed relieved. The tears looked like tears of bitter accomplishment. We knew we were going to lose, the faces and the back-pats said, but hey, didn't we hold it off for a while? (*"Héroïque, héroïque,"* murmured the French commentator.)

The next morning, I slipped in a tape I'd made of the fifth game of the NBA finals, for purposes of comparison. It was a French broadcast, and the commentators announced that the game was a test of truth — *une épreuve de vérité* — for the Utah Jazz. To my surprise, I was, after a week of starvation, used to the austerity of soccer scoring. All those basketball points seemed a little loud, a little cheap. Points coming in from left, from right, cheap points, inspired points, stupid points — goals everywhere you looked, more goals than you knew what to do with, democratic goals, all leveled and equal. It was too much — like eating whipped cream straight. And why had I never before noticed the absurd, choppy, broken rhythm of deliberate fouls and time-outs in the last two minutes of the game?

A few nights later, England-Argentina — to see who would go to the quarter-finals. The match started off with two typically exasperating soccer events. After only five minutes, David Seaman, the English goalkeeper, lunged for the ball, and an onrushing Argentine stumbled over him. Penalty and, inevitably, a goal. Then young Owen, who, with his brush cut, looks as if he ought to be wearing a blazer and beanie, got tripped. He acted out the death scene from *Camille* and drew a penalty himself, which was knocked in by Alan Shearer, England's captain. A few minutes later, Owen raced half the length of the field — really sprinting, huffing — mesmerizing an Argentine defenseman, who kept moving back, back, defeated in his own mind, and then he sent it in: 2–1, England! With fifteen seconds left in the half, Argentina got the ball, executed a jagged, pinball-quick exchange of passes, and, shockingly, the ball was bouncing in the net, and the game was tied.

At the start of the second half, David Beckham, the blond midfielder who is engaged to Posh Spice, was expelled from the game, leaving England, like the Spices, a performer short. Though England scored on a corner, the goal was ruled out by the referee for a meaningless, barely visible (but undeniably real) elbow. Nothing happened in thirty minutes of overtime, and the game went into the self-parody of soccer: a series of penalty kicks. With England needing only one more to tie, David Batty, of Newcastle, stepped up and, rushing his shot, fired it right into the diving goaltender. The Argentine side rushed out into the pitch, weeping with joy and exhaustion.

The game had been marked by everything that can exasperate an American fan: the dominance of defense; the disproportion between foul and consequence, the absurd penalty shoot-out, the playacting. (In England they will be arguing did-he-fall-or-was-he-pushed about the first Argentine penalty for years.) But it had been as draining as any contest I'd ever seen.

Soccer was not meant to be enjoyed. It was meant to be experienced. The World Cup is a festival of fate — man accepting his hard circumstances, the near certainty of his failure. There is, after all, something familiar about a contest in which nobody wins and nobody pots a goal. Nil-nil is the score of life. This may be where the difficulty lies for Americans, who still look for Eden out there on the ballfield. But soccer is not meant to be an escape from life. It *is* life, in all its injustice and tedium: we seek unfair advantage, celebrate tiny moments of pleasure as though they were final victories, score goals for the wrong side. (In the first three nights of the World Cup, three of the seventeen goals were "own" goals: a player would head the ball away and watch it backspin past his own goalkeeper, his face a rapidly changing mask of decision, satisfaction, worry, disbelief, and despair.) A bad play or call in baseball — Merkle's boner or Denkinger's call — hurts, but usually there's a saving air of humor. "We're due," "It's our turn," "Wait till next year" are the cheers of American sport. We are optimists, and look to sports to amplify our optimism.

In soccer, tomorrow is a long way off, even in ordinary circumstances, and four years in these special ones. By then, everything will be different; there are no second chances in the World Cup. It is a human contest on a nearly geological time scale. Grievances, injustices rankle for years, decades, forever. But along with that comes, appealingly, a sense of proportion. Accepting the eventual certainty of defeat in turn liberates you to take real joy in any small victory — that one good kick. If American sports are played in Paradise, soccer takes place after the fall. Even its squabbles have their echoes: *Did he fall or was he pushed?* It's the oldest question.

Finally, on a stray, leaking cable channel, I got to see highlights of Detroit and Washington in the Stanley Cup final. I turned it on with

joy and then found, to my shock, that . . . I couldn't see the puck! It
was too small, way too small — a tiny black spot on a vast white
surface, with huge men in bright-colored sweaters hulking over it.
When a goal was scored (and they do get scored), I knew it only by
the subsequent celebration. I squinted at the set and called in my
wife, a pure-bred Canadian, and asked if she could follow the puck.
"I could never follow the puck," she told me.

Had I been corrupted by the Old World's game or enlightened
by it? Another of the old, unanswerable questions. All I knew was
that I was looking forward to the next big match, between France
and Italy. Anything might happen, or nothing at all.

JONATHAN MILES

Big, Ugly Green Fish

FROM SPORTS AFIELD

NOT SO MANY years ago there existed a bar a step or two south of
the courthouse square in Oxford, Mississippi — name of Ireland's
— where the basement was a poolroom with its walls painted into
a massive Confederate flag; where men drinking away disability
checks would commence their rounds at 11 A.M.; and where, not
infrequently, someone would take offense over something someone else said or did or looked like, and crack a longneck bottle over
that latter someone's head. But it wasn't a bad place, truth to tell. It
was open on holidays, and since I spent my Christmas Eves in that
bar — and for at least two years was hopelessly in love with one of its
barmaids — I bear a wistful affection for its memory.

My telling you this, however, has less to do with the bar than with
its men's bathroom, or, rather, a certain portion of the graffiti on
that bathroom's walls. More precisely, the portion where someone
had drawn, with a black Sharpie marker, an astoundingly exquisite,
detailed, annotated map of Sardis Lake, a 58,500-acre reservoir ten
miles north of town. Choice fishing holes were circled and named.
Boat landings were clearly designated. And the damn thing was
huge — you had to spin your head 180 degrees to view it all. All this
while peeing, remember.

I used to ponder the fundamental, centrifugal why of that map,
cradling a beer. Then one winter night — the sort of bone-cold
night that keeps Mississippi women indoors because absolutely no
one, my dear, can wear that much clothing and still look skinny —
it hit me. I was standing there, engaged in the aforementioned
chore, staring at the map. My eyes glazed over in a dreamy haze.

And then — *poof!* — I was there on the lake, the sun ablaze, warm blue beads of water dappling a stretch of monofilament, the shoreline a verdant strip of green horizon.

I realized then that it was this very image — gilt-edged and summery — that had inspired some half-drunk soul to draw a map of a lake on a barroom's bathroom wall. It was to remind himself of what he loved. Some men tape breasty pinups to the wall; some gaze longingly at Corvette calendars; odd specimens like Balzac painted imaginary furniture on garret walls; and still others — like me, and probably like you — choose to conjure up, however possible, the lakes of summer and the great fish they harbor.

Sardis Lake isn't particularly unique, or even, for that matter, special — your chances of landing a trophy bass are far greater at 33,000-acre Ross Barnett Reservoir, in central Mississippi; and it was at Enid Lake, not Sardis, where the world-record five-pound three-ounce white crappie was yanked from the water — but it is emblematic. Like nearly all the South's big inland waters, its origins have little to do with the Book of Genesis. It was created via the Sardis Dam in the 1940s, its raison d'être being flood control. I suppose, officially, that its raison still is. But not to those of us who fish it, who dip our boats into its waters in the faint light of dawn, or who sit with a bait pail and canepole on the rock cliffs at the spillway, and certainly not to those Legionnaire types among us who wrestle catfish from their lairs barehanded. To us, the lake is about fish. The water is just pretty wrapping paper.

Consider Buddy Jordan. He's a Louisiana attorney in his fifties, flirting with a head of gray hair, an Everyman in a gimme cap. I met Jordan several years ago when the battery on his Ford Explorer went kaput at the lake's Hurricane Landing. His daughter had been at Ole Miss for five years, he told me, working toward "an M.R.S. degree."

For all five of those years he'd been venturing north to Mississippi, toting his bass boat, ostensibly to visit his daughter, though sometimes seeing her for just an hour or so, maybe for lunch, en route to the lake. One August, early on, when his daughter was going through sorority rush, he had caught the largest bass — in south Louisiana fashion, he called it a green trout — of his life. At least thirteen pounds, he said. But he'd caught it by its tail. He was reeling in a lure — a Rattlin' Rapala, he said, damn fish should've heard it coming — when he felt a queer strike. It felt like something big, real big, but the way it was fighting . . . It was strange, running in all the wrong directions.

Upon landing the fish, he understood what had happened. "Treble hook in the ass," he said, somewhat forlornly. You must understand that this wasn't a story told in jest. Buddy Jordan had watched glory pop like a soap bubble. He'd thrown the bass back into the lake, for a man can't claim rights to a fish caught accidentally, and there it remains. Jordan's greatest fear was that his daughter would graduate from college, leaving him no excuse to pursue his lost prize so far from home. I should add that it was Jordan writing the checks for her tuition.

Just a bass, some folks might say — but, please, not to Jordan, not to me, and probably not to you. That the largemouth bass is an ugly fish (and let's be honest, it is) pursued in sometimes ugly places (vast southern impoundments, nothing but water, buttonbush, cypress stumps, and riprap) by occasionally ugly men (them of the portable stereo and cellular phone set, whose boats trail beer cans like honeymoon sedans) makes no difference whatsoever.

Of course I would prefer, for the purposes of this valentine, there to be something mystical and soulful about the pursuit of largemouth bass in the South's big, flat waters — even something subtle would be nice. Alas, it's not to be. The fish are hogs, the fishing is muscular, the philosophy dim. Aesthetics are for trout and their cute clear streams. They have nothing to do with the bass fisherman in a $30,000 glitter-painted boat tearing across the surface of a flood-control reservoir toward some fat-bass willow flats.

A summer or two ago I was out on Sardis Lake with my teacher and pal Barry Hannah, the only man I know of to kill a fish just by looking at it. (The landed bass glanced up at Hannah's face, which is nothing if not kind, and suffered a major coronary. We puzzled about that one for a while, and I think Hannah felt a little bad.) It was a Saturday in June, one of those blustery, cranky, weird-weather days, and the two of us were fishing from Hannah's little plastic tub boat, the sort of watercraft you can carry out of Wal-Mart over your head. Hannah had had a hot tip: there was a cove on the north side of the lake where the bass were thick as butter.

Unfortunately, a storm crashed in from the east just as we were piddling via trolling motor across the vast expanse of wet acreage. It was a biblical storm; our tiny ship was tossed. We pressed on, however, and when the storm passed, fished the dickens out of that little cove. Hannah's hot tip was cold, but that's beside the point. The fact that two grown men would venture out in a boat smaller than the New York City phone book in potentially foul weather just for the chance to snare an ugly greenish fish is both ludicrous and beautiful, and is offered here as merely anecdotal evidence that there is a freakish fanaticism to bass fishing that is awfully hard to explain. Just ask Buddy Jordan.

Ireland's is gone now, which is a shame, and with it went the map on the bathroom wall, But the lake, of course, remains. As summer heightens and intensifies, so too will the activity upon and around it. The die-hard bassers will crowd the boat landings at dawn, sliding their sleek, clean crafts into the water. There will be men with their pals, making lewd jokes; men with their children, instructing them in the art of knots and the science of fishing; and men with their wives, quiet and content. Later in the morning the canepolers will arrive, the old black women with their lawn chairs and stringers and Jesus-faced cardboard fans. Soon thereafter the eighteen-year-olds will come to the water's edge to drink beer and turn up the Memphis country station on their Delco car stereos and flex their tattoos in the hazy sunlight.

If Buddy Jordan was lucky enough to talk his daughter into graduate school, he'll be there too, out in his boat, hoping like hell that he'll finally pull in that thirteen-pound largemouth with the curious scar on its tail. And somewhere too there will be an amateur cartographer who loves the lake so much he once felt compelled to paint it on a bathroom wall, stand back, and grin.

MELISSA KING

It's All in the Game

FROM CHICAGO READER

Eckhart Park, Noble and Chicago

I like my husband, but I love my snowmobile. That's what his T-shirt said. He didn't speak English too well, and I bet he bought the shirt at a thrift store because he liked the color — an appealing purple, actually. Somebody must have told him what "husband" meant, because he had obviously tried to eradicate the word with white shoe polish. You could still see it, but I guess he succeeded in changing the message. *Yo soy heterosexual.*

I don't know his name. I played basketball with him, his brother, and their roommate today. They were new to the game, but they played hard. The most experienced player (also the tallest and the best English speaker) was the one who asked me to play. I had been at the other end of the court shooting baskets, stealing glances at them, knowing they were returning the favor. When you're a thirty-year-old white woman shooting around by yourself in a park populated largely by Latinos, everybody looks at you.

This is the way it works. I shoot around, make a point to have them notice me clandestinely checking them out. I stand tall and swagger a little, as if to say, "I got skills. I play all the time. I know what you're thinking. The question is, are you good enough to play with me?" I can't actually say "I got skills," or "My bad" or "I got next" or any of that stuff. I hate it when white people try to talk street. But that's how I feel.

So I did my little routine and the tall good-English-speaking guy asked me to play two-on-two. My team won both games. And I played some more after that, with another group of guys; the teams just kept melding and interchanging, with new groups of people coming to play. The sun was beating down and a slightly sickening chocolate smell wafted west from the Blommer factory on Kinzie. I played for hours.

Horner Park, Montrose and California

Tori, Melinda, and I got into a discussion tonight about whether or not the person we'd all seen as we walked into the gym was a teenage boy or a woman in her twenties.

Tori was changing into her basketball clothes right there on the side of the court. It was a little brazen, but people hadn't started arriving yet for the Monday night women's open gym.

"It's a guy," Tori said, standing there in her bra.

"She has breasts," Melinda argued.

"He's not wearing a bra."

"So?"

There's a television commercial where Sheryl Swoopes is talking about what she likes to buy with her Discover card. "I'm very prissy," she says, and then you see her playing playground ball with a bunch of men, screaming like a crazed warrior *Put up or shut up!* as she drives the lane.

"I love to get my hair done, get manicures, pedicures, but my greatest weakness is shoes," she says in the next cut, walking through a mall in a trendy outfit.

We never did decide.

John, who for some reason plays with us at the women's open gym, was there; it was just the four of us because it was really too hot to play and no one else showed up. John's not quite as good as he looks like he would be, but he looks like he would be good. A guy I used to date has a poster in his house captioned "Shirts and Skins." It's a drawing of a bunch of black men going up for a rebound, stretched out all long-limbed and elegantly gangly toward the sky, everyone moving in what looks from a distance to be a synchronized unit, like a flock of geese falling in instinctively for flight. John looks like one of those guys.

John likes us. He's there almost every Monday, and I always

notice him listening to what everybody's saying, even though he never says anything. So I said, "John, do you think that person out front is a man or a woman?" He was shooting around, looking like he was in his own world (he's a little cross-eyed). "Boy," he said.

"This guy walked by me once," Melinda said, taking a shot, "and he goes, 'Hey dude.' I told him, I said, 'Hey, I'm a woman.'"

Then Tori said she was in a car wreck once, and while waiting for the ambulance to arrive she was laid out on the floor of a convenience store. People kept coming up to her and looking over her and saying, "What's up with dude?" She said she kept fading in and out of consciousness saying, "Hey, I'm a woman."

I've never been mistaken for a man that I know of, but when I'm going for rebounds, screaming like a karate master, wringing the sweat from my shirt, making faces I probably wouldn't want to see, I feel kind of weird. Sometimes it occurs to me that I'm aggressive. Not "assertive" — aggressive.

Tori said to me once, "Girl, you're like a Reebok commercial. This is your world. You go."

It's a good way to feel.

Wicker Park, Damen and Wicker Park

Sometimes I really like white people. Not always, and you might say not even very often, but sometimes I really like them. Today I rode over to Wicker Park on my bike and got stuck in the rain, and waited it out under an awning. Afterward three white guys came over and played with me. We played two-on-two, and they were so without egos.

As they should have been — they sucked. They were fouling the hell out of each other, totally laughing, having a good time. I think they were a little drunk. This guy, Vince, who had been the first one to come over and shoot around with me, was my teammate. After one particularly good play he stuck both hands behind his back, palms up, while he was running backward down the court, for me to slap him ten. It was stupid, but he knew it was stupid. That's kind of fun. In fact, I think it's pretty evolved.

Another time in this same park I was shooting around with a kid called Orlando. His three friends rode up on two bicycles to watch us. The Gap can only dream of capturing the urban slouch of these kids in their baggy jeans, sitting on two-thirds-enough bicycle.

They kept saying, "Yeah, she's going to the WNBA next week. She got a right, she got a left, she got a shot, got some D." Orlando was teasing me too, pretending he was shoving me around and laughing, saying stuff like, "All right, it's on now" and "You know I'm mad now." I was kidding him back, saying, "Thanks for the warning, Orlando." I like that kid.

I tried to tell Orlando about how, when you're playing defense, you need to look at someone's belly. How you don't look at his face, because he can fake you out with his face but he can't fake you out with his belly. I wanted Orlando to be good. He liked it that I was telling him something, but I think he already knew about the belly.

A group of older guys started playing on the other end of the court. They were playing twenty-one. I hate that game sometimes, because it's so rebound-oriented. I love to get rebounds, but I can't get any rebounds against those guys. "Orlando," I said, "do you think those guys would let me play with them?" Orlando looked at me funny. "I don't think so. They're kind of rough," he said.

Orlando left with his friends. I did my thing, hoping the older guys would ask me to play. They never did, even though I know they saw me wanting to get in the game. I rode home thinking those sons of bitches made me sick. They didn't know if I could play or not.

Vince had written his phone number on my arm with a felt-tip pen after we finished playing. I wrote it down somewhere else when I got home, but I don't know what I did with it now.

Eckhart Park

Snowmobile wasn't there today, but his two compadres were. The court was so crowded I couldn't get out there. The other Snowmobiles were having the same problem, so I sat down on the ground next to them.

It makes me so mad that I can't speak Spanish. I had three semesters of it in college, for God's sake. And I made A's all three times.

So I chatted in English with Snowmobile #2 and Snowmobile #3. They told me they were both taking English classes four times a

week. They kept saying they still couldn't speak English. I told them
yes they could.

I couldn't understand why they weren't getting in the game. I
mean, for me, being a woman, sometimes you just get the sense that
a court is not exactly an equal opportunity situation, but they're
guys. It seemed like any guy should be able to play.

They said they weren't good enough. I told them yes they were.

When I was in college taking those Spanish classes, I used to have
dreams where I could really speak Spanish. In my dreams the words
would just be flying out in whole sentences with a perfect accent.

A young black guy was bouncing his ball around on the side of
the court, screaming at the players in the game: "I'm gonna kick
ya'll's tired asses when I get in there!"

Snowmobile #2 was telling me I could come to play with them
next weekend at this park they play at sometimes where there's
always plenty of room. "They have sodas," he said.

I have those same kind of dreams about basketball. That I'm
making every shot, flying toward the basket, never tired, no one can
stop me. When I wake up I feel like those dogs too old to run anymore. You can see them chasing rabbits in their sleep, their legs
twitching.

Wicker Park

"What's up kittycat?" That's what this old park dude was saying to
me as I sat on my bike scanning the court, seeing if I wanted to play.

"What's up kittycat you gonna shoot some hoops you gonna play
me some one-on-one can you dunk it?"

Damn. I almost turned around and rode off, because I knew this
guy was gonna stick to me the whole time I was there, but there was
an empty hoop and I all of a sudden felt irritated about having to
leave a court because of this old park dude.

The guy I told you about earlier that I used to date, the one with
the poster, used to say I should stay away from the criminal element.
He thought I was reckless. He won't ride the el, and he never
gives money to homeless people on the street. But he volunteers at
homeless shelters around the holidays and sits on the boards of
several charitable organizations.

Park Dude was walking away, so I shot for a while. Then he came

back and started shooting around with me. There's a certain eti-
quette when two people shoot around. One person shoots from the
outside and the other stands under the hoop and rebounds. When
the shooter misses he goes in for a lay-up, and it's the other guy's
turn. Everybody knows that.

Park Dude was not so great to shoot around with. He kept throwing the ball back to me too hard, or over my head or off to the side
so that I had to jump or make a quick move to catch it. Every once
in a while it got past me and I would have to run after it, trying to
stop it before it went onto the other court or rolled into the middle
of the softball game going on twenty feet away. It was really pissing
me off. If I were a male or truly urban I would have said, "Man,
would you *watch* that shit? What's the matter with you? *Damn.*" But
I'm not.

The thing about Park Dude was that he could really shoot a hook
shot. Who the hell shoots a hook shot?

A bunch of kids trickled onto the court. At this particular park I
sometimes find myself in a game with kids of all shapes and sizes.
It's my ball and no one else has one, and I know they want to play,
so I play.

A little white girl asked me how old I was. She nearly fell over
when I told her I was thirty. "How old are you?" I asked her. "Ten."

Park Dude let fly with one of his hook shots, missing the hoop
completely this time. "He's weird," the girl said. "He smells like
beer." He was, he did, I thought, but far as I could tell there was
nothing wrong with his hearing.

Park Dude said he was getting hot, and he took his shirt off. He
had a long, vertical scar running down his rib cage and stomach.

There's a sign in the park that says, WARNING YOU ARE IN A
SAFETY ZONE PENALTIES FOR SELLING DRUGS OR OTHER CRIMI-
NAL ACTIVITY IN THIS PARK ARE SEVERELY INCREASED. I've
seen guys walk past each other making secretive handoffs, or drive
up in separate cars, walk off together, then come back a few minutes later and go their separate ways. The park is segregated, with
the park dudes sticking to the Damen side and the hipsters playing
Frisbee with their dogs in the back corner. All over, savvy little
independent kids are running around.

I worry about what happens to a harmless park dude's brain
when he's treated like dirt by arrogant white girls. My personal

opinion is that inclusion is safer than exclusion, but I'm not positive about that.

All of a sudden I did feel a little reckless, not for being there myself but for being the thing that brought the Park Dude and the little girl together. After the game petered out, I hung around for a while, making sure everyone had scattered before I rode home.

Wicker Park

I wanted to play so bad today. This morning I couldn't get up to save myself. I hit the snooze alarm for an hour.

I muddled through work, came straight home, got on my bicycle, and went looking for a game. I ended up at Wicker Park, shooting around with a little kid, another little kid, and his toddler brother, killing time until a game developed.

I kept grinning at the toddler because he was cute, but his brother didn't grin; he included him. He expected him to play, but he wasn't too rough on him. The toddler just ran around with the ball, happy as could be. He could dribble pretty good for a three-year-old.

All of a sudden a commotion broke out on the other court and we all got still, watching.

"Why you testin' me, nigga? Why don't you test summa these other niggas!" one kid was saying to a shorter kid, pushing him in his face. Two middle-aged guys were standing on the side of the court. They were Park District employees; I could tell because they were wearing those plastic ID holders on their shirts. One of the other boys got between the kids, and then one of the Park District guys walked over and said something. It was about damn time.

"Gentlemen, gentlemen," he said. "Let's just play ball. Gentlemen." But those two kids didn't care about some middle-aged white guy with a pot belly and an ID tag. They just kept on. "Man if you ever touch my shit again, I'll kill you. Come on, nigga, swing! Do it!"

I don't know why it ended, but it did. The taller kid stalked off, daring the other kid to follow and fight him. The older brother on my court looked over at the toddler and said gently, "Boo, wanna go see a fight?" The toddler just laughed, running around in his stiff-legged toddler way, holding the ball.

After a while the game on the other court disintegrated and an older guy asked me if I'd like to play with him and some other guys. I said sure. I was the only woman and the only white person. I played the best I've ever played, only erring a few times, when I misjudged how fast these young guys were and how high they could jump. I'm not that great a shooter, but that night I was. They kept yelling at each other, looking for someone to blame every time I made a shot. "Who's guarding that girl?" They started calling me "little Larry Bird."

We all have our moments.

The guy who asked me to play was an adult; everyone else was a teen. He was intense, and the kids were kind of laughing at him until we started kicking their butts. The guy who asked me to play kept saying to the scoffing teens, "You know I play hard." The rest of them got into it in spite of themselves, though nobody could ever remember the score.

Riding home, I remembered how I used to sit around the house waiting for something to happen. It was good not to be doing that.

Eckhart Park

My friend Laurie used to tell me how she couldn't go to church without about three guys asking her out. It was the biggest pickup situation you ever saw, evidently, because everyone there wanted to meet somebody at church. She would joke that all the single people at her church were "datin' for Jesus."

Well, the same thing happens in basketball. I met a guy on the court today. Let's call him Peter. I saw Peter looking at me all intense from the other end of the court. He made sure he got in the game I was in, and then he hung around afterward and asked if I wanted to go have a drink later. I said I did; he was very cute, and he was a good player. A guy doesn't have to be that good for me to like him, but it doesn't hurt.

The thing about some guys is, the most important thing about you is where they met you. For instance, I met a guy at a dog party once. It was a dog party because it was a party everyone brought a dog to, and it was supposed to help you mingle and meet other dog owners. The dogs kept fighting with each other and trying to get at each other's butts, which was potentially embarrassing for strangers trying to chat, but people just kept acting like they didn't notice and trying to meet one another.

I went to the party with this girl I worked with, who kind of talked me into it. Neither of us actually had a dog, so we borrowed one, that's how hot she was to go. Single women in their thirties are always latching on to me to do stuff like this. We don't even really like each other necessarily, but they need someone to go do these man-meeting things with. It's incredibly depressing, and usually I run the other way when I smell these situations coming, but this time I went, mostly because I was always telling this woman no.

So at this dog party, this guy, Ed, decided he liked me. And he did everything right. He asked me out for a polite date, and I went, and it wasn't too terrible so I said I'd go out with him again. He introduced me to his friends, always asked me for the next date before he left. He was sweatin' me, as they say.

But there was no connection. The only reason he wanted to go out with me was that he could just imagine telling everybody how we met at a dog party. The story was all the cuter because I didn't even have a dog. It was very *That Girl*.

People don't want to say they met in a bar or through the personal ads. There's always got to be some damn cute story or you don't have a chance.

Peter was all over me because he met me the way he always envisioned meeting *the* woman: on the basketball court. That's what he said, "I always wanted to meet a woman on the basketball court." Me personally, I don't really care how I meet someone, so long as one of us doesn't bore the other half to death.

Horner Park

There's this other guy that keeps asking me out too. He plays with our coed group on Wednesday nights. Lucky me, he prefers my butt to all the other Wednesday night butts. I should write him a thank-you note, I guess. But I already heard him say he has a girlfriend, the dumbass. Oh, and guess what: the girlfriend lives in another city.

The thing about men is, they'll ruin every last thing you like if you let them.

Peter and I went out for a week. We rode our bikes to the lake, played basketball, sat on park benches kissing. All very romantic.

He was funny, although he wasn't the kind of funny where he knew he was funny. The day we went riding I met him at his house, and he came out carrying a bottle of wine, some plastic cups, a corkscrew, and two sheets to sit on, all in a white plastic garbage bag. That kind of stuff can be kind of funny.

When he kissed me he was always pulling the back of my hair. I have short hair, and I kept thinking he was wishing I had longer hair so he could really grab on and pull. I really wanted to say, Hey what the hellareya doin', but I didn't.

One night he asked me to come to his house and watch a Bears game. I was a little late getting there, and when he answered his door he just looked at me kind of sternly and said, "You're late."

I think he was drunk, and there were two joints sitting on the kitchen counter. He was talking a mile a minute. In fact, I was starting to notice, Peter was the sort of person who didn't let you get a word in edgewise. And, if he didn't think you were listening closely enough, he would move closer and talk louder.

We sat down to watch the game, and he lit up one of the joints. I hate to admit it, but I smoked some. I used to smoke in college, but I don't anymore. I used to get too paranoid. I'm kind of self-con-scious already and pot just makes it worse.

All of a sudden I couldn't tell if Peter was really stupid or just pretended to be as a joke. And I hadn't really noticed he was stupid before. I mean, he wasn't by any means the smartest guy I had ever run into, but I just thought he was really physical, that he related to the world in a physical way. If I think a guy is kind of cute, and he entertains me at all, and if he seems to like me, I can kind of make excuses for him and overlook a lot of rude and just plain stupid behavior. A lot of women do that. Decent men without girlfriends must really get sickened by it.

So I was sitting on this chair, really stoned, trying to sit up straight. Peter sat down beside me in the chair and put his arm around me, and he was kind of absentmindedly digging his fingers into my arm, hard. It seemed compulsive. It was like he couldn't help himself, it felt so good to him. And then, and this is really embarrassing, Peter got up and started gyrating around like a Chippendale dancer, saying, "So, what should I do . . . do you want me to dance for you?" I just kept hoping he meant to be cheesy, to make me laugh. But I didn't laugh, because I was afraid he was serious. All I could think of to say was, "Man, I'm stoned."

All of a sudden, Peter picked me up and carried me over to an open window. I never like it when guys physically pick me up. I know it's supposed to be all romantic, but I just think it's embarrassing. It's too dramatic unless they're going to laugh and maybe act like you're so heavy they're gonna throw their back out or something.

Then I started to worry that he was going to sort of chuck me out the window. I squirmed to get down without saying why, and then Peter said, "I wouldn't throw you out the window."

That's when I really got scared. Peter's face looked really brutish to me, and when he moved anywhere near me it felt like he was trying to dominate me, not just get close. After I got out of his King Kong–like grasp, he tried to pick me up on his back, like we were going to play piggyback. And his movements were slow and, I don't know, just slow, like a dumb animal's. I got the distinct impression that he wanted to hurt me. That even if I said I would have sex with him he would still want to hurt me. I kept thinking about the post-racquetball scene in *Cape Fear*, the new version, with Robert De Niro. If you saw the movie, you know what I'm talking about.

Peter kept saying, "Why are you so afraid of me, try to have a little self-confidence, why don'tcha . . . I know I can make you feel good," and other creepy stuff like that. I got the hell out of there. I was afraid to drive but I drove home anyway, thinking I was going to go mad the whole time if I had to drive that car one more inch.

But like I said, I quit smoking pot because it makes me paranoid.

Wicker Park

These three girls I had seen before came running over, saying, "There's that girl again!"

They looked like a female version of the Fat Albert gang. I asked them if they wanted to shoot around, and the youngest one, who wore about twenty-five colored barrettes in her hair and jeans about three sizes too big, took the ball.

"I can't do it," she said every time she missed a shot.

"Yes you can, you just need to practice some. Nobody makes it every time."

"Why aren't you shootin'?" she asked me.

"I'm all right, go ahead."

These girls, you had to draw them in. I've never seen any boy worry about if he was keeping you from playing.

One girl wouldn't play at all. We tried to play two-on-two, but she just wouldn't play. She kept saying she didn't know how, and she couldn't make it, and all that stuff. The youngest one's younger brother came up and tried to play. He was running all over the court, never dribbling, a big grin on his face, saying "almost" every time he shot the ball.

The girls didn't play long, but they didn't leave, either. They hung around at the edge of the court, watching. You could see them kind of whispering together and looking at different boys.

"Where's you girls' boyfriends?" I asked them, just to see what they'd say.

"Twanisha got her a man," the little one said.

"Where's Twanisha's boyfriend?"

"He over there with his boys."

"That why you won't play basketball, Twanisha? What's his name?"

She shrugged her shoulders.

They were doing it already, waiting around for something to happen. Damn, it made me sad. It reminded me of this story I saw on TV, on 20/20 maybe, about whether or not little girls could learn as well when they had boys in their class. They couldn't, some researchers had decided, because the boys just got in there first, talking faster and talking louder. I wanted to shake Twanisha and say, "Listen here, young lady, you're gonna spend your life falling for arrogant men and sitting around a dirty apartment waiting for them to call if you don't start taking an interest in some things."

If I ever have a daughter, she'll have to learn how not to be stupid about men. I don't know how I'll teach her, because I don't entirely know myself. But somehow she's got to know early on it's okay to miss some shots on your own, that you can't let other people always do your shooting for you.

I started playing with some adults, so I told a bunch of adolescents who had walked up that they could play with my ball if they took care of it. They had a big game going before long.

One of the guys on their court was mad because one of his peers had defected to play with us. Leon was on my team. He was two feet shorter than almost everyone else out there, but he could play. He was smart and serious about it. This other kid was screaming at him: "Oh, yeah, I see how it is. You wanna play over there with them. Man, I hate people like you!" He was joined by a glaring fellow malcontent who ran up to us and said, really sarcastic, "Can I play?" Suddenly the tension was racial, because most of the adults were white.

Once our ball flew over onto their court, and the loud kid shot it into their hoop like he thought it was the ball from their game, or I should say my ball. He looked over at us and went, "Oh, is that your ball?"

Leon ignored them. He wouldn't even look at them. We just kept playing. I kept looking over to make sure my ball was still there, and sure enough, the next time I looked up, all the kids and my ball were gone.

So as our game was winding down, I asked Leon, "Hey, do you know those kids that were over there?"

"Which ones?"

"Those ones that were playing with my ball over there."

There they were, standing about a hundred yards away with my ball. I wondered if Leon had seen them.

"Come on man, you got that girl's ball! Bring it back! Bring it back now!"

Thomas threw it across the playground at us, and we went back to our game.

Wicker Park

Oh my God, David. That child is pure love. He comes to the park with his mom on Saturdays. She's a good player; you can tell she was really good in high school. She coaches a bunch of girls in the gym at Wicker Park.

I played with her in a pickup game once, and after it was over I shot around and David came over to talk to me.

"Where's your friend?" he asked me.

"What friend?"

"Your friend. She wears black shoes too."

David thought he remembered me from somewhere, I guess, so I told him I didn't know who he meant, was he sure it was me he had seen before, and he said yes, he was sure.

I asked him how old he was. He's five.

"I play with my mama."

"You do? Was she the one who was playing with me a little earlier? She's pretty good."

She came over to shoot around with us.

"She made me in her stomach," David informed me. I said, Really, how 'bout that.

He said something quietly to his mom. "Well, she's pretty good too," his mom said.

A few months later I was playing a two-on-two game and saw David's mom again. She told us to come inside the gym and play if we wanted. After the game, David came running over to me, shouting, "Hi Melissa!"

I couldn't remember his name. What an asshole I am, I thought as I talked to him, said it looked like his front teeth were growing in and asked what he had been doing. Then he ran around all over the gym with kids his age while his mom and I and a bunch of teens played a game.

In the middle of the game David came over and said, "Maaama . . . maaama . . . maaaaaaama!" His mom, the point guard, picked up her dribble and said, "What!"

David hesitated, caught off guard by her attention. "Do you want me?" he asked. He looked at his mom expectantly.

"I want you," she said, "but not right this minute."

Satisfied, David resumed running around, and we went on with our game.

DAVID HALBERSTAM

Jordan's Moment

FROM THE NEW YORKER

THE DESOLATE NEIGHBORHOOD on the West Side of Chicago
where the Bulls play their home games is very quiet these days.
Their gleaming new arena, the United Center, is set down there as
if on a moonscape. All twelve pre-Christmas home games have been
canceled, because of the labor dispute between the owners and the
players, which was initiated by the owners in a lockout described as
a struggle between short millionaires and tall millionaires, or between billionaires and millionaires. The National Basketball Association, which would have entered its fifty-second season this fall,
seems to have fallen victim to its own dizzying success, one that has
seen the player payroll increase by an estimated 2,500 percent
in the last twenty years. The incident that probably triggered the
lockout occurred about a year ago, when the Minnesota Timber-
wolves extended the contract of a gifted young player named Kevin
Garnett, paying him $126 million over seven years. The Timber-
wolves' general manager, the former Boston Celtic Kevin McHale,
completed the deal; unhappy with the direction of the league and
his own part in it, he later noted, "We have our hand on the neck of
the golden goose and we're squeezing hard."

In Chicago, where for much of the last decade the best basketball
team in the country has played, the silence is particularly painful.
The last time games were played here, the Bulls, led by Michael
Jordan, were contesting for their sixth NBA championship and
playing against a favored team, the Utah Jazz. It was an indelible
series, the memory of which serves as this year's only fare — and it
is melancholy fare — for basketball junkies everywhere.

Michael Jordan was thirty-five, and arguably the dominant athlete in American sports, as he led Chicago into Salt Lake City. He
was nearing the end of his career, and he was, if anything, a more
complete player than ever. What his body could no longer accomplish in terms of pure physical ability he could compensate for with
his shrewd knowledge of both the game and the opposing players.
Nothing was wasted. There was a new quality, almost an iciness, to
the way he played now. In 1995, after Jordan returned to basketball
from his year-and-a-half-long baseball sabbatical, he spent the summer in Hollywood making the movie *Space Jam,* but he demanded
that the producers build a basketball court where he could work
out every day. Old friends dropping by the Warner lot noticed that
he was working particularly hard on a shot that was already a minor
part of his repertoire but which he was now making a signature shot
— a jumper where he held the ball, faked a move to the basket, and
then at the last minute, when he finally jumped, fell back slightly,
giving himself almost perfect separation from the defensive player.
Because of his jumping ability and his threat to drive, that shot was
virtually unguardable. More, it was a very smart player's concession
to the changes in his body wrought by time, and it signified that he
was entering a new stage in his career. What professional basketball
men were now seeing was something that had been partly masked
earlier in his career by his singular physical ability and the artistry
of what he did, and that something was a consuming passion not
just to excel but to dominate. "He wants to cut your heart out and
then show it to you," his former coach Doug Collins said. "He's
Hannibal Lecter," Bob Ryan, the *Boston Globe*'s expert basketball
writer, said. When a television reporter asked the Bulls' center, Luc
Longley, for a one-word description of Jordan, Longley's response
was "Predator."

"The athlete you remind me of the most is Jake LaMotta," the
Bulls' owner, Jerry Reinsdorf, told Jordan one day, referring to the
fearless middleweight fighter of another era, "because the only way
they can stop you is to kill you."

"Who's Jake LaMotta?" Jordan answered.

In Utah during the 1977 NBA finals, Jordan had woken up before
Game Five violently ill. It seemed impossible that he would play.
(Whether it was altitude sickness or food poisoning no one was ever

quite sure.) At about 8 A.M., one of Jordan's bodyguards, fixtures in his entourage, called Chip Schaefer, the team trainer, to say that Jordan had been up all night with flu-like symptoms and was seriously ill. Rushing to Jordan's room, Schaefer found him curled up in the fetal position and wrapped in blankets, though the thermostat had been cranked up to its maximum. The greatest player in the world looked like a weak little zombie.

Schaefer immediately hooked Jordan up to an IV and tried to get as much fluid into him as possible. He also gave him medication and decided to let him rest as much as he could that morning. Word of Jordan's illness quickly spread among journalists at the Delta Center, where the game was to be played, and the general assumption was that he would not play. One member of the media, though, was not so sure — James Worthy, who, after a brilliant career with the Los Angeles Lakers, was working for the Fox network. Having played with Jordan at North Carolina and against him in the pros, Worthy knew not only how Michael drove himself but, even more important, how he motivated himself. When reports circulated that Michael had a fever of 102, Worthy told the other Fox reporters that the fever meant nothing. "He'll play," Worthy said. "He'll figure out what he can do, he'll conserve his strength in other areas, and he'll have a big game."

In the locker room before the game, Jordan's teammates were appalled by what they saw. Michael, normally quite dark, was a color somewhere between white and gray, Bill Wennington, the Bulls' backup center, recalled, and his eyes, usually so vital, looked dead.

At first, fans watching at home could not understand how Jordan could play at all. Then they were pulled into the drama of the event, which had by now transcended mere basketball and taken on the nature of an entirely different challenge. Early in the second quarter, Utah led 36–20, but Jordan played at an exceptional level — he scored twenty-one points in the first half — and at halftime his team was down only four points. The Bulls managed to stay close in the second half. With forty-six seconds left in the game, and Utah leading by a point, Jordan was fouled going to the basket. "Look at the body language of Michael Jordan," Marv Albert, the announcer, said. "You have the idea that he has difficulty just standing up." Jordan made the first of two foul shots, which tied the score, and somehow grabbed the loose ball after the missed second shot.

Then, with twenty-five seconds left, the Jazz inexplicably left him open, and he hit a three-pointer, which gave Chicago an 88–85 lead and the key to a 90–88 win. He ended up with thirty-eight points, fifteen of them in the last quarter.

Throughout the 1997–98 season, Jordan had wanted to meet Utah in the finals again, in no small part because after the 1997 finals too many people had said that if only Utah had had the home-court advantage the Jazz would have won. He was eager to show that true warriors could win as handily on the road, and he was also eager to show that although Karl Malone was a great player, whose abilities he admired, there was a significant degree of difference in their respective abilities.

Unlike more talented teams, Utah almost never made mental mistakes during a game, and at the Delta Center, home of some of the league's noisiest fans, a game that was at all close could easily turn into a very difficult time for a visitor. In the Western Conference finals, Utah had gone up against the Lakers, a young team led by the immense Shaquille O'Neal, and with considerably more athletic ability, and yet the Jazz swept the Lakers in four games, making them look like a group of befuddled playground all-stars. "Playing them is like the project guys against a team," Nick Van Exel, the Laker point guard, said after the series. "The project guys always want to do the fancy behind-the-back dribbles, the spectacular plays and the dunks, while the Jazz are a bunch of guys doing pick-and-rolls and the little things. They don't get caught up in the officiating, they don't get down on each other, they don't complain. They stand as a team and stay focused."

Utah was a *team*, smart and well coached, and its players never seemed surprised late in a game. No team in the league executed its offense, particularly the interplay between John Stockton and Karl Malone, with the discipline of Utah. But that was a potential vulnerability, the Chicago coaches believed, for the Jazz were very predictable. What worked night after night against ordinary teams during the regular season might not work in a prolonged series against great defensive players. The price of discipline might be a gap in creativity — the ability to freelance — when the disciplined offense was momentarily checkmated.

Some of this could be seen in the difference between Jordan and

Malone. Each had improved greatly after he entered the league, and each had the ability to carry his team night after night. But Jordan's ability to create shots for himself, and thereby dominate at the end of big games when the defensive pressure on both sides had escalated significantly, was dramatically greater than Malone's. Malone had improved year by year not only as a shooter but as someone who could pass out of the double team. Still, like most big, powerful men, he could not improvise nearly as well as Jordan, and he was very much dependent on teammates like Stockton to create opportunities for him. What the Chicago coaches, and Jordan himself, believed was that the Bulls would be able to limit Karl Malone in the fourth quarter of a tight game but that Utah would never be able to limit Michael Jordan, because of Jordan's far greater creativity.

There was one other thing that the Chicago coaches and Jordan thought about Malone, which gave them extra confidence as they got ready for the final series, and which differed from how most other people in the league perceived Malone. Malone, the Chicago staff believed, had not come into the league as a scorer or a shooter, but he had worked so hard that he was now one of the premier shooters among the league's big men, averaging just under thirty points a game for the last ten years. But deep in his heart, they thought, he did not have the psyche of a shooter like Larry Bird, Reggie Miller, or even Jordan; therefore, it remained something of an alien role. At the end of a big game, they suspected, with the game on the line, that would be a factor.

The Bulls' coach, Phil Jackson, hoped to steal Game One of the championship, in Salt Lake City, because the Jazz had had ten days off and were rusty. But it had taken the Bulls seven exhausting games to beat the Indiana Pacers for the Eastern Conference title, and they came into Game One slow and tired, constantly a step behind in their defensive rotations. Even so, they made up eight points in the fourth quarter to force Utah into overtime before they lost.

The Bulls recovered, however, and stole Game Two, and, with that, the Jazz lost the home-court advantage they had worked so hard for all season. Worse, the series now seemed to be turning out the way the Chicago coaches had wanted it to, with the Bulls' guards limiting Stockton's freedom of movement and isolating Malone, who, on his own, was no longer a dominant presence.

Game Three, in Chicago, went badly for Utah. On defense, the Bulls played a nearly perfect game: they stole the ball, they cut off passing lanes, and their defensive rotations were so quick that Utah's shots almost always seemed desperate — forced up at the last second. It was as if the Chicago players had known on each Jazz possession exactly what Utah was going to try to do. The final score was 96–54, the widest margin in the history of the finals, and Utah's fifty-four points were the lowest total in any NBA game since the introduction of the twenty-four-second clock, in 1954. "This is actually the score?" Jerry Sloan, the Utah coach, said in his post-game press conference, holding up the stat sheet. "I thought it was a hundred and ninety-six. It sure seemed like a hundred and ninety-six."

Game Four was more respectable, with the Bulls winning 86–82. But the Jazz came back in Game Five. Malone, bottled up so long, and the target of considerable criticism in the papers, had a big game, hitting seventeen of twenty-seven shots for thirty-nine points, while Chicago seemed off its game, its concentration slipping. Jackson said later that he thought there had been far too much talk of winning at home, too much talk of champagne and of how to stop a riot in case the Bulls won — and too much debate over whether or not this would be Michael Jordan's last game ever in Chicago in a Bulls uniform.

At this late point in Michael Jordan's career, there were certain people who thought of themselves as Jordanologists, students not only of the game but of the man himself. They believed that they could think like him; that is, they could pick up his immensely sensitive feel for the rhythm and texture of each game, his sense of what his team needed to do at a given moment, and what his role should be — scoring, passing, or playing defense. Would he set an example for his teammates by taking up the defensive level? Would he spend the first quarter largely passing off in order to get them in the game? Over the years, he had come a long way from the young man who, surrounded by lesser teammates, had gone all out for an entire game, trying to do everything by himself. The mature Michael Jordan liked to conserve energy, let opponents use theirs up, and then when the moment was right take over the game.

Now, in Salt Lake City, it was as if he had reverted to the Michael Jordan who had carried that bottom-feeding Chicago team in the early days of his career, the player who effectively let his teammates know they were not to get in his way, because he was going to do it all himself. On this night, he knew that he was going to get little help from Scottie Pippen, who was severely injured — virtually a basketball cripple. Dennis Rodman was a rebounder, not a scorer. Toni Kukoc had played well lately, but he was always problematical. Ron Harper, once an exceptional scorer, had become, late in his career in Chicago, a defensive specialist, and he, too, was sick — apparently from something he had eaten. Luc Longley, the center, was in the midst of a wretched playoff series, seeming out of synch with himself and his teammates. (He played only fourteen minutes of this game, scored no points, and picked up four fouls.) Steve Kerr was a talented outside shooter, but Utah would be able to cover him more closely with Pippen limited.

It was clear from the beginning of the game that Jordan would try to do it all. Pippen was out for much of the first half, and Jordan, with Phil Jackson's assent, rationed his energy on defense; at one point, the assistant coach, Tex Winter, turned to Jackson and said, "Michael's giving defense a lick and promise," and Jackson said, "Well, Tex, he does need a bit of a rest." By all rights, the Jazz should have been able to grind the Bulls down and take a sizable lead, but the Bulls, even with their bench players on the floor, never let Utah break the game open. On offense, Jordan carried the load. He was conserving his energy, playing less defense and doing less rebounding than he normally did, but at the half he had twenty-three points. Utah's lead at the half, 49–45, was not what any Jazz fan would want against such a vulnerable Chicago team.

Later, Jordan said that he had remained confident throughout the game, because Utah did not break it open when it had the chance. Jordan's former teammate B. J. Armstrong, watching at home, thought that Utah was blowing it, leaving the game out there for Michael to steal. Armstrong and Jordan had been friends, but it had often been difficult for Armstrong to play alongside Michael. The game had come so much more easily to Jordan than to anyone else, Armstrong felt, and Michael had often showed his impatience with his more mortal teammates — indeed, at one point a frustrated Armstrong had checked out of the library several books on genius, hoping that they would help him learn to play with Michael.

One of Jordan's particular strengths, Armstrong believed, was that he had the most acute sense of the tempo and mood of every game of any player he had ever seen. A lot of players and coaches can look at film afterward and point their finger at the exact moment when a game slipped away, but Jordan could tell instantly, even as it was happening. It was, Armstrong thought, as if he were in the game playing and yet sitting there studying it and completely distanced from it. It was a gift that allowed him to monitor and lift his own team at critical moments and to destroy opposing teams when he sensed their special moment of vulnerability.

Now, watching the second half of Game Six, Armstrong had a sense that Michael regarded the game as a potential gift. The Jazz, after all, could have put it away early on by exploiting the obvious Chicago weaknesses. But they hadn't. If they had, Armstrong thought, Michael might have saved his energy for Game Seven. But instead the Jazz were leaving Game Six out there for the taking.

As the fourth quarter opened, the Utah lead was marginal, 66–61; the low score tended to favor the Bulls, for it meant that they had set the tempo and remained in striking distance. Slowly, the Bulls began to come back, until, with under five minutes to play, the score was tied at 77. Jordan was obviously tired, but so was everyone else. Tex Winter was alarmed when Jordan missed several jump shots in a row. "Look, he can't get any elevation," he told Jackson. "His legs are gone."

During a time-out two minutes later, Jackson told Jordan to give up the jump shot and drive. "I know," Jordan said, agreeing. "I'm going to start going to the basket — they haven't got a center in now, so the way is clear."

Once again, it was Michael Jordan time. A twenty-foot jumper by Malone on a feed from Stockton gave Utah an 83–79 lead, but Jordan cut it to 83–81 when he drove to the basket, was fouled by Utah's Bryon Russell, with 2:07 on the clock, and hit a pair of foul shots. Back and forth they went, and when Jordan drove again he was fouled again, this time by Stockton. He hit both free throws, to tie the score at 83, with 59.2 seconds left.

Then Utah brought the ball up court and went into its offense very slowly. Stockton worked the ball in to Malone, and Chicago was quick to double-team him. Malone fed Stockton, on the opposite side of the court, with a beautiful cross-court pass. With Harper rushing back a split second too late, Stockton buried a twenty-four-foot jumper. That gave Utah a three-point lead, 86–83. The clock showed 41.9 seconds left as Chicago called its last time-out. The Utah crowd began to breathe a little easier.

Dick Ebersol, the head of NBC Sports, watched the final minutes in the NBC truck. He had started the game sitting in the stands, next to the NBA commissioner, David Stern, but had become so nervous that he had gone down to the control truck. Ebersol liked Michael Jordan very much, and was well aware that he and his network were the beneficiaries of Jordan's unique appeal. Jordan's presence in the finals was worth eight or nine million viewers to NBC. Ebersol was delighted by the ratings for this series so far — they would end up at 18.7, the highest ever. At this point, though, Ebersol was rooting not for Michael Jordan but for a seventh game, and that meant he was rooting, however involuntarily, for Utah. A seventh game would bring NBC and its parent company, General Electric, an additional ten or twelve million dollars in advertising revenues. Jordan's exploits had brought many benefits to the NBA over the years, but he was such a great player that no NBA final in which he was involved had gone to the ratings and advertising jackpot of a seventh game.

When Stockton gave Utah the three-point lead with 41.9 seconds showing on the clock, Ebersol was thrilled. He was going to get his Game Seven after all. "Well, guys," he told the production people in the truck, turning away from the screens, "we'll be back here on Wednesday, and the home folks" — the GE management people — "are going to be very happy."

During the Chicago time-out, Jackson and Jordan talked about what kind of shot he might take, and Jackson reminded him that his legs were tired and it was affecting his jump shot. "I've got my second wind now," Jordan answered. "If you have to go for the jumper, you've got to follow through better," Jackson said. "You haven't been following through." Tex Winter drew up a variation on a basic Chicago play, called Whatthefuck — actually an old New York play, from Jackson's time on the Knicks. It called for the Bulls to clear out on one side, in order to isolate Jordan against Bryon Russell. As it happened, Jordan took the ball out near the back-court line, moved in a leisurely fashion into his attack mode on the right side, and then, with Utah having no chance to double him, drove down the right side and laid the ball up high and soft for the basket. The score was 86–85 Utah, with thirty-seven seconds left. It was a tough basket off a big-time drive.

That gave Utah one wonderful additional possession — a chance either to hit a basket or to use Malone to draw fouls. Stockton came across the half-court line almost casually. He bided his time, letting the clock run down, and finally, with about eleven seconds left on the twenty-four-second clock, he worked the ball to Malone.

Buzz Peterson, Jordan's close friend and college roommate, was watching Game Six with his wife, Jan, at their home in Boone, North Carolina. In the final minute of the game, Jan turned to him and said, "They're going to lose." But Peterson, who had played with Jordan in countless real games and in practice games when the winning team was the first to reach 11 and Jordan's team was behind 10–8, knew all too well that moments like this were what he lived for: with his team behind, he would predict victory to his teammates and then take over the last part of the game. Peterson told his wife, "Don't be too sure. Michael's got one more good shot at it." Just then Jordan made his driving lay-up to bring the Bulls within a point. The key play, Peterson felt, was going to come on the next defensive sequence, when Utah came down court with the ball. Peterson was certain that he could track Jordan's thinking: he would know that Utah would go to Malone, hoping for a basket or, at least, two foul shots. He had seen his friend so often in the past in this same role, encouraged by Dean Smith, the North Carolina coach, to play the defensive rover. Peterson thought that Michael, knowing the likely Utah offense every bit as well as Malone and Stockton, would try to make a move on Malone.

As soon as Malone got the ball, Jordan was there. Sure where the ball was going and how Malone was going to hold it, he sneaked in behind him for the steal. Jordan's poise at this feverish moment was fascinating: as he made his move behind Malone, he had the discipline to extend his body to the right and thus get the perfect angle, so that when he swiped at the ball he would not foul. "Karl never saw me coming," Jordan said afterward. There were 18.9 seconds left on the clock.

The crowd, Jordan remembered, got very quiet. That was, he said later, the moment for him. The moment, he explained, was what all Phil Jackson's Zen Buddhism stuff, as he called it, was about: how to focus and concentrate and be ready for that critical point in a game, so that when it arrived you knew exactly what you wanted to do and how to do it, as if you had already lived through it. When it happened, you were supposed to be in control, use the moment, and not panic and let the moment use you. Jackson liked the analogy of a cat waiting for a mouse, patiently biding its time, until the mouse, utterly unaware, finally came forth.

The play at that instant, Jordan said, seemed to unfold very slowly, and he saw everything with great clarity, as Jackson had wanted him to: the way the Utah defense was setting up, and what his teammates were doing. He knew exactly what he was going to do. "I never doubted myself," Jordan said later. "I never doubted the whole game."

Incredibly, Utah decided not to double-team Jordan. Steve Kerr, in for Harper, was on the wing to Jordan's right, ready to take a pass and score if Stockton left him to double Jordan. Kukoc had to be watched on the left. Rodman, starting out at the top of the foul circle, made a good cut to the basket, and suddenly Bryon Russell was isolated, one on one, with Jordan. Jordan had let the clock run down from about fifteen seconds to about eight. Then Russell made a quick reach for the ball, and Jordan started his drive, moving to his right as if to go to the basket. Russell went for the bait, and suddenly Jordan pulled up. Russell was already sprawling to his left, aided by a light tap on the rear from Jordan as he stopped and squared up and shot. It was a great shot, a clear look at the basket, and his elevation and form were perfect. Normally, Jordan said later, he tended to fade back just as he took his jumper for that extra degree of separation between him and his defender, but because his previous shots had been falling short, he did not fade away this time — nor did he need to, for Russell, faked to the floor, was desperately trying to regain his position.

Roy Williams, the Kansas coach who had heard about Michael when he was back in Laney High School, in Wilmington, North Carolina, was at his camp for high school players, in Kansas, and was watching the game in the coaches' locker room. He remembered saying after the steal, as Jordan was bringing the ball up court, that some Utah defender had better run over and double him quickly or it was going to be over. You forced someone else to take the last shot, he thought — you did not allow Michael to go one on one for it. But no one doubled him. What Williams remembered about the final shot was the exquisite quality of Jordan's form, and how long he held his follow-through after releasing the ball; it was something that coaches always taught their players. Watching him now, as he seemed to stay up in the air for an extra moment, defying gravity, Williams thought of it as Michael Jordan's way of willing the ball through the basket.

There is a photograph of that moment, Jordan's last shot, in the magazine *ESPN,* taken by the photographer Fernando Medina. It is in color and covers two full pages, and it shows Russell struggling to regain position, Jordan at the peak of his jump, the ball high up on its arc and about to descend, and the clock displaying the time remaining in the game — 6.6 seconds. What is remarkable is the closeup it offers of so many Utah fans. Though the ball has not yet reached the basket, the game appears over to them. The anguish — the certitude of defeat — is on their faces. In a number of instances their hands are extended as if to stop Jordan and keep the shot from going in. Some of the fans have already put their hands to their faces, as in a moment of grief. There is one exception to this: a young boy on the right, in a Chicago Bulls shirt, whose arms are already in the air in a victory call.

The ball dropped cleanly through. Utah had one more chance, but Stockton missed the last shot and the Bulls won, 87–86. Jordan had carried his team once again. He had scored forty-five points, and he had scored his team's last eight points. The Chicago coaches, it turned out, had been prophetic in their sense of what would happen in the fourth quarters of this series, and which player would be able to create for himself with the game on the line. In the three close games, two of them in Salt Lake City, Jordan played much bigger than Malone — averaging thirteen points in the fourth quarter to Malone's three. Jordan should be remembered, Jerry Sloan said afterward, "as the greatest player who ever played the game."

THOMAS BOSWELL

For Timeless Player,
It Was Time

FROM THE WASHINGTON POST

CAL RIPKEN and his inspiring streak of 2,632 consecutive games ended tonight in the one way that few within baseball expected.

Perfectly.

Neither injury nor old age, nor lost skill, nor clubhouse intrigue, nor any bitter controversy snapped The Streak.

Instead, Ripken ended it himself. The legendary Baltimore Orioles third baseman did it with exquisite timing — not too soon and not too belatedly. Ripken managed this nationally awaited moment with no fanfare or self-celebration. At the last minute before a game against the New York Yankees, he told Manager Ray Miller: Not tonight.

Best of all, Ripken ended his streak — which he had more than enough clout and health to continue indefinitely — voluntarily. It was in the best interests of the team and its future. So he did it.

"It's time to change the subject. It's time to return the focus to the team. . . . I'm a realist. The timing was right," said Ripken, who even stunned his teammates with a decision he had thought about for weeks, but kept secret until thirty minutes before game time. "Every time I told somebody before the game, they got that stare in their eyes that a deer gives you when your headlights hit him."

Over the sixteen years since he missed his previous game, in 1982, many of his teammates have asked, jokingly, what would Ripken do with himself if he couldn't play? Tonight, they got their answer. By the fourth inning, he was out in the bullpen — the only place where a player can interact with fans without breaking a rule or interrupting the game.

Ripken was signing autographs.

By the sixth inning, he was warming up the outfielders by playing catch between innings, like a bullpen catcher or an old coach. In the seventh, with a warm-up jacket on, despite a warm evening, so he could hide his famous number 8 and not cause a commotion, Ripken was out in center field beyond the wall, shaking the hands of bleacher fans.

"I wanted to scream and yell and say thank you to everyone. And tell them it was okay. Don't be sad. Be happy," Ripken said. "I wanted to celebrate it, not mourn it."

Sad? Who's sad? When you do everything right for your entire career, then end your milestone streak on your own terms and in your own low-key, classy style, that's just a different kind of beauty.

Of all the records set in baseball, perhaps Ripken's mark, more than any other, deserved a clean, untarnished, and dignified ending. Yet, hard as it is to believe, that same incredible mark was one that baseball insiders worried would end with ugliness, embarrassment, or recriminations.

One of Ripken's greatest strengths is his absolute stubbornness — a family trait. Would he *ever* see the wisdom of missing a game? Or would a manager, general manager, or even owner Peter Angelos, who has shown a mean streak at times, order him benched? Several days ago, a prominent member of the Orioles' organization told me, "I hope Cal takes a day off *this* season before somebody *makes* him take one next spring."

That might have been in the cards. And Ripken might well have sensed it. No player understands every aspect and nuance of the game better than this son of a career coach and manager. No one knows better than Ripken how significantly his stats have slipped this season.

His .273 batting average is just three points below his career average. And, with only nine errors this season, he's one of the best fielders at his position in the game. He's played every game this season for a good reason: the Orioles have had nobody better. In that sense, his streak has not been tainted at all.

But Ripkin's long-formidable power is almost gone — fourteen homers and sixty-one RBIs. In an era of mammoth offense, he's one of the worst run producers among major league third base-men. In recent days, he's resorted to a desperation batting stance too grotesque to describe. At midseason, he was asked, "Is your old power gone for good?" He didn't blink or duck. It was a baseball question. "In the past, I've never known when it'll suddenly come back. Hitting is timing. We'll see."

Nonetheless, it hasn't returned. "Cal looks like he's cheating to get to some pitches. And when he does hit it, the ball doesn't jump off his bat anymore," said one scout at tonight's game. "There's no shame in that. He's thirty-eight. And he's still a solid player."

Ever since he broke Lou Gehrig's mark of 2,130 straight games on September 6, 1995, in one of the most moving events in base-ball in the last quarter century, Ripken has claimed he'd "know when it was time" to snap the skein. Many times he explained that the streak would end "within the context of the game."

In other words, there would come a moment when it would be obvious that, if there were no streak, it would be normal baseball procedure for him *not* to play. Most assumed the ultrafit Ripken, who has never been trimmer or stronger, was referring to an injury.

Now, we know that injury and age never got the last word on Ripken. And neither did hubris, that other bane of normal men. Suddenly, tonight, everything came together to make it obvious to Ripken that this was a suitable end.

It was the Orioles' last home game of the season. The night's opponent was a mighty Yankees team, worthy of Lou Gehrig or Babe Ruth. The Orioles had been (realistically) eliminated from the wild-card race. At such times, it is considered good form for veterans to step aside and let the organization's top prospects and late-season call-ups show their stuff and get their cleats wet. The most prominent of all Orioles prospects is, ironically, a third base-man — Ryan Minor.

Ripken scratched himself from the lineup. Minor played.

One final piece of timing made this evening perfect. Ripken may have lost some of his timing at the plate, but not in his heart, not in his sense of what's right for his game.

On the night of 2,131, baseball needed Ripken as its standard-bearer more than the sport had needed any player at any time since Ruth saved the game with his home runs and his smile in the wake of the Black Sox scandal of 1919. Ever since that moment, as Ripken hit home runs in numbers 2,129, 2,130, and 2,131, he has signed more autographs — no one disputes this — than any other modern player. Maybe any five modern players.

In fact, long after midnight, Ripken returned to the Camden Yards field tonight to wave, shake hands, and sign for the thousand fans who simply would not leave.

No interview, no charity appearance to promote adult literacy, no opportunity to help revive baseball has been too much for Ripken.

Now it's Mark McGwire and Sammy Sosa's turn. Ripken showed them, and everybody else in the sport, how to act in the spotlight, how to grow larger when history demands it of you, and how to enjoy the game and its adoring fans as they deserve to be appreciated.

Ripken's time on top — as the greatest power-hitting shortstop in American League history and as the Iron Man — has come to an end.

However, one distinction is still left to Ripken. Baseball has never had a more universally beloved player. Nor has it ever had one who was raised up as the embodiment of the game for better reasons.

That has not changed. That's a streak that will go on forever.

JOHN HILDEBRAND

Coming Home

FROM HARPER'S MAGAZINE

THE VIEW FROM Five Mile Bluff on the west bank of the Chippewa River in Wisconsin extends beyond five miles, so that looking down the gun sights of the valley, one sees across a vast canopy of swamp white oak, soft maple, basswood, and river birch to where tangled bottomland forest gives way to open hayfields and prim white farmhouses with matching barns and the tall Harvestore silos known as "big blues." It is a vista of the kind that kept landscape artists of the nineteenth century busy illustrating such themes as the marriage of wilderness and cultivation or, on a loftier level, a young nation's limitless possibilities. Above its mouth, the Chippewa River splits into two unequal channels: the main channel skirts the bluffs, braiding itself like a glacial stream around sandbars and wooded islands, while Beef Slough, the lesser channel, runs a parallel course to the east before unraveling altogether. Between the channels lies a wedge-shaped floodplain twelve miles long by two and a half miles wide. From ground level — that is, to anyone slogging across it on foot — the Tiffany Wildlife Area is a dire swamp, a Mesopotamia of deadwater sloughs and pothole lakes interconnected with beaver canals, islands within islands, where the most pressing possibility is the possibility of getting lost. Every year, hunters manage to lose themselves in this pocket of wilderness, some more permanently than others.

On an Indian summer day in October 1970, a thirteen-year-old from nearby Durand became lost while duck hunting with his father and older brother. It was the boy's first hunt, a rite of passage in these parts, and he had wandered off in a light jacket and tennis shoes. By evening the temperature had dropped below freezing, and the search for the missing boy intensified. Being lost is usually a temporary setback, more a loss of equilibrium than self, since it's not you that's been misplaced, only the sense of terra firma that comes from knowing where you are in the world. On the other hand, to remain lost for long is to court more drastic synonyms: defeated . . . abandoned . . . departed . . . dead.

"The best thing, of course, is not to get lost," the Boy Scout manual advises in its avuncular way. "But there may come a time when you are temporarily 'bumfuzzled' and don't know where camp is. Here are a few things to do. Sit down on a rock, or under a tree, and think the whole thing over. In fact it's a good time to think of a few funny stories. In other words calm down, and don't be afraid. If you let your imagination run away, you will run away, and probably run in a circle and come right back to where you started."

Did the lost boy sit down on a rock and tell himself a funny story? More likely he let his imagination run away and then gave frantic chase, because three weeks later the boy's body would be discovered lodged against a marker buoy in the navigation channel of the Mississippi River. He must have fallen into a slough and the current carried him away, swept him miles downstream, far from home and all that he would ever know of this world; it swept off his tennis shoes, but a handful of shotgun shells would be found in his jacket pocket. In the painful interim, the search escalated, drawing more and more searchers into the swamp. At one point, more than five hundred volunteers spread out at arm's length to form a human chain and walked the length of the bottoms from channel to channel, bushwhacking through thickets and scaring up deer and a few massasauga rattlesnakes but no lost boy. Sentiment began to turn against the tangled landscape itself. An editorial in the *Durand Courier-Wedge* accused the state of maintaining the Tiffany Wildlife Area as "a private jungle," a metaphor wrong on both counts, though it must have seemed timely, especially when one of the searchers told the newspaper, "I never realized we had a Vietnam so close to home."

These woods have a long memory. Twenty-two years later, Kia Xue Lor, a Hmong immigrant from Laos, lost his way in a blizzard while deer hunting in the Tiffany with his son and a friend. Ten inches of snow had fallen the night before, and the three hunters,

none standing much over five feet tall, waded through drifts up to
their knees. Occasionally they'd cut a deer trail in the snow, always
headed in another direction, but there was no sign of other hunters. About noon, the younger men decided to hunt elsewhere and
agreed to meet Lor in the same spot a few hours later. Lor hiked
east through a monotonous winter landscape of windfalls and
prickly ash until he came to a frozen pond. Circling the pond, Lor
assumed he would intersect his own tracks and follow them back,
but they eluded him. By four o'clock, the winter sky was darker than
the snow-covered ground, and Lor frequently stopped to listen for
traffic on Highway 25 to the east. He could see bluffs above the tree
line, though he was so turned around now that he had no idea what
side of the river they were on or if he'd passed them earlier that
morning.

Thoroughly "bumfuzzled," Lor scraped away snow beneath a
large tree and sat down to wait for his son to find him. He had no
food. His hunting outfit consisted of three pairs of pants, a nylon
jacket, and a pair of moon boots. Heaping brush together to make
a windbreak, he made a fire and then lay beside it, alternately
roasting and freezing. In Laos, he had slept alone in the jungle
many times during the protracted war with the North Vietnamese
and the Communist Pathet Lao, sometimes drinking a potion
made from the bladders of wild pig and deer that enabled the
sleeper to awaken at the slightest sound. He had a great fear of
waking to loud noises.

The next morning, he followed an airplane and ran into two
local hunters, who called the Department of Natural Resources to
pick him up. As other members of the search party drifted back to
the landing, one ran into a Hmong who said he'd just been threatened in the woods. A local hunter had promised to cut the Hmong
man's dick off if he ever caught him hunting in the area again.

"But to return to our back settlers," J. Hector St. John de Crèvecoeur wrote in 1782, "I must tell you that there is something in the
proximity of the woods which is very singular. It is with men as it is
with the plants and animals that grow and live in the forests; they
are entirely different from those that live in the plains. . . . [T]his is
the progress; once hunters, farewell to the plough. The chase renders them ferocious, gloomy, and unsocial; a hunter wants no

neighbor, he rather hates them because he dreads the competition. . . . Thus our bad people are those who are half cultivators and half hunters; and the worst of them are those who have degenerated altogether into the hunting state."

Crèvecoeur, the agrarian optimist, was describing an America newly wrestled from the wilderness. What could he possibly have made of Buffalo County, Wisconsin, at the twilight of the twentieth century, where the plow is finishing a poor second to the chase? Ever since outdoor magazines began listing it as the top county in the nation for trophy white-tailed deer, farmers have been selling off their hilly woodlots to outsiders for more than the cultivated fields are worth. Working farms are a vanishing act even as blood sport occupies their former occupants. Crowded into public hunting grounds such as the Tiffany Bottoms, the landless locals face increased competition from newcomers like the Hmong and grow ever more "ferocious, gloomy, and unsocial."

On the opening day of hunting season, I saw no deer in the river bottoms but plenty of small men in makeshift tree stands calling to one another in a language as high-pitched and fluty as birdsong. Hmong hunters are easy to pick out: anyone standing five feet tall or so, carrying a single-shot shotgun, and wearing sneakers. Obviously they were seeing deer, because there was no end to the gunfire. In the late afternoon, sun low in the trees, I ran into a local hunter climbing down from his metal tree stand after a pointless day. Shrugging off his bad luck, he began to praise, rather elaborately I thought, a Hmong tree stand he'd found in the woods.

"Oh, it was beautiful. Like something out of *Swiss Family Robinson.* Bent limbs for railings going up the sides. A seat fashioned out of a log." He shook his head and winked. "Big wind blew it down." The wink was conspiratorial, because he'd played the role of the wind.

On the way home, I stopped in Durand to chat with a man who had grown up on the last farm in the Tiffany before the state bought up the land and let it revert to swamp. A skilled woodsman, he'd trapped and hunted there all his life, but not anymore.

"My boys and I used to hunt the bottoms the week before Thanksgiving. Got some big bucks out of there. Now I don't even bother. You see *them* at the Ella boat landing in pickup trucks and boats that we paid for!"

A grin flickered at the corners of his mouth when he spoke of the path the DNR had recently cut through the Tiffany. He called it the Ho Chi Minh Trail.

Not wanting to be one of Crèvecoeur's "bad people" who hates his neighbor because he dreads the competition, I drove out to see Kia Xue Lor, the man who'd been lost in the blizzard. He lives in a public-housing complex off a cul-de-sac on the north side of Eau Claire. The decor of these apartments is interchangeable: a few pieces of furniture, school pictures of the immigrant's children, and a black-and-white photograph of a young man, usually deceased, in the slightly operatic uniform of the Royal Lao Army. Lor is a wiry, intense man in his early fifties with slicked-back hair and a few gold teeth. We sat on his living room couch, an interpreter between us, while Lor poured out the past. He had been a soldier all his life, his career following the fortunes of the Armée Clandestine. At fifteen he joined the army, and he fought the Pathet Lao and North Vietnamese for the next fifteen years until the Americans pulled out of the war and left him behind. He knew the Communists would kill him for collaborating with the CIA, so he moved his family into the jungle and for five years fought with a local resistance group before fleeing across the Mekong River. A photograph on the wall showed Lor and his family a month after their arrival at Ban Vinai refugee camp in Thailand, donated clothes hanging in folds around them. After eight years in the camp, Lor came to this country through the aid of a church group, but without English and somewhat disabled by war wounds, he couldn't find work.

A steady stream of kids had flowed into the living room until a dozen or so sat cross-legged on the floor watching a video of Disney's *The Lion King*. Lor whispered something in Hmong to one of the little girls, who announced to the others, in English, "Shut up." I'd considered asking Lor if we could hunt together sometime, but it struck me that a person who must address his children's friends through a translator remains, in many vital respects, lost.

The six-hundred-year-old Kingdom of a Million Elephants and One Parasol did not enter the American imagination until a civil war between Laotian government troops and the Pathet Lao and their North Vietnamese allies turned into a test of the Kennedy administration's Cold War resolve. After the Geneva Accord of 1962 guaranteed Laos's neutrality, operations there became strictly covert, fought largely by a Hmong army of the CIA's own devising, supplied from Air America bases in Thailand, and overseen by case officers with such jaunty noms de guerre as "Bag" or "Mr. Clean" or "Mr. Hog" or "Kayak." It was the agency's largest operation, a secret conflict, a campaign of surrogates that maintained the fiction of neutrality. Former CIA director William Colby called it a "non-attributable war."

In late 1965, a small plane carrying Colby, then chief of the CIA's Far East Division, bumped down on the dirt airstrip at Long Chieng, a remote valley in northern Laos. It was an otherworldly place, surrounded by mountains and weird limestone outcroppings, a thatched-roofed village to one side of the airstrip and a complex of corrugated metal buildings at the other. Colby had come to visit General Vang Pao, leader of the Armée Clandestine. Vang Pao had risen from a thirteen-year-old jungle runner to the highest-ranking Hmong officer in the Royal Lao Army. His hill tribes engaged the North Vietnamese in exactly the kind of guerrilla war that they themselves waged so successfully across the border. During summer monsoons, his army took full advantage of the landscape, attacking enemy operations mired down in the mud on the Plain of Jars, an expanse littered for three thousand years with eleven-foot stone vessels of debatable origin; in the dry season, the Hmong disappeared into the surrounding mountains. Colby, who had parachuted behind enemy lines in Europe with the OSS, understood the value of an irregular force engaged in a limited campaign on their own territory. For him, Laos was a people's war against a foreign aggressor, and in Washington he argued to increase support for Vang Pao. Yet the nature of the war would soon change. "Some immutable principle," Colby wrote in his memoir, "provides that a barefoot guerrilla force must inevitably grow to become a conventional army."

The "immutable" in this case was Vietnam. At its height, Vang Pao's guerrilla army grew to thirty thousand men, with so many CIA advisers that Long Chieng became known as "Spook Haven." The purposes for which they fought were increasingly dictated not out of concern for a "neutral" Laos but to support an expanded American presence across the border. Vang Pao's army tied down North

Vietnamese divisions that otherwise would have faced American forces in South Vietnam. Hmong soldiers guarded a secret radar installation, which, until it was overwhelmed, allowed the all-weather bombing of North Vietnam. Hmong road-watch teams attacked the labyrinth of supply lines running along the Annamese Cordillera between Laos and Vietnam known collectively as the Ho Chi Minh Trail. To these ends, Vang Pao's army sustained enormous losses and became increasingly dependent upon American air power and massive bombing. Still, one could argue that the Armée Clandestine was an unbelievable bargain. The CIA spent in a year (Hmong soldiers earned about three dollars a month) what the military spent in a day in Vietnam, and no American boys were being drafted to die in the misty mountains of Laos.

The Chippewa stretches a quarter of a mile across at the Ella boat landing unless the river is cottoned in predawn fog, in which case it seems as wide as an ocean. A dozen of us stood at the landing on an early September morning, poking flashlight beams into the mist and waiting for a boat to ferry us across. In the distance, a cow bawled like a foghorn. While the others joked among themselves in high-pitched monosyllables, I felt myself lost in a dense cloud of language that would part unexpectedly when, for instance, someone boomed into the darkness, "Where are you, Grampa?"

The Eau Claire telephone directory lists forty-nine entries under X, all of them Xiongs. Two generations were represented at the landing, and a third was lost somewhere in the fog. Joe Bee Xiong had invited me squirrel hunting with his family, and it was his father who was missing. When an hour passed and the boat still hadn't appeared, we launched my canoe to look for him. Joe Bee held a flashlight in the bow, illuminating snags and sandbars recently emerged from the river, as we drifted downstream. Ahead, through tatters of fog, we spotted a skiff dead in the water, its sole occupant straining against an oar. Northern States Power, which operates a series of hydroelectric dams upriver, had cut the flow of water on the weekend to save for peak power demands and, in the process, had stranded Joe Bee's father on a sandbar.

Unlike the *Walpurgisnacht* of the opening weekend of deer-hunting season, in squirrel season the Hmong have the woods to themselves. The Xiongs had carved their camp out of thick brush between the riverbank and the abandoned track bed of the Chicago, Milwaukee, St. Paul, and Pacific Railroad. The rest of the party, having arrived the night before, lounged on sleeping bags beneath a green tarp or else hunkered over a smoldering fire. The older men have the short legs, barrel chests, and sloping shoulders of weightlifters, whereas their teenage sons look lank and reedy — the difference, I suppose, between a youth spent hoeing mountainside fields and one spent sitting in a classroom.

In the montane forests of north-central Laos, the Hmong raised rice and corn by slash-and-burn farming; they also hunted the surrounding jungle at every opportunity. Arriving in this country as refugees, they settled in cities and made forays into the countryside on weekends to hunt. Wardens sometimes arrested Hmong for having blue jays, chipmunks, and robins in their game bags. When the DNR translated its game regulations into Hmong, it was a difficult task, for the language had no written script until the 1950s, no equivalents for such terms as "recycling" or "composting" or "outdoor recreation." The manual jumps back and forth between a taxonomy of the familiar and the strange. Listed under "Protected Species" are "Bitterns, Canada yij Spruce Grouse (poi yij), cormorants, cranes, eagles, falcons thiab plas, great blue herons, grebes, gulls, hawks, kingfishers, loons, mourning doves, plovers, prairie chickens, ravens, sandpipers, swans, yam tsiaj uas tsis tsim kev kub ntxhov thiab tsis ntshai." In Laos, the Hmong had traditionally hunted songbirds, squirrel, red deer, buffalo, wild pig, and monkey with homemade arrows and bamboo crossbows. In the 1960s, they used M-1s, M-16s, hand grenades — the full arsenal of democracy.

Joe Bee Xiong, his thirteen-year-old son, Lar Zeng, and I followed the railroad tracks south through a canopy of overgrown bottomland hardwoods. At some distance from camp, we stopped so that Lar Zeng could practice shooting his father's new .22 rifle at a maple leaf tacked to a tree trunk. Every time the boy worked the bolt action, Joe Bee would announce, "Safety first!" in a manner so grave and quietly deliberate that it took me a moment to realize he wasn't repeating a hunter safety slogan but merely telling his son to push the safety forward so that the rifle would fire.

The first time I met Joe Bee in his office in the Eau Claire County courthouse, where he worked as an employment specialist, he wore a dark blue suit and an American-flag lapel pin. Now he looked dressed for an insurgency, in fatigues and carrying armament that included, besides the .22, a shotgun and a bayonet blade. At thirty-five, he was old enough to have fought in the "secret war" against the Pathet Lao and young enough to have graduated from an American high school. It's hard to imagine which was the more trying time. Having shared the defining experience of two generations, he is in the unique position to mediate between the elders, whose lack of English isolates them from the larger society, and the young, who've grown up on TV and hip-hop. As a Xiong clan leader, Joe Bee is responsible for an extended family of more than three hundred, not to mention eight children of his own. He is both a traditionalist who believes the landscape is animated by spirits and a consumer with an eye for the latest gizmo.

"Thirty-five degrees northeast," said Joe Bee, consulting a compass on a lanyard around his neck before we plunged into the woods. The fog had burned off, leaving the forest dappled in leaf-light. For their part, the squirrels stayed hidden or else danced momentarily across the crowns of the tallest trees. Lar Zeng's job was to circle the tree and chase the squirrel into the open so that his father could plink it with the .22.

I didn't see the squirrel until it was free-falling, an acrobat who'd lost his grip, tumbling through thin air to land with a soft *humph* among the fallen oak leaves. A couple more joined it in Joe Bee's knapsack before we headed back to camp. We bushwhacked north through stinging nettles and prickly ash, then along the stinking shore of a deadwater slough caked in duckweed. It seemed a perfect jungle to me. In the distance, we could hear the tattoo of small-arms fire.

How was this different, I asked Joe Bee, from hunting in Laos?

"No tigers."

Joe Bee grew up in Mong Cha, a village in Xieng Khouang Province. When he was a child, a tiger came into the village and killed some of the family's chickens. The next evening, the tiger returned and carried off a pig. Joe Bee's father took the boy along to follow the tiger because the older man's hearing had been damaged in the war and he needed his son's ears for the pursuit. Through the jungle gloom they followed the pig's strangled cries until they reached a spur of Phou Bia massif, at nearly ten thousand feet the tallest mountain in Laos.

"I was younger than my son at the time. My father asks me which way the tiger is going. I say, 'That side of the mountain.' My father says, 'That's impossible. Are you sure?' I say that I am certain, but I didn't understand the echo from the mountain. So we lost the trail. The next day we followed the right trail, and all we found of the pig was its head lying on the jungle floor. My father was angry at the loss of the pig because he knew the tiger would keep coming back until all our animals were gone. So he wired a hand grenade to the pig's head. That night I woke up to an explosion off in the jungle. When my father followed the trail the next morning, he found the tiger had lost its head."

In Hmong folklore, the tiger symbolizes evil. It is the stock villain in cautionary tales in which children who wander too far from the village are greedily devoured. A master of guile, the tiger can also appear in disguise or transform itself into human shape to trick widows into believing their husbands have returned from the dead. In a jungle full of bears and snakes, the tiger is the most feared creature not only because of its great strength but because it possesses the dangerous ability to metamorphose, to change its stripes, to be one thing one day and something else another.

In 1973, Joe Bee Xiong took his father's place in Vang Pao's army at its mountain headquarters at Long Chieng. He was twelve years old and did not look out of place. As Hmong casualties mounted, the army's ranks were filled with boys and old men; most everyone in between was dead. Flooded with refugees from an uprooted rural population, Long Chieng had become the second most populated city in Laos, but the spooks were gone. The secret war, always a shadow of the larger conflict across the border, was winding down. Shortly after signing the Paris peace agreement with the North Vietnamese, Henry Kissinger arrived in Laos to persuade the royalist prime minister to reach a similar agreement with the Pathet Lao. But without the American presence, this attempt at reconciliation collapsed when North Vietnamese troops captured a town in Laos. In May of 1975, Joe Bee, having returned to his own village, heard the news that General Vang Pao and his closest supporters had been evacuated from Long Chieng to Thailand.

The Pathet Lao sent thousands of loyalists — including the former king, queen, and crown prince — to "seminar camps," from which they never emerged. The Hmong in particular were marked for retribution. In the following years, as many as 150,000 fled across the Mekong River into Thailand; others took up arms buried since the cease-fire. The center of resistance was Phou Bia, the fog-shrouded massif whose foothills had once hidden Joe Bee's tiger. After his own village came under attack, Joe Bee went to the mountain to join Chou Fa, the same resistance group Kia Xue Lor had fought with in the jungle, a movement whose leaders claimed to be able to foretell the future and to possess a powerful magic that would protect soldiers in battle. Sometimes the magic worked, sometimes it didn't. In late 1977, North Vietnamese and Pathet Lao forces converged on Phou Bia, bombarding it with artillery and T-28 airplanes. Survivors accused the Communists of dropping chemical/biological weapons on Hmong villages, though corroborative evidence remains sketchy and experts have dismissed the "yellow rain" as everything from bee pollen to defoliants left over from American stockpiles.

Joe Bee, who had escaped the attack by moving to his cousin Doua's village, joined thousands on a month-long exodus south through the mountains and bamboo forests to the Mekong River. A few days away from the Thai border, those who survived ran into a North Vietnamese army patrol, and in the ensuing firefight one of Joe Bee's friends was killed and five were wounded. Scouting ahead of the main party, Joe Bee and a few others reached the river, which stretched more than a mile across, wide enough to dwarf the water buffalo on the other side. Beyond it lay refugee camps and an uncertain future. Centuries ago, when the Hmong lived in China, they had a saying: "If you don't see the Yellow River, your heart will not be saddled." Joe Bee understood this to mean that the courage of ignorance is stronger than the swiftest current. Waiting until dark, the men kicked across, using bamboo poles as floats. For an entire generation of Hmong, crossing the Mekong would be as common and significant an event in their history as steerage passage across the Atlantic was to emigrants of the last generation.

Back at our hunting camp, a pot of rice steamed on a portable gas stove. Tupperware containers of sticky rice and hot peppers lay open on the ground while a young man sat beside the campfire gutting squirrels with a jackknife. There was a whiff of something acrid in the air.

"This is how we cook squirrel," said Joe Bee, and he tossed a squirrel onto the fire, where it smoldered until the fur ignited in a blaze. Turning the squirrel with a stick, he scraped away the burnt fur until the bare carcass was thoroughly scorched. Deprived of fur, the squirrel looked even less appetizing, its long whittled nose and whip-like tail more a caricature of a rodent. It looked, in short, like a burnt rat.

"The smoke," said Joe Bee, "is what gives it the flavor."

The blackened squirrel was cleaned and chopped into pieces before being thrown into a stewpot with red peppers, lemon grass, and ginger root. When the stew was ready, Joe Bee took a spoonful, whispered something in Hmong, then tossed it into the brush. It was a kind of grace before meals, he explained, an invitation to whatever spirits inhabited the woods and a request that nothing bad would happen while we hunted there, though I gathered that the midwestern landscape had nothing on the Loatian highlands when it came to ghosts.

The stew was delicious. We ate it with sticky rice dipped into a pepper sauce that made my lips vibrate. For dessert there were sweet cucumbers from the garden, peeled and eaten like ice cream cones. Everyone ate seconds except Doua's son, who had been stung by a wasp and lay moaning under the tarp, his mouth swollen shut. I felt stuffed, but at Joe Bee's urging I ladled the last helping from the pot into my bowl. Bits of squirrel meat floated anonymously among the vegetables, all but unrecognizable, all but one: a pale globe of bone papered in flesh.

"Ha! You got the head!" said Joe Bee, as if I'd plucked out a golden ring. "The Hmong say: If you don't get the squirrel, you eat the head. The next time, you'll outsmart the squirrel."

It made roundabout sense, the notion of outwitting the thing that you desired by becoming it. Joe Bee, I noticed, had a skull in his bowl too.

The Hmong Mutual Assistance Association occupies a red-brick building in downtown Eau Claire directly across from an auto-body shop and the local Jobs Service. In February, the streetlights blink on by late afternoon, illuminating a ridge of dirty snow between sidewalk and curb. Inside, older Hmong sat at a table studying to become citizens. The walls are decorated with *National Geographic* photographs of villages perched on mountain ridges, turbaned

women in black pajamas pounding rice by hand, fields walled in by
jungle — the world left behind. Afraid of losing their government
benefits, the older men and women crammed for the naturaliza-
tion exam:

> In order to vote in the United States, a citizen must —
> A. own property
> B. have a steady job
> C. speak English clearly
> D. be old enough

Upstairs, a handful of Democratic Party veterans and political
innocents, myself included, were mapping out a campaign strategy
to elect Joe Bee to the city council. Five seats were up for grabs, yet
there was no single compelling issue at stake. The possible exception was Joe Bee's candidacy itself. A Hmong candidate had run for
the school board two years before and lost. The good news was that
Eau Claire's Hmong community, which had grown from twelve or
thirteen refugees in 1976 to nearly three thousand, were solidly
behind Joe Bee. The bad news was that only a hundred or so were
registered voters.

The main question tonight was whether Joe Bee's résumé —
family man, employment specialist, former police reserve officer,
businessman — should also include his military service.

"I'd strongly advise against it," said an older committee member.
"Might put people off, especially in the Third Ward."

The Third Ward is where I live, a university neighborhood where
the Vietnam War is still a tricky topic and mere mention of the CIA,
no matter how distant the connection, brings an involuntary shud-
der. Whether Joe Bee's service was a campaign plus or a liability
depended upon the larger question of whether the Hmong were
our forgotten allies or hired mercenaries engaged in an illegal war.
Either way, the Hmong presence in this country is inextricably
bound up with the war, and their cool reception here may reflect
the lack of magnanimity one feels toward partners in a failed venture who show up, years later, as reminders of the loss.

On a cold spring night, Joe Bee's campaign workers gathered at
the committee manager's home to eat spring rolls and watch the
election returns trickle in on the television. The competition included a bank vice president, a realtor, two retirees, and a former

assistant superintendent of schools in a race that clearly favored incumbents. At 8 P.M., Joe Bee was in second place. An hour later, he'd dropped to third. The early totals represented only a few districts, so there was still hope. By midnight the tide had turned and it was all over.

Joe Bee received 5,879 votes, winning a seat on the city council and the distinction of being the first Hmong elected to any city office in Wisconsin. He threw a victory celebration at the local VFW, giving new meaning to the concept of "veterans of foreign wars." Afterward, those who'd worked on the campaign were invited to Joe Bee's one-story home near the airport. Tables had been set up in the basement, and the women brought more noodles and spring rolls and sticky rice. We toasted Joe Bee and one another with warm beer: the Happy Toast, the Thank-You Toast, the Welcome the Guests Toast. An old *txiv neeb,* or shaman, wished Joe Bee a life as long as an unending river and the strength of a mountain so that when the wind blew he would remain unmoved. A *hus plig* ceremony followed, each of us tying a cotton string around Joe Bee's wrist for his good luck. I was happy because my candidate had won. Joe Bee, a solid cuff of cotton strings on his wrist, was happy despite having taken on even more responsibility. But Yong Kay Moua, head of the first Hmong family to settle in Eau Claire, seemed the happiest.

"It really means that this is our hometown. We came to America twenty years ago, and we've been waiting for some word, for someone to say, 'Your home is our home. Welcome.' This election shows that this is a hometown for the Hmong and not a temporary place."

Four days after the victory party, somebody smashed the right side windows of Joe Bee's Toyota van. The next night, the left side windows were broken and, for good measure, a window on his wife's car. The evening after that, someone shot out a window of Joe Bee's younger brother's car with a pellet gun. Police staked out the neighborhood, but after two nights without incidents they left.

Blind routine in the face of reason is a hallmark of the chronically stupid. Late the following night, two men were trying to rip the plastic off one of the broken windows when they were surprised by a group of Hmong spilling out of Joe Bee's van, in which they had been taking turns as lookout. Joe Bee's brother chased them while the others called the police, who stopped a red Dodge Omni shortly after 4 A.M. The driver of the Omni was a twenty-year-old white female; her accomplices were seventeen and nineteen. Eventually, police linked the trio to twenty-three cases of criminal damage to vehicles and eight cases of theft from autos, but clearly they had felt something special for the Xiongs.

The classic struggle in American society is never competition for the top — a foregone conclusion — but the kicking and shoving over who will occupy the bottom rung. Fear of personal slippage drives the most outrageous acts of bigotry. "The chase renders them ferocious, gloomy, and unsocial." The immigrant is despised not for his cultural differences — his strange language and impossible cuisine — but for driving a better car. The Hmong, however, are unique among immigrant groups in that the cold shoulder they sometimes got may be linked to our own ambivalence about Vietnam. Perhaps the teenagers who trashed Joe Bee's car had absorbed the dark brooding of adults who could not bear strangers returning home in place of sons and brothers lost in the war.

Yong Kay Moua, who'd reached Eau Claire before any of his countrymen, understood the frustration better than most. "Maybe you didn't come home with the same people but with different people. Different color. Different size. Different shape. Maybe coming this way changes their faces. Maybe you were expecting someone else, but some people came back and you should welcome them."

In late May, Joe Bee attended a convention of Hmong war veterans in Fresno, California. On the last day, he joined nearly five thousand middle-aged veterans in camouflage fatigues performing close-order drills on the playing field of Cal State's Bulldog Stadium. A handful of ex-Raven and Air America pilots flew T-28s over the stadium in the missing-man formation, a gesture that couldn't have been more relevant to the men on the ground. They were an army in exile, parading before the flag of a kingdom that no longer existed. In this country, nationalism gives way to ethnicity, which soon becomes memory and finally ritual. Even if the Communist regime falls in Laos, few Hmong of Joe Bee's generation would be returning except as tourists.

The event had been billed as Lao Veterans of America Recognition Day, but it was largely self-recognition. Ex-CIA personnel and former Air America pilots showed up, but few of the invited government officials. The most noticeable absence was the late William Colby, whose presence was evoked by a makeshift shrine in front of the dais that held photographs, a bowl of fruit, and the blue shield of the CIA. The man who had kept the agency's operation in Laos a secret for so long spent his retirement trying to make up for that anonymity by speaking to Hmong groups across the country. One might argue that he was as responsible as anyone for the Hmong being here instead of there. Colby had planned to attend the conference in Fresno but had disappeared two weeks earlier while canoeing on the Wicomico River, a tributary of the Potomac. For eight days he was presumed lost until searchers discovered his body floating in shallow water half a mile from his vacation home. Apparently, he had fallen into the river and died of hypothermia.

When someone dies, the Hmong believe that person's soul must return to the original village where he was born. Mourners play a song on the *qeej*, a woodwind made of six bamboo pipes fitted with copper reeds, to guide the spirit over mountains and rivers on this backward journey. The song's duration depends on the age of the deceased and his or her travels through life; it can often take several hours before a dead person's soul finally reaches home. Since the Hmong language is tonal, the musician literally speaks through his instrument, giving directions. So it may not have been coincidence in Fresno when two men dressed in kilts played a dirge for Colby on Scottish bagpipes, the only instrument that rivals the *qeej* for sheer eeriness. The song they played was "Amazing Grace." It's a song of repentance, of course, but an ironic choice under the circumstances, what with its plaintive reference to one who "once was lost, but now am found." Joe Bee, an accomplished *qeej* player, thought the melody appropriately sad but hardly long enough for so extensive an itinerary as a soul might require to find its way home.

JOHN McPHEE

Catch-and-Dissect

FROM THE NEW YORKER

THE BOATS COME IN through Petit Bois Pass, make an arcuate turn in Mississippi Sound, and line up on final in the Aloe Bay Channel. The afternoon sun is behind them. The boats in the middle distance are indistinct, and the far ones are lost in summer haze. They are like airliners coming in from the west, descending in an endless queue.

Willy Bemis is waiting at the dock. The judges' stand is behind him. In the fish bin there — on five tons of solid ice — are redfish, lookdowns, stargazers, amberjacks, and kings, not to mention congers, morays, spadefish, ladyfish, catfish, bonitas, barracudas, and guaguanches. In the sense that he means to pay nothing, Willy is begging fish. As the competitors tie up and reveal their entries in the Alabama Deep Sea Fishing Rodeo — twenty-seven hundred competitors, in eight hundred boats — Willy casts a selective eye on the catch. When he decides he wants something and makes a pitch for it, his line is so incongruous that most of the fishermen seem to grant him the benefit of the doubt. Dressed in shorts and sandals and a T-shirt covered with sharks and other fish, he tells them that he is a professor of ichthyology from the University of Massachusetts, and that his purpose in coming to the rodeo is to collect skeletons.

As American fishing tournaments go, this rodeo is, in various respects, at or near the number one: number of boats, number of fisherwomen, number of fishermen, number of species. The last is what attracts Willy. Most tournaments award prizes in one category, and some in four or five categories. These fish, though, are coming from the Fertile Crescent, the fishery piñata of the Gulf of Mexico, in forty-five thousand square miles of which the action takes place; the catch is brought here to Dauphin Island, at the mouth of Mobile Bay; the prizewinners are in thirty categories; and they will range in length from four inches to eight and a half feet.

In the manner of a major golf tournament, a large leader board keeps the crowd informed. Among the categorical leaders of the moment are Robert Groh, with a 156-pound tuna; Creighton T. Parker, with a 33-pound wahoo; Melvin Dunn, with a 33-pound barracuda; John Holley, with a 51-pound grouper; Michael Burgess, with a 6½-pound flounder; and Jeff Gaddy, with a gafftopsail catfish a hair under 8 pounds. Competitors are out there in twelve-foot homemade johnboats fishing "inshore" for redfish, flounder, and speckled trout. Competitors are out there in big cruisers that carry 450 gallons of gasoline and troll along the lip of the continental slope. With fourteen rods in rod holders, brass reels, the big boats, as they come in, bristle like porcupines. Ladders go up to their flying bridges, where other ladders go on up to tuna platforms. They have outriggers, gin poles, venturi windshields, and fighting chairs that would not attract attention in a barbershop. The occupants of these vessels tend to be wearing one-way sunglasses that flash carnival colors — red, green, orange, purple, and blue. When these fishermen are milling about the dock, it appears to be a disco. Other fishermen have big tattoos and no sunglasses.

Resting on the bridge of Willy's nose are two clear lenses, surrounded by gold circles. His hair falls long in all directions from a bald spot at the top. He is a professor with an inquiring mustache, and enough extra weight to make him seem trustworthy — enough to help him float. More, he is amiable, straightforward, and benign. He explains his way of working the fishermen. "I just stand here and see how badly they want their fish." After a moment, he adds, "We came to get tarpon, ladyfish, and sharks, but we'll take as much diversity as we can handle."

Now comes Steve McConnell, in *Play 'N' Hookie,* with a hammer-head shark. *Play 'N' Hookie* is powered by a 225-horse Johnson outboard, and is twenty-one feet long. The shark is nearly nine feet long. Steve — compact, wiry, his hair close cut — presents his ticket to the Mobile Jaycees who officiate the tournament. A portable crane on a bright red truck moves toward the dock. It lifts the hammerhead out of the boat and moves it to a fish rack, a wooden arch twelve feet tall — a gibbet. There the hammerhead is hung, ogled by the crowd, and weighed (163 pounds). It looks a little like a steer and a little more like nothing else in the world, this creature with a widespread rectangular cranium like the bar antenna on a spinning radar. Jerry Walden, the crane operator, has been coming here ten years and has picked up some heavy fish. He remembers a fisherman who came in with a 300-pound shark longer than his boat.

And now a man in sandals with sharks on his shirt appears before McConnell mentioning marine science, mentioning the possibility that McConnell's great fish could find a home in Massachusetts. So far, McConnell's day has included getting out of bed at 4 A.M. and fighting a shark for two hours. He was thirty miles off Dauphin Island, using fifty-pound-test line, a fifteen-hundred-pound-test leader, and two hooks baited with a ten-pound bonita. The hammerhead hammered it. And when all was over, and the fish, exhausted, neared the boat, McConnell saw that a ling, or cobia, about twenty-five pounds, had come up with it, and a second shark was chasing the ling. McConnell's wife and two friends were with him. They went to the rail to see the second shark. Immediately, they all stepped back and clustered in the middle of the boat. The second hammer, as McConnell would describe it, was the largest shark he had seen in fifteen years of shark fishing — "a monster." Now, contemplatively, McConnell looks at Willy Bemis. "Massachusetts?" he says, and donates his fish. An Ohioan who was trained at Cornell, Michigan, Berkeley, and Chicago, Willy is a world-class ichthyologist — coauthor, with Lance Grande, of a 690-page book called *A Comprehensive Phylogenetic Study of Amiid Fishes (Amiidae) Based on Comparative Skeletal Anatomy* — but he is only in his second year at Dauphin Island, and this is his first hammer ever. The crane lowers the fish into Willy's pickup. The nose is near the cab and the tail is out the back. Willy says, "If I live to be a hundred, there's nothing like the first hammerhead you have as a specimen."

Willy adds other species — including a white sea trout and the gafftopsail catfish — and takes off for his lab. The dorsal fin of this catfish will rise so far and so acutely that it closely models the highest sail on the mainmast of a schooner. Otherwise, the cat looks like an ordinary bullhead, barbels and all. The fish ride three

miles down a palm-lined boulevard to the old Army post around
Fort Gaines, beside the mouth of Mobile Bay, where floating mines
were ignored by David Farragut, in 1864, when he sailed through,
saying, "Damn the torpedoes, full speed ahead!" People now pronounce the name of the island as if it were "dolphin," which, as it
happens, is the primary meaning of *dauphin*. The Army post has
become the Dauphin Island Sea Lab, marine-science laboratory of
a consortium of Alabama colleges and universities. In a breezeway
between two buildings, Willy has created a dissection room, with a
floor of crushed shells, screen walls at the two ends, and a four-foot
belt-driven fan. With the help of two assistants, he has dug two offal
pits, found a darkroom sink and plumbed it himself, and set up an
operating table with a surface area of twenty-four square feet.

The hammer is on the table, cater-cornered. Nonetheless, it over-
hangs. Willy picks up a Rapala filleting knife, its thin blade eight
inches long — the same kind of knife I use at home to fillet shad
that weight five pounds. Also on the table are razor blades and a
scalpel. Idly, he slides the palm of one hand away from the shark's
head and along its flank; gingerly, he moves the hand in the other
direction. "It's smooth one way, but like rose thorns and will tear
your flesh the other way. This is caused by a shagreen of denti-
cles. Placoid scales. The skin of the hammerhead was used like
fine sandpaper at one time." The wallet in Willy's pocket is made of
carp skin.

The hammerhead is male. It has two claspers — hard penis-like
pelvic appendages. "That is really, really, really fancy," Willy says
admiringly. "They penetrate the female and shoot." Internal fertili-
zation, standard for sharks, is not uncommon in other fishes, he
remarks, and he slides his knife through the big shark as if he were
cleaning a cod. "You're taking off a hundred pounds before you
dry the skeleton." A large mass of muscle plops onto the table.

"Every few years, a guy makes a name for himself by claiming to
find bone in a shark. The consensus is that there is no bone."

"So how can you be collecting the skeleton? What is the skeleton?"

"Calcified cartilage. The distinction between this type of cartilage
and bone is somewhat subtle. True bone has bone cells, calcified
cartilage does not. You would need a microscope." Another muscle
mass falls off the fish, joining the first one on the table. The shark's

vertebral column is becoming well exposed. "The hammerhead has negligible rib structure," he observes, and, with a heavy cut, he starts another blob on its way to the pits.

Ready for finer work, he picks up a large steel kitchen spoon and uses it as a scraper, working rapidly, removing berms of shark tartare. Hammerheads will kill people. Normally, they eat fish, squid. He drops the spoon and opens the mouth wide, demonstrating its great flexibility, displaying its dental coronet and the hyoid arch. "The hyoid arch is suspended from the jaw by the interhyal, which allows the hyoid arch to move independent of the jaw. It's the only joint that connects the hyoid arch to the rest of the skull." Snap. He goes back to work with the spoon. The Navy became very interested in sharks and shark repellents after the USS *Indianapolis* disaster, in the Second World War, he says, and much of what we know about the sensory biology of sharks — their brains, their nervous systems — we owe to Navy funding. Look at that weird head — leading the fish like the crossbar of the letter T — with eyes at the extremes, nearly half a meter apart. The hammerhead's vision is stereoscopic. The nostrils are long slits, also well separated, like leading-edge grooves near the tips of a wing, allowing three-point olfactory discrimination, receiving scents from great distances. All over the roof of the skull are the gray peppery speckles of the ampullae of Lorenzini, which detect electric fields, maybe including the earth's magnetic field. "These animals live in a very different sensory world than people do. They're detecting things we never detect. The lateral line — a distant sense of touch — senses movement in the water column by detecting changes in water pressure. The hammerhead has a very large brain, comparable to some mammals'. People think of sharks as 'swimming noses.' There's a lot about them they don't understand."

Lateral lines are thin tubes along the sides of fish. A submarine passing fifty fathoms below a ship will feel the pressure of the ship, and note it with instruments less sensitive than a hammerhead's lateral line. The *Indianapolis* was the heavy cruiser that delivered the fission bomb Little Boy to Tinian. After the ship left Tinian, alone, it was fatally torpedoed. Sailors were in the water for as much as ten days. Of the 883 who died, a great many were killed by sharks.

Eric Hilton, who is completing his Ph.D. under Willy at U Mass, removes from the hammerhead a plug of flesh to be studied for its DNA. Hilton's rufous ponytail and pharisaical beard offset the barbered hairlessness of Willy's other assistant. Tall, bare to the waist, he is an undergraduate named Mark Grgurovic. Dangling from a chain around Mark's neck is a golden fish.

Willy opens the hammerhead's body cavity. The liver, brought out on the tabletop, is a large scale model of Oahu. Why so much of it?

"It contains a lot of lipid material, which is light. It is thought to help with the fact that sharks have no swim bladder. They are very agile in the water column. They have to be neutrally buoyant to be agile. The liver helps that happen."

Would Willy comment on the conventional wisdom and litigatory metaphor that sharks can never stop swimming, have to remain in motion as long as they live, because they have no air bladder?

"A lot of sharks stop swimming. A lot of sharks are bottom feeders."

The shark's stomach is now on the table, too, and it is such a gross and loaded bag that it could easily have inside it something I would prefer not to see. As Willy slices into it, I nearly look away. It contains large hunks of large fish — whole severed segments of twenty-pound, thirty-pound fish.

Opening a thick tube about fourteen inches long, he reveals the hammerhead's spiral-valve intestine, which corkscrews around a string-like membrane in the axial center of the tube. "Food goes down the spiral, which has a tremendous surface area. It's a Slinky inside of a pipe."

Willy now opens the penetrating end of a clasper, the part analogous to the glans of a penis. He slices it the long way and spreads it out to show the range of its ability to expand. "Doesn't that look nasty," he comments. "Claspers go in the cloaca and then spread out."

The shark is so long that Willy and Eric break the skeleton into five pieces before putting them into a tub of alcohol for drying. The tub is half of a fifty-five-gallon drum — sliced the long way, like the clasper. The alcohol draws nearly all the water from the tissue, making a great stride in the skeleton's advance toward an exhibition cabinet — exactly what happens in a person who drinks like a fish.

The collection of fish skeletons at the American Museum of Natural History, in New York, is in many respects unrivaled, and can be compared only with skeletal collections in London, Paris, and Chicago. There are more than ten thousand fish skeletons in the American Museum, and about a quarter of them came from the Alabama Deep Sea Fishing Rodeo. Most of these specimens were dissected and prepared by Gareth Nelson, an American Museum ichthyologist, who, over the years, scraped and dried on Dauphin Island more than 2,500 skeletons representing 253 species. A year ago, on the verge of retirement, Nelson brought Willy Bemis with him and showed him how to work the rodeo. Then Nelson went off to Australia. The American Museum, in Willy's words, "is out of the fish-skeleton-collecting business now," and Willy has an obsessional dream. He sees in his mind's eye a Massachusetts Museum of Natural History. He has already sketched a logo for it. He has designed an MMNH green-and-gold flag, which is flapping even now on a pole within a few feet of the space in which he is dissecting. He knows just where on the UMass campus, in Amherst, he intends the building to be. Already, he has raised $1.3 million. He needs twenty.

Sponsored fishing teams are in the rodeo. Young, photogenic pros, they go from tournament to tournament, representing boat makers, engine makers, or tackle companies. Appearing on the dock in essentially identical clothes, they look like assistant basketball coaches: Team Big Boy, in green and gold; Ranger Sportfishermen, in blue. Their boats are as showroom-fresh as they are.

Second afternoon, and *Blue Monday* ties up — a homemade boat flying two Confederate flags. She is skippered by a competitor who is also a commercial fisherman. He has shrimp stickers on his wheelhouse and trawl doors aft. *Blue Monday,* imperfectly fashioned from quarter-inch steel plate, is possibly a sister ship of the *African Queen.* The skipper's face is quizzical and darkly bronzed. His eyes seem to be narrowing on something they can't quite hit. He says he has asbestosis. He says he has been shot eleven times, mainly in Vietnam. He says he has had a heart attack and lung disease, and each day he lives for the day. Crediting a bumper sticker, he says veterans sleep under bridges while a draft dodger sleeps in the White House. His bluefish and red snappers are not going to appear on the leader board. He casts off resignedly, and leaves.

Ynot comes down the Aloe Bay Channel. *Ynot* is a Fountain, a thirty-one-foot open fisherman, with a fineness ratio (length to width) of such elegance that it seems to slice — rather than part — the quiet water. Watching it approach, Jerry Walden remarks that it's "a high-dollar boat." Two people are aboard: a man, at the wheel, and a smiling — not to say exuberant — young woman eyeing the dock. They are father and daughter. Five feet tall, wearing shorts, a T-shirt, and New Balance boat shoes, she is as trig and pretty as the boat — blond and fine-featured, with the shape of a gymnast. *Ynot* waits for an opening and then moves into a slip.

They got up at four, at their home, near Pascagoula, Mississippi, and at six were trolling off the Chandeleur Islands in thirty-five feet of water. Due south of Biloxi Bay, the Chandeleurs are seventy-five miles east of New Orleans. The skipper on this run was John Colle (kól-ē), and the fisherwoman Natalie Colle. With two drift lines and a third line on a downrigger, she was fishing for king mackerel. On each line she used a single hook and a treble hook and a hundred-pound-test metal leader. ("Mackerel have such sharp teeth.") The bait on each line was a ribbonfish, "which we call a silver eel, a skinny eel — the single hook goes through its mouth and nose and the treble hook goes on its back to make it seem to be swimming right, even though it's dead." The line itself was thirty-pound-test, appropriate for a king. Each rod was seven feet long — "a king/ling rod, a standard king-mackerel rod." The rods were held vertically in hardware rod holders.

Off the curving Chandeleurs, the Colles were following birds. ("Where there's birds, there's baitfish; where there's baitfish, there's fish.") They trolled around the feeding schools. ("It was real slick water, real calm. We could see the schools.") Suddenly, one of the drift lines moved. Natalie picked up the rod. For forty-five minutes, the fish on the line held her off. It felt sizable, and Natalie wondered how it might place among the tournament kings. When the fish came to the boat, though, it was a blacktip shark, about five feet long, with three sharksuckers riding on it. She released it, and rerigged the line.

Something hit heavily at noon. The rod was in a rod holder. The reel, on light drag, started "zinging."

"We had the clicker on. Tournament rules — you reel it in yourself. I went to the rod, put it in my rod belt. I'm thinking, It's a big

king. A real big king. The prize king! Before long, it jumped. It
shook in the air. It was a tarpon! Again, he jumped. He twisted in
the air. We call it skyrocketing."

What Natalie had on her line was like this — described for all
time by Thomas McGuane, in the collection he titled *An Outside
Chance:*

> The closest thing to a tarpon in the material world is the Steinway piano.
> The tarpon, of course, is a game fish that runs to extreme sizes, while
> the Steinway piano is merely an enormous musical instrument, largely
> wooden and manipulated by a series of keys. However, the tarpon when
> hooked and running reminds the angler of a piano sliding down a
> precipitous incline and while jumping makes cavities and explosions in
> the water not unlike a series of pianos falling from a great height. If the
> reader, then, can speculate in terms of pianos that herd and pursue
> mullet and are themselves shaped like exaggerated herrings, he will be
> a very long way toward seeing what kind of thing a tarpon is. Those who
> appreciate nature as we find her may rest in the knowledge that no
> amount of modification can substitute the man-made piano for the real
> thing — the tarpon. Where was I?

When her tarpon jumped, Natalie saw a spray of blood leaving
the gills. This was neither the scene nor the fish she had imagined,
and she felt an impulse to cut the line and let the tarpon go. Her
father, John Colle, suggested that she stay with it. In all his years, he
had never caught a tarpon. His father's dream had been to catch a
tarpon. He never did. And now his father's granddaughter had a
tarpon firmly hooked — a fish at least as big as she was. The tarpon,
in a sense, was hanging by a thread. Her monofilament line was
thirty-pound-test.

An hour passed as Natalie dealt with the tarpon. "He fought and
fought. He would surface and jump. He stayed strong the whole
time. I'd huff and puff and reel and get him in close, and he'd take
off again. At least ten times he did that. I thought the rod was going
to break. It was totally bending over. Then he would sound, and sit
there like a dead weight. Every time he did surface, he would take
my line back out and just sit there."

John Colle had shut off the engines. Now and again, the tarpon
pulled the boat. This way. That way. Several times, Natalie walked
completely around its periphery "trying to keep him clear."

After an hour and fifteen minutes, little had changed. "Was I exhausted? No, I'm in pretty good shape. I work out a lot. I do triathlons. I got, if anything, kind of bored. You have to keep the rod tip up the whole time. I'm kind of a hyper person. My attention span isn't real long. When he sat there, I could not reel him in. So I just sat there, too. Each time, he came up a little more slowly. He would make an arch and go down again. When he was making the arch, you could see the brilliance of his body shining off the water. I thought, This is a beautiful animal and he's fallen into a terrible trap. He came close to the boat four times, regained energy, and went off. After an hour and a half, we missed him twice with the gaff. The third time, my father and I hoisted him into the boat together. My first tarpon. My first time, for sure. I had no plans to catch that fish."

She decided to go in and enter the fish "before he loses a lot of weight" — fifty miles to Dauphin Island. As *Ynot* reached the sound and swung into the Aloe Bay Channel, she was, as she would later describe herself, "beaming with excitement." She was thinking, This is going to be great. Maybe I'll set a record. Maybe as a woman angler I've accomplished something. It all seems worthwhile — the heat, the sun, the effort.

Now *Ynot*, after waiting its turn, at last nudges the dock. A Jaycee says to Natalie, who is standing in the bow, "You have a kill permit — right?"

"A kill permit?" she repeats.

"A fifty-dollar tarpon kill permit. You can't enter the fish if you don't have one."

"But I didn't know I was going to catch it — I wasn't trying to catch it."

The Jaycee says he is sorry.

"We were not aware of it."

The Jaycee repeats that he is sorry.

Her great surprise is not as great as her palpable disappointment. Her triumph in vapor, she is struggling to deal with the psychological bends, and in this moment is confronted by a professor from Massachusetts saying, "Can we have your fish? We're marine scientists. We're going to do research."

She is bewildered but she gives him the tarpon. "All right," she says slowly. "You can have him. At least, it's good for research." The tarpon is lifted by two men and carried in a trough to a large scale. Ninety pounds. The tarpon is driven off in an ATV.

Tarpon permits are a requirement of the State of Alabama. Over the years at the deep-sea rodeo, tarpon permits have not been required, because they have always been superseded by the "permit for scientific collecting" that pertained to the American Museum of Natural History. Because Gareth Nelson retired and the tournament was not sure that anyone would be here to replace him, the tarpon permit is mentioned on the competitors' tickets this year for the first time — mentioned, as Natalie Colle sees it, "in little bitty writing."

The Colles might have won prizes for most beautiful boat, most beautiful competitor, most beautiful fish, but those are not categories in this tournament, and *Ynot* goes up the channel into the haze. She is heading back to Pascagoula, the largest deepwater port in Mississippi, where a tugboat named *Natalie* is one of seven vessels in the fleet of Colle Towing — "the place with the big American flag" — where her great-great-grandfather worked, and where she works now. What Natalie Colle doesn't know is that her tarpon's complete and bushy structure, mounted on mahogany, is destined for a wall at the Massachusetts Museum of Natural History.

"If we do a nice job with this fish, it's a major exhibit piece," Willy remarks at the dissecting table, knife in hand. "This is the largest living representative of a group that hasn't changed much in a hundred and twenty-five million years. They are the fish-like elopomorphs, and are generally thought to be closely related to eels. Eels and tarpon have similar larvae — leptocephali — so thin they're almost transparent. I mean big larvae, some of them like a foot long. As larvae metamorphose either into eels or into fish-like elopomorphs, they shrink. It's counterintuitive. Bonefish and ladyfish are elopomorphs. The group also has an interesting fossil history and is probably among the most primitive of the teleosts. We study them to get that insight."

In a day or two, Natalie will send her tarpon's measurements ("I'm sixty inches, he was nine inches longer") to J. T. Reese Taxidermy, Inc., in Fort Lauderdale, Florida, which will feed the data into a computer and reproduce the tarpon in glass and fiberglass, and send it to Pascagoula. Willy, meanwhile, at the dissecting table, begins to remove the tarpon's skin. With the knife, he is as slow and careful now as he was swift and casual in addressing the shark, because the tarpon has three thousand bones, including six sets of intermuscular bones, the tips of which touch the skin. Eventually, he holds up what appears to be a vest of chain mail. A single tarpon scale is nearly as large as a playing card, and the third of it that is not overlapped by other scales is covered with what appears to be silver plate. You can read the age of the tarpon in the rings of the scale. This one is thirteen years old. Tarpon scales are deciduous — lightly attached, easily removed — and are almost pure bone. People collect them as souvenirs and paint seascapes on them where they are shell white, above the silver.

The flesh looks wine red, but the red muscle is only a veneer over a white inner mass. When fish swim idly, routinely, steadily, Willy says, they are using red muscle, but when, for any reason, fish require great speed they use white muscle. The flesh of the tarpon, like the flesh of an orange, is divided into segments. In this tarpon, each segment is about half an inch wide. The intermuscular bones are ossified connective tissue between the flesh segments. The intermuscular bones are attached variously to ribs and to the vertebral column. They are so numerous that the skeleton, to a remarkable extent, will resemble the complete fish. With the filleting knife, Willy makes long slices between the intermusculars — angling with them toward the tail — and then begins scraping with the cooking spoon, driving shredded flesh along and off the bones as if he were cleaning a pitchfork.

Detaching the skull from the bony curve that is known as the pectoral girdle is not easy without an axe, but Willy patiently succeeds, commenting as he works: "Fishes have a loose pelvic girdle, just floating, whereas the pectoral girdle is attached to the back of the skull tightly — the reverse of land creatures like us, tight in the pelvis and loose in the shoulders."

Now he has the tarpon's head in his two hands and, with a little pressure, causes the mouth to open so wide that a small car could park inside it. Or so it seems. "The hyoid drops down, the top of the head comes up, then the two sides go out. What an incredible expansion! It flares the suspensorium!" Between the lower jaws is a bone called the gular, common in fossil fishes but rare in the modern world. Also evident, with steel connective wire, are Natalie Colle's hooks — one in the urohyal bone, ventral to the gill arches, and the other in connective tissue between the urohyal and the lower jaw.

Going into the tarpon's swim bladder, Willy removes a thick, spongy cord that resembles lung tissue. "These fish come up to the surface and gulp air," he comments. "It's because of this special tissue in the swim bladder. In the Florida Keys, tarpon come up, breathe air, and eat what tourists feed them."

With a wire brush, he scrubs the cavity of the tarpon along the bottom of the backbone, locus of the kidneys. You could knit a wool sweater with two tarpon ribs. Not long ago, Willy was diving in the Cayman Islands, and he went into a natural tunnel in a reef. The tunnel was full of tarpon. Hundreds of tarpon. "They are not skittish," he says. "They are so peaceful. They let you swim around them." Much like caribou.

Albert Reynolds, a Mobile stockbroker who is a former chairman of the rodeo, takes me out to the action in his twenty-two-foot single-engine Grady-White. Through early morning air too thick to be haze, too thin to be fog, we go to the western tip of Dauphin Island and then run south about seven miles. Suddenly, in the cottony seascape, looms a great standing structure, more than two hundred yards long, in three parts joined by long aerial footbridges. Rising through fifty-seven feet of water and continuing on up ten stories, the Triple Rig, as the fishermen call it, is Chevron 864MO, largest of the numerous platforms that collectively produce a hundred million dollars' worth of natural gas in this area of the Gulf each year. Broad and squarish, the central structure resembles an oil refinery, with Erector-set skeletal girders. Three pipes come up beneath it, because it is the center of three radial wells. Its highest point is a long, crane-like tilted arm, whose upper end is abloom with orange flame. A safety device, it is known on the rig as "the flare." Signs wherever you look say "Danger Poison Gas H_2S." The tower at one end supports a three-story house, the crew's quarters. The tower at the other end accommodates a fourth well. Under the connecting footbridges are passages of open water, where boats can go through the platform. Eight boats are fishing here. A couple are tied to the structure. Most are trolling. Like shuttles going back and forth in a loom, ours and the other trolling boats woof the Triple Rig. The oil and gas platforms of the Gulf have the same effect as artificial reefs. In a soft-bottomed environment unappealing to invertebrates, they offer hard surfaces for the likes of barnacles and

clams, which in turn attract reef fish and transient species. Out of
sight of land, out in the marine wild, one of the best places to go
fishing is under the Chevron flare.

One boat, surprisingly, is *Play 'N' Hookie*. Where we are fishing
earnestly for prizewinning kings, Steve McConnell has stopped off
to fish for shark bait. He is fishing for bonitas to take to deeper
water and drag past the noses of hammerheads. The symbiosis
between oil or gas platforms and recreational fishing is personified
in Steve McConnell. Half his time, he lives on a rig. He is an
operator of oil rigs. Every other week, he leaves his home, in Mobile, to spend seven nights headquartered on Eugene Island 42,
about fifteen miles from land, south of Morgan City, Louisiana, at
the Atchafalaya Basin Sea Buoy. Frequently, he fishes from the rig,
catching king mackerel, red snapper, dolphin. Employed by Sonat
— a company that sells its crude oil to Shell, Chevron, Mobil, and
Exxon — he runs seven other rigs, too, across four hundred miles
of the Gulf. Every day, he flies from rig to rig in a helicopter, and
fishing rods are always aboard.

If you float a wooden plank, fish will be attracted to its shadow
and shelter. You can fish productively near the plank. If you don't
have a plank, try an oil rig. The public-relations benefits of rig
fishing have not been lost on the energy companies. Chevron, in
fact, has a "Rigs to Reefs" program, in which rigs that have ceased
to produce oil or gas are disengaged from the seabed, toppled
onto their sides, and, in many cases, dragged to appropriate fishing
sites.

Albert Reynolds has three lines out, thirty-pound-test, with stain-
less-steel leaders, and fishes them close to the boat, scarcely ten
yards back. He outlines the thought processes that go on in king
mackerels' brains: "Near the boat, they think they've got to get it
and run. Way back there, they look it over and think something's
wrong and go away." As baitfish he is using blue runners — foot-
long jacks locally known as hard tails. Gentle-mannered and quietly
bemused, now in his upper sixties, Albert Reynolds has been fishing the rodeo forty-five years. He once took a second prize with a
speckled trout but "can't remember when." His boat is *Shazam* and
his wife calls him Captain Marvel. He has been successful enough
as an investor for this to qualify as a reference to his work. "You
catch the right fish, you can make a lot of money," he remarks

about the rodeo. It may not be the All-American Futurity at Rui-
doso Downs, and it's not the PGA championship, but as fishing
tournaments go it has attractive money. There's a prize worth
$30,000 for most overall points, a $5,000 jackpot for the biggest
king, and another $120,000 spread through the various categories.
Rocky Marciano fished here.

Something hits a hard tail, and a reel zings. It is my turn to pick it
up. The reel is rigged for right-handers, so I try turning it upside
down, which makes Reynolds chuckle. It also doesn't work, and I
fish right-handed. The thing on the line feels heavy. It is active in
the water column. It is stronger than a bluefish. It feels like a big
roe shad. As I hold up the rod tip toward the Chevron rig and the
billowing flame, I pass the time, mentally, at an ATM in New Jersey
depositing the $5,000. Nice fish. You can tell. You can feel it. Baby
grand. And after eight or ten minutes it is out of the water and into
Shazam. King mackerel. Forty-six inches long. Nineteen pounds,
ten ounces.

I remember Willy Bemis saying about kings, "They're aggressive,
torpedo-shape, fantastic animals. They're running very strong right
now, fifty-pound size." I have at least caught dinner.

All afternoon at the judges' stand, fishermen arrive with long insu-
lated white vinyl bags, like bulky ski bags zippered up for travel.
These are king bags, so called, and the zippers open to reveal
torpedo-shaped fantastic animals: a fifty-four-pound king, a sixty-
one-pound king, a sixty-three-pound king. Robert Shipp, one of
the judges, says, "The big kings are more than a hundred miles
offshore. Fast boats go sixty miles an hour to get them. It is not
uncommon for them to run a hundred and fifty miles to weigh
'em in."

Shipp, an ichthyologist at the University of South Alabama, is the
author of *Dr. Bob Shipp's Guide to Fishes of the Gulf of Mexico.* Long
before he became an official of the tournament, he came to Dauphin Island every summer to teach his marine-vertebrate course at
the academic sea lab. The immemorial judge of the tournament
was Roy Martin, mayor of Panama City Beach, Florida. Over time, as
prizes grew larger, and decisions with them, the mayoralty of Panama City Beach became an insufficient qualification for the rodeo
bench. There came a great question: Is this a very small blue marlin

or a very large white marlin? Roy Martin took the Fifth. The tournament's underwriting bankers asked Bob Shipp if he would become assistant judge. Sure, he said. A student of the population biology of fishes, he was interested in the tournament for the fish. A question even more controversial soon arose as well: Is this a young king mackerel or a Spanish mackerel? Spanish mackerel have spots, and so do young kings, which resemble mature Spanish mackerel. This was all sort of academic until the jackpot prize for the biggest Spanish mackerel approached and then surpassed a couple of thousand dollars. Shipp — gray hair, equanimous mustache, handsome as a tenor — was addressed one day by a fisherman he describes as having "one or two teeth, breath of beer and garlic, and bloodshot eyes." The fisherman laid a fish before Shipp and said, "That beauty is a Spanish mackerel."

Shipp said, "I'm sorry. It's a small king."

The fisherman said, "I've got Dr. Bob Shipp's book in my boat. I'll get it and show you."

One of the rodeo's prize categories is Most Unusual. It illuminates the tournament, because a fish of any size can win it. A fish four inches long can be honored beside a tarpon. The winner is determined by what Shipp calls "unofficial subjective calibration." Shipp picks the winner.

The Most Unusual category was introduced in the middle eighties. Tony Stuardi, a marlin fisherman, caught on early. He went so far out in the Gulf — at least a hundred miles — that he laid up overnight. Most Unusual, he thought as he lay there, rising on the swells, and he got up and baited two bream hooks — ordinary small hooks of the sort more accustomed to dangling in a pond — and dropped them on a long line over the side. He was dropping them into DeSoto Canyon — two thousand feet of water, off the edge of the continental shelf. He caught a six-inch fanged mackerelet. By anyone's calibration, it was a clear winner. The next year, Stuardi came in with something equally odd, and Shipp again awarded him the prize. Then he told Stuardi that in years to come Stuardi could show up with anything from an oilfish to a bearded puffer but he was not going to win.

The blacktail moray lives so obscurely in deep water that it was not even described taxonomically until 1980, when it was known from only twenty-five specimens found in the world. Since then,

however, six blacktail morays have appeared in the Alabama Deep
Sea Fishing Rodeo, three of them this year. Shipp no longer thinks
them unusual. Subjectively, they haven't got a prayer. He looks for
"something never entered before, and if it's a legitimate catch we'll
move it up to the top of the list." Three-two-one on his present
list are Wendy Kennedy's short-fin mako shark, Don Henderson's
smooth dogfish, and David Simms's blunt-nose jack — a fish that
Shipp has never seen anywhere.

The geographical boundaries of the tournament were established after a competitor fished off Costa Rica and flew to Dauphin
Island with the catch. Money may not have been the whole motiva-
tion. It is not always simple to fathom what makes a fisherman
cheat. Why did Marcus Antonius, the Triumvir, cause dead lunkers
to be draped on his hook so he could lift them from the water in
the presence of Cleopatra? For the prestige? Did he actually think
so little of her? According to Plutarch, she sent a servant swimming
under Antony's boat with a dried, salted fish from the Black Sea.
The servant put it on Antony's hook. When Antony pulled up the
fish, he was drenched by all present with derisive laughter. "Impera-
tor," she said, "you had better give up your rod."

The late Roy Martin, when he was the rodeo's judge, opened the
stomach of a fish scoring high on the tournament scale. A chunk of
lead fell out. That was not an isolated moment. Over the years,
enough lead has been discovered in rodeo stomachs to suggest a
new link in the food chain.

There were fishermen who came in every year with entries of
frozen red snappers. And a clergyman in the tournament brought
to the scale an amberjack that weighed ninety pounds. It was full of
frozen blue runners — stuffed with frozen bait. In recent times, the
tournament has acquired a Torrymeter, a machine that tests flesh
to see if it has been frozen. "Electrodes pass current through a fish,"
Shipp explains. "If cells have been ruptured by freezing or deterio-
ration, the current is stronger. A computer chip translates it to a
number." The tournament has also introduced a polygraph. Competitors agree to its use when they buy their tickets. When the
polygraph was first contemplated, a mailer was sent out asking if the
competitors would approve. Eighty-five percent said yes. In the first
polygraph year, a winner failed the test miserably and was disquali-
fied. He sued the Alabama Deep Sea Fishing Rodeo, but soon

withdrew the suit. In the summary words of Bob Shipp, "He was a lyin' sumbitch and they got him."

As a Confederate cannon ends the tournament, spectators are ten deep straining to look into the fish bin. A woman leaning over a vermilion snapper is wearing a green bikini. Jingling in her navel on an extremely short gold chain is a green pendant scarab. She is not alone in her choice of wardrobe. All the way down the back wall of the bin are women leaning forward in bikinis, resting on the cinder block their soft-rayed pectoral fins. We have come here for purposes of comparative anatomy, and we're getting what we came for. I mean this as a compliment: these women are almost as good-looking as the fish. Before them on the ice are whitebone porgies, whitespotted soapfish, wahoos, black drums, gags, and snake eels. Striped burrfish. Gray triggerfish. Violet gobies. Rainbow runners. Bearded brotulas. Sailfish. Tarpon. Horse-eyed jacks. Literally, it's a ton of fish, and only a small fraction of all the competing fish not retained in the bin by the judges.

The rodeo has been criticized for killing so many fish, which is, among other reasons, why Willy is particularly welcome here. The aura of research tends to mute criticism. One of my sons-in-law is the skipper of a trawler in the Bering Sea. He fishes for cod, for Alaska walleye pollock. Both in metric tons and in numbers of fish, he will often catch in a single pass, in five minutes, the equivalent of all the fish caught in the Alabama Deep Sea Fishing Rodeo.

Willy is now lecturing the crowd on pelvic and pectoral fins. He is actually in the bin himself, standing, in his sandals, among the fish on the ice, because he knows that spectators will soon be taking the fish, and he is keeping an eye on specimens he has chosen for the lab. Pectoral fins, which spread to either side just below and behind the head, are for steering and braking, he says. The pelvic fins are anti-roll devices. Anti-roll devices on ships include stabilizers and flume tanks. Commercial fishing boats will extend their booms to both sides and lower into the water delta-shaped weights known as flopper-stoppers. Their flop-stopping ability may be considerable but cannot approach the efficacy of a pair of pelvic fins. Dorsal fins, in erection, supply some power and are helpful with anti-roll and steering, but more often they are social: they attract or repel other fish. The caudal fin — the tail fin — is for power. A tall, forked tail is for high speed. A squared tail is for easy going, moseying near the bottom.

A boy about four feet tall wants to know if he is as long as a king snake eel. Willy measures him with an eel. He is not.

A man in camouflage pants and a sleeveless red T-shirt reaches into the fish bin and picks up specimens one by one. He opens the mouth of each fish, looks down into it, and asks Willy what it is. "Almaco jack," Willy says. "*Seriola riviolana*. Pretty unusual." This one? "Cubyu. *Equetus umbrosus*." This one? "Tilefish. *Caulolatilus chrysops*. See how the teeth are angled backward? If the guy bites into food, it's not going to come out." In the mouth of the short-fin mako shark are two sets of teeth. "They are made to cut and then slice," Willy says. "Which is really cool." The sailfish, with that long hard bill, stuns prey by hitting it as if with a ball bat, which it does with a whip of the head. "Blacktail moray," Willy says, moving on. "*Gymnothorax kolpos*. '*Gymno*' means naked. It hasn't got any scales. You can look at it and right away make a lot of predictions based on its anatomy. That eel-like body can live in cracks and crevices. Those tubular nostrils allow him to sample water farther away than would otherwise be the case. There are no paired fins. They don't need anti-roll devices."

Back in the lab by 6 P.M., Willy works through the evening without dinner, putting off until midnight the cooking of fillets of dolphin and sailfish. In three days, he has collected 52 species and 115 specimens. Fifty of the smaller fish are on the table now. Where to start?

He picks up a five-inch tattler bass. It was caught on squid bait three hundred feet down. Coming up so fast caused its air bladder to move into its mouth like a cherry. "These are serranids," he says. "This family has interesting reproductive biology. Females reverse to males, and vice versa. In the spawning rush, one tattler will release an egg, another milt. Next time, each does the opposite. Sex reversal is not uncommon. Some fish are born alive, but not these."

He fillets a one-pound leopard toadfish. There's not a lot to cut. The toadfish is 75 percent head. It looks like a boulder with a tail. Its flesh is pure white. "Which is what you would expect in a fish that does almost nothing but sit and wait for something to go by." It is doing less than that when it pursues an oyster. That bouldery head, with its small molar-like teeth, is a shell crusher. Willy removes the jaw muscles. They are the size and shape of two golf balls. "Are those the coolest jaw muscles you ever saw, or what?" he says. "But here's what's even more cool about this fish." He removes a diaphanous spheroid that looks very much like a calf testicle — a mountain oyster. It is the leopard toadfish's swim bladder, wrapped in a veneer of sonic muscle, which the toadfish vibrates to make sound. "Some fish produce sound for social communication," Willy says. "Some species make sounds with their fins, with their teeth, with their gill arches. This one does it with the swim bladder."

After three days and nights, Willy's body is hurting; his hands are puffy and sore. What drives him on is that everywhere he looks he sees another golden chance. He has worked in the Tana River, in Kenya; in the Brisbane River, in Australia; in the Comoro Islands, off East Africa; in the ponds of the Osage Catfisheries Company, in Osage Beach, Missouri, which are full of paddlefish, sturgeons, and gars. "It's an unparalleled opportunity," he says, once more sharpening his knife. "I couldn't collect like this anywhere in the world."

RANDALL PATTERSON

The Trophy Son

FROM THE HOUSTON PRESS

IN HER IMMACULATE KITCHEN, remembering the saddest day, Mrs. Sonja Rutherford's lip began to tremble. "It makes me cry even now," she said, sniffling. "Sorry." And she reached for the Kleenex.

They had such hopes for that day. It was May 17, 1996, and Kyle Rutherford's whole family — his mother, Sonja; his father, Scott; his brother who had driven from Austin; an aunt and uncle from Fort Worth; another aunt and uncle from North Carolina — they had all come out to watch Kyle pitch. It would be the last game of his senior year, unless Cypress Falls High won. Kyle's parents believed college scouts would be watching. His mother called it "the game of his life."

They were waiting for this game to begin, this ultimate contest that would return glory to their home, when Mr. Rutherford saw Kyle, his would-be hero, not walking onto the field but plodding off of it, speaking those horrible, unspeakable words.

Benched again, said Kyle.

Mr. Rutherford became despondent then. Mrs. Rutherford began weeping. And sitting nearby, the football coach seems to have simply been waiting to watch a baseball game. Wayne Hooks had been through more than thirty high school football seasons, but he had never been to a baseball game like this one.

The Rutherfords shared their pain with the principal, who called the football coach down from the stands and asked him to explain what had happened on the baseball team. He said he could not, and the principal shrugged.

Kyle's brother and one of his uncles stepped forth. They told Coach Hooks that he was, among other things, one "sorry individual." Violence seemed imminent until the principal threatened to call the police. After they departed, Coach Hooks was just relaxing again when he was approached by a friend of Kyle's and was told he was "not much of a man." In fact, the coach was "the most despicable man" the fellow had ever met.

Hooks took all of this into consideration, but it was the confrontation with Mrs. Rutherford that made the deepest impression. If she'd had a gun, she probably would have shot him, she said later. Instead, with her face contorted in anger and the tears streaming down, Mrs. Rutherford shouted, "When are you going to leave our family alone? This is not over! We'll see you in court!"

And somewhere, out on the field, there was a baseball game. Kyle Rutherford stayed on the bench as the Golden Eagles went through four pitchers and lost, 8–4. The trainer drove a truck over to the dugout. The football coach and the baseball coach were smuggled off to safety.

The Rutherfords live in a Cypress-Fairbanks subdivision called Hearthstone, where the houses are large and the cars are new, but where dreams die young and people trudge through ordinary lives with utterly no hope of playing big-league ball.

The death of Kyle's particular dream left the Rutherford family in agony. As a result of the benching of May 17, 1996, and related tragedies, Mr. Rutherford is said to have become a "social recluse." Mrs. Rutherford suffered sleeplessness, extreme stress, and "general weepiness." And Kyle Rutherford did not get a college scholarship and grew depressed.

Several months after the game, the Rutherfords recited these woes in filing a federal lawsuit. They alleged that Wayne Hooks, who was Cy Falls' athletic director as well as football coach, was the mastermind of a conspiracy that violated Kyle's constitutional rights, cost him a scholarship, and caused all of them "severe emotional damage." The family asked for damages in the amount "the court deems appropriate."

The Rutherfords, in the meantime, continue to mourn. Mr. Rutherford has only recently begun reentering the larger world. At home, he and his wife sit in their soft armchairs, watching the pros screw up on television. Mrs. Rutherford will say, "Gee, Kyle could have done better than that." And Mr. Rutherford answers curtly, "Yup." She still occasionally weeps. When the basketball player La- trell Sprewell choked his coach, Mrs. Rutherford understood how he felt.

"Choking's too good for them," she said.

As for Kyle, he had to settle finally for an academic scholarship at Texas Christian. The lawsuit that bears his name was not his idea, and to avoid talking about it, he rarely comes home. His mother and father fight on without him. Mrs. Rutherford admits the case has become her obsession. "We're doing this for Kyle," she says, and the same energy she once spent helping Kyle's teams, she now devotes to suing his coaches. Some nights, she stays up until 3 A.M., reading depositions, scribbling comments in the margins ("liar!"), pounding out letters to the lawyer. She spoke at length for this story. When the school's lawyer advised the coaches not to cooper- ate, Mrs. Rutherford provided their depositions.

More than anything, she wants to be understood. After the benching, the Rutherfords tried not to discuss it with acquain- tances, but after making it a federal case, they were happy to talk with the entire world. The lawsuit, if anything, seems to have made the whole situation *less* embarrassing for them. Its message, after all, is that Kyle was never benched for any shortage of ability. He was only the victim of extremely wicked coaches.

Their story was picked up by the Associated Press, and eventually appeared in a syndicated column called "News of the Weird." Mrs. Rutherford quickly fired off a letter to the author. "How can you," she wrote, "make a mockery out of our attempt to fight for justice?"

Which is to say, how can you laugh? If anyone in the Rutherfords' circle had been able to laugh, then maybe the family wouldn't have found itself in federal court. But laughing would have required a sense of humor, which would have required perspective. And in all the passion of Texas high school sports, perspective is often lost.

"If you knew the important issues at stake," Mrs. Rutherford went on, "you would not be making a joke out of our son's painful experience."

She is a small, nervous woman whose mouth in repose wears a look of dread. Returning to his former self, Mr. Rutherford is amiable, with a Texas twang, and seems like the insurance salesman he is.

He doesn't know if his children could have grown up without an interest in sports. Mr. Rutherford's father, who was the water boy in high school, always threw balls at his boy. In time, Mr. Rutherford became a high school quarterback and a pitcher and even earned a football scholarship to Rice University. Deep on the depth chart, he quit the team in his sophomore year. More than twenty-five years later, he still spends part of every day regretting this.

The Rutherfords married while still in college and, after graduation, quickly settled into conventional roles. She became the homemaker, and he the breadwinner. He always managed to work in jobs that allowed ample time at home. When they began having children, they both agreed their priority, as Mrs. Rutherford said, was "raising decent human beings."

Like his own father, Mr. Rutherford threw balls at his children. The first of their trio was a good athlete but preferred solitary sports. He grew up to become a golf pro in Austin. Kyle was next: he was built like his daddy, and right away his daddy noticed his "awesome" hand-eye coordination. Everyone seemed to notice. In the front yard, Mr. Rutherford pitched plastic balls to his two-year-old, and a neighbor said, "That kid's coordination is great!" It was the kind of story the Rutherfords never forgot.

They recall the victories of Kyle's early history as others might remember the heroics of Babe Ruth. Kyle was just six when he chipped the ball in from the sand and won the eight-and-under golf tournament. "That was a big moment!" Mrs. Rutherford said. He was seven and seeded tenth when he won his division at a swim meet. After he began playing T-ball, he hit so many home runs that even Mrs. Rutherford got bored.

Kyle never had a problem with his coach until his coach wasn't his father. Coach Rutherford always taught the fundamentals of the game, but above all, he said, he stressed teamwork. Nothing irritated him more than "a kid who thought he was a star and screamed for the ball." His own son was a team player "one hundred percent," said the coach.

"He lived a charmed life," Mrs. Rutherford said. "He was always the little star."

Like many boys, Kyle grew up wearing NFL jerseys, but also developed a stylized signature, suitable for autographs. When he got to high school, just like his daddy, he became a quarterback and a pitcher.

As Kyle led his team on the field, his parents led the supporters on the sidelines. Since Cy Falls was a new school, Mrs. Rutherford didn't want Kyle to suffer from its lack of tradition. Together, she and her husband founded the booster club. For two and a half years, they spent nearly every spare hour raising money, setting up the concession stand, selling ads for the weekly program. They didn't mind. Their son was the quarterback.

Kyle's father talked about football wherever he was — in the insurance office, at lunch, in the locker room of the country club where he played golf. More than anywhere, he talked about it at the dinner table. Until the next game, the last game was just about all he had to discuss with his son. "High school football's about the most fun you'll have in your entire life," said Mr. Rutherford.

On game days, all the parents would sit together with their programs and binoculars and video cameras. Mrs. Rutherford said it was very exciting to be the mother of the quarterback, "but I kept telling myself, Don't let it go to your head!" Kyle's status could change at any time, she knew, but it was always injury that she feared ("You read about broken necks, you know"). During the games, each time an opponent would lay hands on her son, Mrs. Rutherford would lay hands on her husband, shrieking and slapping him until Kyle rose unharmed. It was such a distraction to Mr. Rutherford that he chose eventually to sit apart from his wife.

Mr. Rutherford enjoyed his place among the parents. He was grateful when someone told him the coach had said Kyle was the best freshman quarterback he'd ever seen. Mr. Rutherford believed it. He came to believe that Kyle had a gift: he could throw a football better than anyone in town.

"I know I'm his father," Mr. Rutherford said, "but I'm objective when it comes to this."

They had two glorious years, during which the young Golden Eagles crushed nearly everyone they played. Perhaps on the strength of these seasons, Kyle began receiving form letters from college recruiters, including one from Texas A&M that read, "You are now the focus of our recruiting efforts."

The Rutherfords seem to have interpreted these as promissory notes, as though it were just a matter of time. In Kyle's junior year, the school fielded its first varsity squad, and it was then that everything changed. Coach Hooks and his assistants became much more serious. Every time Kyle came off the field, they seemed to have a new complaint. From the stands, the Rutherfords could see the coaches red in the face, shouting at their boy. They hesitated to complain. They feared the coaches would retaliate by scuttling the scholarships.

Anyway, Kyle began to falter. He threw critical interceptions. When the rush came, he panicked, exhibiting what the coaches called "shaky feet." After the seventh game, when he threw four interceptions, the coaches told Kyle Rutherford to have a seat.

He played in none of the final three games. Mr. and Mrs. Rutherford began to suffer the "severe emotional damage" of which they would later complain. When the season was over, they finally sat down with Coach Hooks. They told him he was a bad coach. To any trained eye, Kyle was obviously more talented than his replacement. Surely, Hooks saw this. The Rutherfords came to view him not as an incompetent coach but as a crooked one. They saw only one way to explain the fact that Kyle sat on the bench: his replacement was the nephew of a former superintendent, who must have cut a deal with Coach Hooks. "I don't know how else he could play. It was not ability," said Mr. Rutherford. (The player in question would later make the All-District team.)

Mr. Rutherford extracted from Coach Hooks a promise that Kyle would be treated fairly the next year. When Hooks gave his word on that, Mrs. Rutherford was skeptical, but Mr. Rutherford was fully assured Kyle would again be Cy Falls' starting quarterback.

He was. He wasn't. And then he was. Mr. Rutherford, who was in the hospital for the first game, had the tape brought to him and was dismayed. Coach Hooks had decided to alternate Kyle with the other quarterback from series to series. Hooks said later that Kyle had worked hard for four years and deserved to play some, but the Rutherfords were not consoled.

At home, the grief began setting in. Kyle would try to talk football with his father, but his father would only grunt. "Talk to him!" Mrs. Rutherford pleaded privately with her husband. But Mr. Rutherford said, "It's too depressing."

Kyle stayed in his room with the door closed. Mr. Rutherford saved his words for God. "Lord," he prayed, "you've blessed him with so much ability — why won't you let him use it?"

Still, their star did not shine. Kyle felt worthless on the bench. In the field, he was rarely allowed to pass. The Golden Eagles were losing nearly every week, and in the middle of the sixth game, Mrs. Rutherford watched Kyle trudge off the field and knew their football dream was over. She borrowed the keys of the parent who had driven them, and she went to cry alone in the van.

Later, Kyle and the team listened as Hooks explained that they were losers. Then Kyle stepped into the coach's office and told him football just wasn't fun anymore, and well, "I guess I quit." Hooks shouted for the assistants to clean out Rutherford's locker, and that was that.

Walking into the night, Kyle found his father waiting for him. For the first time in his life, Kyle saw his father cry. Kyle cried, too. In the parking lot by the gym, they cried together.

Grief fell over the Rutherford home like a wet blanket. "It was like someone died, almost," said Mrs. Rutherford. "We all took it hard."

The Rutherfords quit the booster club and threw away the plaque they received for their service. They shut themselves inside their home. Without football to speak of, Mr. Rutherford quit his golf club and avoided the restaurants where once he had held forth so proudly. "I just got tired of going around people, trying to answer questions I can't answer," he explained. Mrs. Rutherford, by then, was fully afflicted with "general weepiness." At night, she lay awake thinking about her son, who lay awake, just thinking.

In the darkness of mourning, the only hope the Rutherfords saw was that some recruiter might pick up what Coach Hooks had put down. And then as January arrived, there were thoughts of baseball. Baseball always brought glory. Kyle was a pitcher with an eighty-five-mile-an-hour fastball, said Mr. Rutherford.

"And a knuckle drop," Mrs. Rutherford added.

Baseball gave them many reasons for hope, not least of which was a coach who still believed in Kyle. From Kyle's freshman year right through the lawsuit, Coach Archie Hayes continued to believe Kyle was "a great kid," though one who sometimes made mistakes and had to learn from them. Such was the coach's faith in Kyle that before Kyle's senior year, Hayes sent a letter to college recruiters urging them to take a look at "the heart and soul of our pitching staff," a player who would be "an asset to anyone's program."

Kyle was supposed to have a wonderful season, but he and his family had problems forgetting football. Coach Hayes noticed that Kyle didn't practice as hard as before. Kyle blamed Coach Hooks. The baseball season hadn't yet begun when Kyle came home and announced, "When is Coach Hooks going to leave me alone?"

"What do you mean?" Mrs. Rutherford asked.

"Mom, I didn't get captain!"

"*What!*"

The Rutherfords saw no other way to explain it: since Coach Hayes liked Kyle, and Kyle's leadership qualities were evident to anyone, Coach Hooks must have rigged the players' election of their captain.

In nearly everything that went wrong that baseball season, the Rutherfords found the football coach to blame. He became to them a large, looming Satan of sports, bent on the destruction of Kyle, simply because his parents had dared question a coach.

For some time, the Rutherfords bore their injuries well and soldiered on. The damage football had done to Kyle's psyche he seems to have concealed. His mother said, "He's very humble. He isn't the kind to strut." But in the stories from that season, he seems to swagger.

In one game, he raved at an umpire to the point that his teammates and coach rushed forth to calm him down. In another, after throwing the final pitch, Kyle shouted to the opposing team, "Number one, my ass!" He was an aggressive designated hitter; from across the field one day, Hayes heard him yell, "Coach, use your damn head and let me hit!"

A precedent was set when Kyle stood on the mound, ignoring his coach's pitching signals. "I know how to call my own pitches," Kyle said later. "I had been pitching since I was eight years old." He had given up five runs in the first inning before Hayes strolled out for a chat. "Kyle threw a temper tantrum," the coach recalled in his deposition, "and began accusing me of trying to put him down."

Which Coach Hayes did, of course. Kyle sat out the rest of that game, and as punishment, the next one, too. For one infraction or another, he sat on the bench during four games.

The family finally had to accept that all interest in Kyle as a football prospect had dried up. Maybe this was because Kyle had ceased to be a football player, but it was easier to believe that Hooks had slandered Kyle to the recruiters.

"They must have said something about me," said Kyle, "to all of a sudden make everyone quit talking to me."

From baseball scouts, though, Kyle was still receiving "Dear Prospect" form letters from such places as Lamar University in Beaumont, Southwest Texas State in San Marcos, Baylor, and Texas Christian. The Rutherfords were sure Hooks was trying to kill these hopes, too, when they received news that Kyle had been named to the all-district team *only* as a designated hitter.

"I guarantee you," Mr. Rutherford explained, "that Coach Hooks said, 'You don't let Kyle be captain and don't nominate him as pitcher for all-district.' And Hayes, he got around it by nominating Kyle for designated hitter."

The injustice of it all finally brought Mr. Rutherford to express himself again. Mrs. Rutherford, because of her work with the football programs, had been asked to help organize a farewell book for the graduating seniors. There would be ads from parents wishing their children the best — Kyle's would be one of the few full-page ads — and there would be "wills," in which seniors would take parting shots at those they were leaving behind.

The wills were supposed to be exclusively from seniors, but Mr. Rutherford later confessed to authoring two anonymous bequests. One, "to all football parents," offered the number of a good real estate agent: "Call 444-MOVE!!!" Another left Coach Hooks "a new set of earplugs so you can't hear the other coaches in the district laughing at you."

Mr. Rutherford also had a suggestion for Kyle's will. As Mrs. Rutherford recalled, Kyle said, "But Coach Hooks will get mad, won't he?"

"Well, what can he do to you?" asked Mr. Rutherford. "You're out of school. You'll never see him again."

"Well, okay," Kyle said, and he sat down to write the will that would change his life. To one comrade, he left "some of my blazing speed"; to another, "some of my smarts I don't use"; and to a third, a can of Skoal. And just as his daddy told him, Kyle wrote, "To Coach Hooks, I leave a $40,000 debt. I figure you cost me that much with your 3–7 season."

The will was electric. It was, without dispute, pure and genuine insubordination. A certain Coach Raffield seems to have taken delight in handing it to Hooks and to Hayes, gauging their reactions and spreading the word.

Coach Hooks abandoned a recruiter he was speaking with and went directly to complain to the principal. A student should never be allowed to speak of a teacher in this way, he believed. What most annoyed Hooks was that Kyle had called it *his* 3–7 season, when actually the coach was not responsible.

"You know," Hooks said in his deposition, "I didn't get any shin splints from playing. I didn't play."

It must have been interesting to watch Coach Hayes read the will. "I felt," he said later, "like my heart had been ripped out."

Meanwhile, Kyle was preparing for the regional quarter-final game. According to the custom Mrs. Rutherford had maintained since he was a little boy, she kissed him and said, "Hit me a grounder and throw strikes!"

Alas, it was not to be.

Perhaps, on that last day of school, there truly was a small conspiracy to bench Kyle Rutherford. In the court record, Hayes and Hooks swore they never saw each other that day; other coaches, in turn, swore they did. It is just as possible, though, that Hayes, as he said, acted alone. For four years, he had tried to teach Kyle to be a good sport. Now here was Kyle's last act — the dissing of the football coach and athletic director.

Coach Hayes and Kyle went for a long walk down the left-field line. Hayes confirmed that Kyle would again be riding the pine. As the coach recalled in his deposition, he told Kyle he had always stood up for him, "at times when a lot of guys didn't think real high of you . . . [but] I cannot back you when you make comments like this."

Kyle pleaded. He fumed. It was established in depositions that he uttered "the F word." When he saw that all was lost, he told Coach Hayes, "You will be hearing from my parents."

"I'm sure I will," said the coach.

It did not help that Kyle graduated the next day with a nearly perfect grade point average, or that he'd been nominated Outstanding Senior. High school had been a disaster for him, his parents believed. "Everything that could go wrong, did," said Mrs. Rutherford.

The Rutherfords pleaded for their son for four months within the school system. They told their sad story three times — to the principal, a disciplinary committee, and the school board — "substantiated" by many documents and letters. These included Kyle's report cards back to elementary school ("This young man is not a troublemaker!"); newspaper stories of his exploits; a letter from his grandmother to Coach Hooks ("I hope no one ever does to your grandsons what you did to mine"); a letter from a receiver complaining he wasn't thrown the ball enough to receive a scholarship offer; and a letter from this receiver's father, who believed his son's time with Coach Hooks was "the biggest misuse of talent ever experienced."

The baseball game could not be replayed, but the Rutherfords were determined, as they later wrote, "to prevent this catastrophe from befalling another unsuspecting student." Mr. Rutherford spoke to the officials with authority; Mrs. Rutherford spoke with emotion.

Though Cy Falls High School was only four years old, two hundred students had left just to escape Coach Hooks, Mr. Rutherford told the disciplinary committee. He didn't explain how he knew this, but he did say there was no way to confirm it, since the kids were probably all too scared to talk.

The only solution, as he saw it, was the "termination" of Coach Hooks. Toward that end, Mr. Rutherford related every evil he had heard about the coach: installation of an underground power line without district permission, personal use of an inflatable cast bought for the team by the booster club, and most significantly, using a walkie-talkie to eavesdrop on an opposing coach during a game.

The Rutherfords went on and on. The principal, the disciplinary board, and the school board — each level of command was attentive and polite. The transcripts and records show no evidence of wisecracking or merrymaking, or of agreement. The coaches were always quickly exonerated. The most supportive reply the Rutherfords received came from Assistant Superintendent Charles Goodson: "Thank you for the interest demonstrated in the education of your son."

Mrs. Rutherford was boggled. Did these people think they were *liars*, that they were just making it up? Just how large was this conspiracy?

"My goodness," she said, "this is surreal. I feel like I'm in the Twilight Zone."

And so the matter of Kyle Rutherford was finally lifted away from the ballfields, out of the schools, and dropped into the soft, capable palms of lawyers. As he filled out the check for $6,000, Mr. Rutherford said farewell to the annual Florida vacation, and hello to a believer.

Larry Watts has spent many years suing school districts, often on constitutional grounds. In a building set among the cheap shops along the far reaches of Harwin, his office is decorated with portraits of old Texas heroes and with a plaque bearing the words of George Bernard Shaw: "The reasonable man adapts himself to the world. The unreasonable one persists in trying to adapt the world to himself. Therefore, all progress depends upon the unreasonable man."

Certainly, there are reasonable men who would not have taken the Rutherford case, which would have left the Rutherfords nothing to do except to go on looking for less reasonable men, or maybe to get on with their lives. But after listening to the conspiracy theory, Watts was convinced, and he even added a twist of his own. The case he saw was fraught with First Amendment violations — infractions of the worst, most outrageous kind. Kyle's role models, the people he was supposed to respect, were punishing him for simply exercising his American right to speak his mind. And through Kyle, these people were also punishing his parents for speaking theirs. The case was absolutely surreal.

"It seems to me what we have here is the world turned upside down," said the lawyer. Naming as defendants every school functionary who hadn't seen the merit of the Rutherford case, Watts filed the lawsuit. As a *federal* civil rights lawsuit, it would allow him to sue the other side for additional attorney's fees.

And Lisa Brown was outraged, too, when word of this lawsuit traveled up to the twenty-fourth floor of the Pennzoil Tower, into the firm of Bracewell & Patterson. Brown is one of the firm's eighteen lawyers dedicated to the defense of school districts. She says there are beautiful schools in this world, and there are struggling ones, but all of them are simply trying to educate people. "Then somebody comes in and tries to sue them," says Brown, and for about $150 an hour, she shows up to defend against greed.

The two lawyers were righteous as only those who are paid to be righteous can be. Watts saw the Event (or Non-Event) of May 17, 1996, as recrimination against free speech. Brown saw it as discipline. They were old foes, and quickly they locked into their death grips.

"And isn't it true," Brown inquired of Kyle in depositions, "that during the course of many baseball games your senior season, that you used the word 'fuck'?"

"Excuse me just a moment," Watts interrupted. The use of vulgarities "certainly is out of character with the high regard I have for you, Ms. Brown." And could she please refer to it as "the F word"?

This was easily done, but later, Watts found it more difficult to interrupt. "Are you ignoring me?" he asked. And Brown replied, "I was." Their courtly manner eventually crumbled. "Your sarcasm is not appreciated," said Watts. "Don't yell at me!" said Watts. "I have never had reason to doubt your word. I now do," said Watts. "I apologize," said Watts, finally. "I have always had the highest regard for you."

There were other dramatic moments, such as when Watts complained of Coach Hooks's "winking at me and grinning at me, the whole bit." Hooks and Hayes attended some of the depositions, and in time were themselves deposed. Watts asked, "Do you have an idea what the First Amendment is all about?"

"Not right offhand, no sir," Coach Hooks replied.

Mrs. Rutherford wept through much of her deposition, but Mr. Rutherford told her, "This is what we paid our money for." He was eager for the confrontation, and under fire proudly defended his conspiracy theory. And the papers piled up with the billable hours, and slowly the evidence was collected.

In constructing her argument, Brown managed to dig up a pertinent case originally filed by Larry Watts. In *Gary Piwonka v. Tidehaven Independent School District*, Watts had argued that a student had a constitutional right to a fair cheerleading tryout. U.S. District Judge Sam Kent disagreed. "A remarkably overblown litigation exercise," he called it.

The Galveston judge dismissed the cheerleading claim "as asinine on its face." He threw out all claims of civil conspiracy and intentional infliction of emotional distress. He wrote, "This court will not waste its valuable time and limited resources on exploring the constitutional implications of whether or not someone gets to be a cheerleader. . . . The court is not in the business of micro-managing middle schools."

"I never realized one physical activity could mean so much to my life," wrote Kyle in a college essay, "[until] it was taken away from me. Ever since the time I quit football, the same questions race through my mind every day. I wonder what might have been if I had kept playing. I wonder if anything would actually be any different. . . . Most of all, I wonder if I would be happier."

It was Kyle's mother who asked him to speak with a reporter. From his room at Texas Christian, he mumbled reluctantly into the telephone. He said he tries not to remember high school. Recalling some of it anyway, he clamped his hand over the receiver and snarled to his roommate, "I hate talking about this shit!"

He's majoring in business and is having to get used to playing sports only in intramurals. In his freshman year, Kyle walked onto the TCU baseball team, but last August, as word of his federal lawsuit was still spreading, he was cut.

His mother says that he called, crying hysterically. "'What if I'm a failure in the business world, too?' he said. And I said, 'Kyle, don't let this carry over into your future. You're Kyle the person, not Kyle the athlete.'"

Mr. and Mrs. Rutherford ache for their son. Though Kyle was cut with four other pitchers, his parents are sure TCU is part of the conspiracy. "No way we can prove it," Mr. Rutherford said, "but that was all a setup deal."

They no longer see themselves simply as parents defending their child, but as leaders of a movement. Though they've received angry anonymous mail, and though some football parents won't talk to them anymore, they also get letters and calls from parents across the country with coaching problems of their own. "You're representing a lot of people out there," one caller told them.

Shortly before he was cut from the college team, Kyle asked his mother and father if they would please drop his federal lawsuit. Mrs. Rutherford said, "Kyle! We can't just drop it! We opened this can of worms!"

It was their lawyer who told the Rutherfords they had to sue for a dollar amount. Mrs. Rutherford says she doesn't want the school system's "stinking money," but only for Hooks to be removed. If the case gets to trial, Mr. Rutherford believes, "we've got them! There's not a jury in the world that won't see their lies." If, on the other hand, Judge Rainey dismisses the case, then Mr. Rutherford will lose his faith in the justice system.

But they have never considered quitting. The lawsuit is their obligation as parents. "You know, we love our kids," says Mr. Rutherford. "This whole thing, it isn't fun, but Kyle's done, you know. They ruined his whole life."

Kingpin

FROM GQ

"I AM NOT A DICK," says the greatest bowler in the history of bowling.

He has had a couple of beers, and he's now on his third Seven & Seven. When he's not bowling, he golfs. When he's done golfing, he drinks. Sometimes things seem clearer after a few drinks. "When I have a little buzz on, my eyesight gets better" is how he puts it.

This is what the great bowler sees now: cool green hills; loose knots of sweating, fleshy men and lean, tanned women; puddled shadows and the midday sun. He watches through a window from the bar at the Bogey Hills Country Club, near his hometown of St. Louis. The people here smile at him, greet him by name. This matters to the bowler. Once, when he was rich and famous and his enormous gifts were no more remarkable to him than breathing or walking, he didn't care what people thought. Now he's just famous. Now there's talk of the enormous waste the bowler has left behind, of the people he has hurt. He wants another chance. Now he wants to be understood.

"I don't want to be remembered as the guy who destroyed his father's name," the great and tortured bowler says. His eyes are filling. He orders a fourth Seven & Seven.

"I am not a dick," he says. "I am not an asshole. That's all I want. I don't want to be remembered as an asshole."

Pete Weber made $1 million faster than any other bowler in history. He is one of two men who have made more than $2 million bowling. (He holds the sole distinction of having spent nearly all his gains.) He is neither the best-liked nor the hardest-working bowler ever to play the game. Yet he employs a huge backswing, and he imparts a subtle spin to his bowling ball that results in a vicious hook. The backswing and the hook delight the most casual bowling fan; the spin fascinates and baffles the lanes' cognoscenti.

He is manic and furious, and this is why all but the most emotionally detached bowling fan either adore or despise him. He bowls with extravagant desperation. He has slammed ball-return devices with his open palm and kicked foul posts and grabbed his genitals, though he can't remember ever doing the latter. He cussed out an old lady during a pro-am tournament. He is one of the most fined, suspended, and disciplined bowlers in the history of the Professional Bowlers Association. But his desperation is fascinating in the way that self-immolating greatness can be. When the PBA wants to draw fans, it knows Weber will bring them. When CBS or ESPN is going to televise a bowling tournament, the producers root for Weber to make it to the finals.

In the spring of 1998, at the Tucson Open, he draws more people than ever. Some want to see redemption; others hunger for rough justice. Some want to see the Pete who bottomed out in 1995, when he earned only $39,795 bowling, winning exactly zero national tournaments. He divorced for a second time that year. He was broke, in debt, still drinking after three stays in drug and alcohol rehabilitation centers (or four stays, depending on who among Pete's friends and family is telling the story).

Others want to see the Pete Weber of 1996, bowling's comeback kid, who, after a third marriage, rediscovered his magical hook and the delicate spin and started winning again.

Going into the Tucson Open, Pete was the third leading money earner on the tour for 1998 (more impressive considering he was thirty-five, old by professional-bowling standards, and that he was suspended during the first three tournaments of the year for complaining about lane conditions), and he held the third-highest average in the PBA.

Will Pete Weber be remembered as the prodigy who squandered his talents or as the courageous maverick who defeated his demons? Bowlers have wondered about this for a few years now. Going into the Tucson Open, Pete's family and friends wondered, too. So did Pete.

Pete Weber cocks his bowling ball so far back that it sometimes rises above his head, which looks especially dramatic because Pete is five feet seven and weighs 127 pounds. Like a lot of pro bowlers, Pete sports a mustache. His nose is thin and long, and his hair is swept back in a pompadour he keeps in place with regular applications of hair spray. He has grayish blue eyes that are soft and almost feminine after he has had a few beers but that go narrow and flat when he is angry or frustrated, which is most all the time when he is bowling. They are narrowed and flat now, and he is puffing his cheeks out. He glares at the ground, as if the ground had delivered him some grievous insult. It is late Wednesday morning, the first round of qualifying at the Tucson Open, and Pete Weber has just knocked down nine of ten pins, leaving the nine pin, which sits in the back row, second from the right. In bowling terms, Pete has left a "hard nine." Hard nines make Pete puff his cheeks out and narrow his eyes. They make him hold his arms out and his palms up, or suck air in through his pursed lips, or just scan the bowling crowd with a wide-eyed, wild-eyed look his father once described as "something out of the weird movies." Hard nines can also lead to rosin-bag flinging and genital grabbing.

It's not only hard nines. A bowling ball that hooks too much disgusts Pete Weber, as does a ball that hooks too little. Leaving a seven-ten split makes him ready to quit. Spares in general make him think about pushing the rerack button and giving up on the frame and having a few drinks. (He did that once. It was his fourth "ethical misconduct violation" in a year's time, which led to an automatic six-month suspension from the PBA.) Left-handed bowlers get to Pete, because he thinks they possess an unfair advantage (their side of the lane is less scuffed and smeared), though he likes some personally. Leaving a ten pin (the rightmost one in the back row) standing, or "tapping ten," makes him want to throw in the towel. Let's not even talk about gutter balls. The PBA tournament committee nauseates him. "They look out for just themselves. I've said that to them. In fact, I said, 'You guys are a bunch of self-serving motherfuckers.'" Even some strikes make Pete want to puke. Especially lucky strikes when he "goes Brooklyn," which is to say, the ball hooks too much and hits the head pin from the left (thus Brooklyn) side.

Pete goes Brooklyn and hits a strike. He spins around, kicks the ground, stares down the offending patch of wood. "Mother*fuck*," he mutters.

"Pete has got a little bit of an attitude problem," says Don Fortman, a fan who has driven from Willcox, Arizona, to watch Pete bowl in the Tucson Open. "He gets a lucky break, he doesn't smile. Now, a lucky break like that Brooklyn, that puts a smile on most anyone."

But how can Pete smile? How can anyone expect the Greatest and Most Troubled Bowler in the World to bowl for something as simple as fun? Pete hasn't bowled for fun in about twenty years. He says the day he retires from the pro circuit will be his last day in a bowling alley. "He doesn't even like to go in a bowling center now unless he's in a tournament," says his wife, Tracy, who also bowls. "To get him to watch me bowl, I've got to beg." Pete has three rounds in Tucson to make it to the top twenty-four, then three more rounds to "make the show," to bowl with the top four finishers on television Saturday for one shot at the Tucson Open's $16,000 first prize.

Pete bowls to pay his child support, his mortgage, and his taxes. He bowls to beat other bowlers. He bowls to show the PBA's self-serving motherfuckers that no one tells him what to do. He bowls because "I've never done anything else." He bowls because that's what he is — a pro bowler — and because if he doesn't bowl well, *that's* what he is.

Just one year ago, the greatest bowler in history, the man who had already earned twenty-one PBA bowling championships, won the Tucson Open, at these very lanes. Right after he accepted his trophy, this is what he said about his victory:

"It tells me I'm not a loser."

Many of the bowlers throwing strikes this afternoon are built like Fred Flintstone. This undercuts the PBA's insistence that bowlers are finely tuned athletes. All the bowlers who chain-smoke, like Pete, don't help the PBA party line, either. And not that facial hair has anything to do with athletic performance, but many of the bowlers, like Pete, sport mustaches that call to mind porn stars from the seventies and dentists through the ages. Dentist/porn-star mustaches simply do not scream "finely tuned athlete."

The PBA wants to attract larger, younger, richer audiences. Which is understandable, because as the desert sun beats down on Tucson's Golden Pin Lanes (right across the street from Courtesy Towing and Tucson Awning & Screen), and as 108 men with a statistically significant number of extra-large guts and dentist/porn-star mustaches throw strikes, sluggish little pockets of hunched white-haired men and women move from lane to lane watching, many of them chain-smoking, some missing teeth, a few with walkers. The air reeks of cigarette smoke and stale beer and disinfectant and sweat.

To counteract this unfortunate impression, the PBA has hired a public-relations company in New York City. Now the PBA is using gold-colored pins and slow-motion cameras on its weekly television show. These efforts to burnish bowling's image make the bowlers happy.

On Wednesday afternoon, the PBA's greatest hope and most fearsome nightmare is throwing strikes on lane twenty-four of Tucson's Golden Pin Lanes. Another hard nine. "Mother*fuck*," Pete Weber hisses.

Imagine the Greatest and Most Troubled Bowler in the World as a surly thirteen-year-old. He is scrawny and longhaired, and he pulls his sixteen-pound ball (the heaviest made, just like the pros use) back, back, above his head, flings it down the lane and watches it teeter and hang on the right gutter then hook with murderous intent. Everything about the kid's delivery — the backswing too high, the release too snapped, the hook too hard — is wrong, almost intentionally different from bowling's classic five-and-a-half-step, shoulder-high delivery.

Which is much more than merely weird, because in 1975, when the kid is flinging strikes, the most famous practitioner of classic bowling, and not incidentally the most famous bowler in the world, is Pete's father, Dick, or the Legendary Dick Weber, as he was and is unfailingly referred to by bowling fans and bowling writers. The Legendary Dick Weber is as renowned for his easy charm, quick smile, and supreme self-control as he is for his bowling prowess. He is sometimes referred to in bowling circles as "bowling's greatest ambassador" and "the Babe Ruth of bowling," a spokesman for and embodiment of the politeness, grace, commitment to hard work, and all-around cheerfulness that the chain-smoking thirteen-year-old with the goofy backswing doesn't seem to lose a lot of sleep over and that the Professional Bowlers Association so desperately wishes people would associate with the sport. (Actually, PBA officials would be delighted if more people would *think* of bowling as a sport.)

It's not that Pete doesn't get along with his dad. No, Pete loves Dick. He especially loves Dick's life. What thirteen-year-old wouldn't? Pete's been on the road with his dad, seen him buy drinks for his bowling buddies, witnessed the fun they have, the parties that never seem to stop.

The thirteen-year-old wants that life for his own. That's why he's flinging that big hook at Dick Weber Lanes. He works on his release, on different angles, on different ways to play different lanes. He throws strikes from each arrow on the lane, six hours a day, seven days a week. Is he good enough to think about hitting the road and buying drinks for the house and hosting the parties that never end? Does he worry about measuring up to his father? He doesn't want to worry about that. He knows what that worry can do. He has watched Richard, his oldest brother, take his sixteen-pound ball and his monogrammed bowling shirt, which unfortunately says DICK WEBER, JR., and follow the Legendary Dick Weber on the tour, a dutiful son with an understated, classic bowling style, just like Dad's. "He'll never be as good as his old man," the bowling fans say, until Rich starts worrying, starts wondering, and quits. Pete watches John, the next Weber, as he packs the bowling ball and the WEBER bowling shirt and follows his pop into the family business. John uses the same classic, understated bowling style as his dad, and people talk, and John worries and wonders, and then he quits, too.

Pete was different. "It just made him mad," says Pete's mother, Juanita, whom everyone calls Nete. "It just aggravated him." Pete made a promise to his mother. He told her he'd make people forget about Dick. Told her that one day, when people saw Dick walking down the street, they'd say, "There goes Pete Weber's dad."

A chain-smoking little old lady wants an autograph, so when the second round of qualifying is over on Wednesday afternoon, she makes her move. But it's not Pete she makes her move on.

"Walter Ray," she calls out. "Oh, Walter Ray," she calls out again, and then a third time, until a big, shuffling blond man with a beard looks her way. Only one bowler in history has earned more money bowling than Pete Weber, and it is this man, Walter Ray "Deadeye" Williams, Jr.

Williams has a physics degree and a savings account and vague plans to teach high school mathematics someday and six world championships in horseshoes. He throws the ball with graceless efficiency, and he has a little hitch in his delivery that makes bowling aesthetes wince. ("Have you seen him bowl?" one of them asks rhetorically. "It's ugly. It's just brutal.") Williams wins, though, and he possesses a placid demeanor on the lanes that bowling's older female fans particularly adore. But when he signs his name for this fan, he neither smiles nor talks. In fact, Williams, the PBA's adored Abel to Pete's very public Cain, scowls slightly, then turns and gives this little old lady his back, which makes her gasp, then pucker her lips, almost as if one of her grandchildren had thrown some freshly baked tollhouse cookies in her face.

She turns to Pete. The older women who frequent bowling alleys are fierce creatures, but she is speaking more softly now. Maybe she has seen Pete react explosively to a few too many hard nines. Whatever the reason, she is positively timid when she approaches Pete.

"Would you mind?" she murmurs, holding out a piece of paper.

"Hey, how ya doin'?" Pete says. "Where are you from?"

She tells him, but warily. Little old ladies — even those who frequent bowling alleys — tend to speak cautiously around men they have watched kick the air while screaming "Mother*fuck!*"

Pete asks how she's enjoying the tournament. He admits that he's having some problems with the lanes. But, yep, he sure hopes he'll improve as the week goes on.

Emboldened, or maybe shell-shocked, she says, "You know, I used to watch your father all the time."

"Oh yeah," Pete says, "he was the greatest. He is the greatest. Greatest bowler of all time."

They talk for five minutes.

As she leaves, she reaches for Pete's forearm. It is a gentle, tentative gesture, as if she is trying to convince herself that what just transpired involved flesh and bone and was not some miraculous apparition made up of cigarette smoke and fluorescent lights and beer fumes.

"Thank you," the little old lady says to Pete.

"No," he says. "Thank *you*."

He turned pro at seventeen, a tenth-grade dropout married to a girl he had met playing Frisbee in the parking lot of his dad's bowling alley.

The other bowlers on the tour invited the kid to the bar. They knew he liked to drink, so they patted him on the back and bought him drinks.

They bought him drinks because bowlers drink. Even the Legendary Dick Weber had knocked back a few. Actually, more than a few. "Dick got drunk from one coast to the other," Nete says, "and no one ever wrote anything bad about *him*."

They bought him drinks because pro bowlers are generous. "Back in the day of Dick," says a high-ranking PBA official, "no one made money, because whoever won the tournament hosted the party in the bar that lasted until they packed up and drove to the next tournament."

And they bought him drinks because pro bowlers might be a lot of things, but one thing they are not is stupid. This scrawny little longhair might have good bloodlines, but how many of those vicious hooks could the foul-mouthed little punk roll after he was pumped full of those sweet-smelling, girlie-sounding drinks he liked?

Trouble was, he could roll a lot of 'em. A whole lot. Trouble was, as the pro bowlers found out, not only was Pete an exceedingly nasty drunk (unlike his father, who was a gentle, fun-loving drunk when he drank), he was also without question the greatest drunk bowler in the history of bowling.

So Pete would suck back two or four or, on a couple of occasions, eight or ten Long Island iced teas, which was one of his favorite drinks in those days, then he would cock that arm back above his head and let fly, all the while taunting opponents and cussing hard nines and grabbing his nuts and screaming at the world and in general making PBA officials and other pro bowlers regret that Richard Jr. and John had been too sensitive and mild-mannered to follow in the big, deep classic five-and-a-half-step-delivery paw prints of the Legendary Dick Weber.

His first year, Pete was named PBA Rookie of the Year.

Pete cocks, flings, hooks. He taps ten. "Fuck," he mutters in a tone of voice that is almost pleasant, considering his range of intonations. Then he picks up the spare.

A fan named Jack Iaci nods grimly. "The game is cruel to you," he says with the existential weariness that seems to infect a certain type of bowling fan. "It will rob you. Pete, though, he's the ultimate bowler. He's an artist."

It is Thursday morning, the final round of qualifying. Pete is in twelfth place, and if he bowls well this morning, he'll make it to match play tonight. Some of the other bowlers at the Golden Pin Lanes are flinging the ball as hard as Pete, but they are bigger, stronger, heavier, and younger. They pump iron, jog, take care of themselves. Pete's limbs are skinny, his chest sunken. Some of the other bowlers call him Bird Legs.

Yet Pete throws the ball so hard, hooks it so dramatically, and imparts such intense forward rotation to it (he's got a "big hand," in bowling parlance) that in the past year he had to switch from a sixteen-pound ball to a fifteen-pound one, because the heavier one was driving too powerfully through the pins, not deflecting enough from pin to pin and leaving far too many hard nines. A right-handed bowler with a big hand will inevitably leave hard nines. (Left-handers with big hands leave hard eights.) Pete leaves more hard nines than almost anyone.

"No one throws a ball like Pete," says Brian Berg, a former pro bowler who now works for Storm Bowling Products, Pete's sponsor, and who serves as Pete's friend, equipment manager, and apologist. "Never has. Never will."

"Pete has unlimited talent," says fellow bowler Mike Aulby, the third-winningest bowler of all time, behind Deadeye Williams and Pete. "There's nothing that can stop Pete but himself. And he's done a pretty good job of that."

By the end of the session, Pete is in eighteenth place. He's made it to match play. Two more days to make it to the show.

In the spring of 1984 — a year in which Pete earned $115,735, turned twenty-two and used cocaine — Pete checked into a drug

and alcohol rehabilitation center in Lonedell, Missouri, after a
drunken argument with his then wife, DeeDee. He stayed twenty-
eight days. Dick told people his son had a sore wrist.

By 1989 Pete had earned $1 million faster than any other bowler
in history. He was twenty-six, divorced, seeing a woman he had
met in a bowling alley (and whom he would later marry), in debt,
drinking again, paying child support, and fined and punished
more times than he or the PBA officials wanted to think about.
(The PBA had never named him its Player of the Year, and Pete was
convinced it was partly because the self-serving motherfuckers flat-
out didn't like him.)

Even his fans considered Pete a crazed natural, a strike-flinging
phenom pissing away his greatness. People commented on his tan-
trums. Bowling writers called him the John McEnroe of bowling.
Pete is a lot like McEnroe, but in ways the writers probably didn't
intend. Like McEnroe, with his command of spin and pace and
angles, Pete is a master of his sport's subtleties, and he "reads" pin
falls and lane conditions as well as anyone on the tour. (Also like
McEnroe, Pete hates to practice and seldom does.)

The phenom was approaching thirty, and the genital-grabbing
tirades notwithstanding, he was beginning to worry about his reputation. He wanted to be remembered. But he didn't want to be
hated.

In 1991 he wrote an article titled "Uncontrolled Emotions Don't
Mix with Victory" for *Bowling Digest*. He told the magazine, "I finally
got it into my head that liquor and Pete Weber don't mix."

In 1996, after a second divorce and a third marriage, to Tracy
Goettel, and a few more attempts at sobriety and a lot more discipli-
nary actions against him, Pete was bowling a pro-am tournament in
Tacoma, Washington, while he drank Seven & Sevens.

The bartender, an older woman, told him he'd had enough.

And that's when the author of "Uncontrolled Emotions Don't
Mix with Victory" said, "You can take your fucking bowling center
and your fucking tournament and you can shove 'em up your ass."

Turns out she was the mother-in-law of the bowling alley's owner.
The PBA put Pete on five years of probation, which he is still
serving.

Pete wishes he had a beer, but the hamburger and fries will have to
do, because, as Tracy says, "We don't cut loose till the weekend.

That's just the way it is." Last night they ate peanut-butter-and-jelly sandwiches in their $99-a-night hotel suite, which is more than they usually like to spend. But now it's Thursday afternoon, and Pete has made it to the top twenty-four, and someone else is buying, so for lunch they splurge. Tony Roma's. Tracy goes for the ribs.

They're both slightly preoccupied. Tracy knows it costs them between $1,100 and $1,400 a week to bowl on the road, including the $400 tournament entry fee, and that if Pete doesn't bowl well in the next three sessions in Tucson, they'll lose money this trip. Pete's first wife is suing for more child support, even though, Tracy says, "I went through the checks he wrote last year, and I found another $11,000 that he spent on the kids, including paying for their braces." She knows Pete's a soft touch, always lending money to his friends and even to some people Tracy doesn't think are his friends. She knows how Pete is about paying bills and that he loves to gamble and that he once won $25,000 in a single night and that he can lose just as big. She knows that he spends most of his afternoons back at the Bogey Hills Country Club, which she doesn't like, but what can she do, other than make him promise to call her to pick him up so at least he won't be driving drunk. She knows golfers bet $1,600 in one afternoon at Bogey Hills. She knows that not too many years ago the PBA had to send Pete's tournament checks straight to his mother. "We bailed him out two different times," Nete says. "Had to do that. He owed the IRS $43,000 one year, and we helped him. We also had to pay his American Express bills."

Tracy knows all that, and that's why she shops for peanut butter and jelly and Wonder bread. That's why she buys Pete's hair spray for $2.48 a bottle at Walgreens. That's why she keeps the books and keeps him out of bars and off the golf course during tournaments. "I worry about him drinking when he's golfing, and besides, these guys might say they're his friends, but they're bowling against him, too, and I wouldn't trust one of them. I mean, who would you like to knock off the tour?"

Pete grabs a french fry, describes his typical day on the road. "I bowl, then I eat lunch, then I go back to my room and don't think about bowling. Then I bowl again."

"Yeah, babe, you're bowlin' great," Tracy says. Pete works over his burger. Tracy dispatches a baby-back.

Tracy knows all about Wayne Webb, the PBA's twelfth all-time earnings leader, who is better known to bowlers and bowling fans as "the King of Karaoke." That's because Webb, a forty-one-year-old with a diamond stud in his left ear and a blond dentist/porn-star mustache, has for three years been lugging his karaoke equipment from tournament to tournament, setting it up in bowling-center bars, where he serves as master of ceremonies three nights a week. He gets $250 a night.

Pete finishing his career manning a microphone in a bowling-alley bar? Tracy doesn't think so. Not if Tracy's around. And she plans to be around. Tracy knows how much she loves Pete. But what she doesn't know is what will happen if Pete doesn't keep winning, if Pete doesn't start saving.

"That's a scary thought," she says. "No, I don't know."

"The King of Karaoke!" the PBA guy shouts into a microphone, and Wayne Webb trots onto lane thirty-two and squints into the spotlight. It's Friday night, the final eight games of match play, and the PBA is doing its best to ratchet up the tension. The fluorescent lights are turned off, rock-and-roll music is pumped up, and the PBA guy is shouting player introductions with all the manic energy he can muster. A new group of bowling fans has shown up for the final night of match play. They are younger, mostly men, and they wear sleeveless shirts and baseball caps. Some have tattoos.

When a bowler is introduced, the young men yell. "One of only three players ever to convert the seven-ten split on national TV!" the PBA guy screams, and Jess Stayrook waves, and the young men yell "Yarghhh!" "The comedian of the tour!" the PBA guy hollers, and Randy Pedersen waves, and the young men yell "Yarghhh!"

Most of the players sit in groups, with friends, and they laugh and cheer and make fun of whoever happens to be the bowler in the spotlight. Pete sits alone, smoking. He knows what's at stake. So do the bowling-ball companies, which pay incentives to those fortunate four who make the show.

Pete is in ninth place, 109 pins from the show. He yawns. "Because I'm not bowling," he says.

Friday night, with four games left, Pete still has a chance for the show.

He strikes.

"Atta babe," Tracy says softly, because she is his wife and she loves him. Also, she wants a new outfit. "That's the deal. If he makes the show, I get a new outfit to wear on it."

He strikes again.

"Yeah, Pete," Brian Berg says, because Pete is his friend and his favorite bowler and because if Pete makes the show, Brian gets an incentive check from Storm.

He strikes yet again.

"Yarghhh!" yell the young guys in the sleeveless shirts, because they know that when Pete's on TV, if he's hitting strikes, he'll sometimes imitate Diamond Dallas Page, his favorite professional wrestler, and he'll make the Diamond Dallas Page hand sign (it's a diamond) for the crowd, and he'll also do the Schwarzenegger pump-you-up flex thing every once in a while, too. And though the young bowling fans haven't yet learned to articulate their existential weariness, they yell "Yarghhh" because Pete embodies the disaffected, free-floating rage they admire, and they don't like the self-serving PBA motherfuckers any more than their hero does.

Pete strikes again, pumps his fist.

"Atta babe," Tracy says.

"Yeah, Pete," Brian says.

"Yarghhh!" the guys in sleeveless shirts yell.

But bowling is a cruel sport, and it will rob you.

Four games to prove he's not a loser and Pete goes Brooklyn, leaves four pins. Then he hooks too early with his spare ball, leaving a pin. An open frame. For a pro bowler, a disaster worse than a gutter ball.

Brian Berg stares at Pete, then at the remaining pin. "His attitude stinks right now," Berg says. "That spare he chopped? He didn't even try."

Pete won't make the show, and he knows it. The last game Pete bowls in Tucson is a meaningless 222. After one strike, for the first time on the lanes all week, he smiles.

He's had four beers and two Seven & Sevens, and his eyesight is good. Friday night in the Golden Pin Lanes bar, less than an hour after match play concludes, and this is what Pete sees: Tracy, sitting across from him, working on her second screwdriver; the King of Karaoke twirling dials and gesticulating; bowlers at the bar, drinking and waiting for their checks; and in the front of the room eight young women in halter tops and shorts, singing a giggling, wiggling version of "Harper Valley P.T.A." "Here's some girls looking to meet a bowler tonight," Tracy says, with a hard smile at the singers.

The PBA tour director enters the bar waving a wad of checks for the twenty finishers who didn't make the show. Tracy snatches Pete's $2,100 check for his tenth-place finish. "We got gambling money for next week in Reno," he shouts.

When the teenyboppers sit down, Brian Berg takes the mike and eases into "Mack the Knife." A pro bowler turned bowling-ball-company representative who can wring beauty from a song is a rare thing, and with each phrasing and pause, another patron of the bar seems to realize his precious luck, until the room is quiet and attentive as Brian nails the big ending of the song. And then bowlers holler, and bowling groupies scream, and Pete and Tracy drink up, and Mackie's back in town, and here at the Golden Pin Lanes bar no one is suing anyone else for an increase in child support, and no one's mother-in-law is cutting anyone off, and seldom is seen a hard nine. The King of Karaoke invites another singer to the mike, and Pete and Tracy order another round. Just one more. Well, maybe two, and then, Pete says, "We'll probably go to the hotel bar. We'll probably close the bar, actually."

The greatest bowler who ever lived has another ten years to earn some money, put some away, leave whatever bowling legacy he's going to leave and get on with the rest of his life. Even though Pete will be inducted into the PBA Hall of Fame this month, even though he was a huge hand, even though Pete is the greatest drunk bowler in history, he is still going to be looking at more seven-ten splits and open frames in the next decade. "And ten years is pushing it," Dick Weber says. "Being forty-five, trying to keep up with these twenty-year-olds, especially now — that's tough."

Sometimes Dick blames himself. He remembers times he let little Petey watch him drink with his pals and wonders if it all looked like too much fun. So he and Nete try not to drink in front of their youngest son. It saddens Dick when people think unkindly of Pete, "that he's a violent person, because he's not. I would say, yes, they're right, when he drinks. But when he's Pete, he's the most kind, the most generous person going. I mean, we didn't believe in the tough love. I guess we're just not that kind of people. So I don't regret not doing the tough-love thing. I still couldn't do it."

Nete wishes Pete would quit drinking. "But what Pete does he does and will admit it. And what he says, you can bank on it being the truth. And he doesn't sneak around and do things. And I happen to know a lot of the bowlers out there who do the same things Pete does and nobody notices it. In fact, I wrote a letter to the PBA once telling them what some of their 'nice guys' did."

("Have a player tell Juanita to get fucked," says a PBA official, who wisely requested anonymity, "and then see what happens.")

"What do I want people to know about Pete?" Dick Weber says. "That he's loved by his family. He's just so loved by his family. We just love him to death."

Pete Weber is sitting in the bar of the Bogey Hills Country Club. He has had two beers and four Seven & Sevens. He has expressed a wish that people not judge him too harshly. He has said he would like to be remembered as a "nice guy." He has fought back tears. In an hour or so, he will call Tracy, who will have to drive out to pick him up. But now he is studying the glass of merlot in front of him, telling the story of his life, remembering how it began, wondering what might have been.

"If it wasn't for bowling," he says, "I would have ended up dead."

DAVID REMNICK

American Hunger

FROM THE NEW YORKER

ON THE NIGHT OF February 25, 1964, Cassius Clay entered the ring in Miami Beach wearing a short white robe, "The Lip" stitched on the back. He was fast, sleek, and twenty-two. But, for the first time in his life, and the last, he was afraid. The ring was crowded with has-beens and would-bes, liege men and pugs. Clay ignored them. He began bouncing on the balls of his feet, shuffling joylessly at first, like a marathon dancer at ten to midnight, but then with more speed, more pleasure. After a few minutes, Sonny Liston, the heavyweight champion of the world, stepped through the ropes and onto the canvas, gingerly, like a man easing himself into a canoe. He wore a hooded robe. His eyes were unworried, and they were blank, the dead eyes of a man who'd never got a favor out of life and never given one out. He was not likely to give one to Cassius Clay.

Nearly every sports writer in Miami Beach Convention Hall expected Clay to end the night on his back. The young boxing beat writer for the *New York Times,* Robert Lipsyte, got a call from his editors telling him to map out the route from the arena to the hospital, the better to know the way once Clay ended up there. The odds were seven to one against Clay, and it was almost impossible to find a bookie willing to take a bet on him. On the morning of the fight, the *New York Post* ran a column written by Jackie Gleason, the most popular television comedian in the country, which said, "I predict Sonny Liston will win in eighteen seconds of the first round, and my estimate includes the three seconds Blabber Mouth will bring into the ring with him." Even Clay's financial backers, the mandarin businessmen of the Louisville Sponsoring Group, expected disaster, perhaps physical harm; the group's lawyer, Gordon Davidson, negotiated hard with Liston's team, assuming that this could be the young man's last night in the ring. Davidson hoped only that Clay would emerge "alive and unhurt."

At ringside, Malcolm X, Clay's guest and mentor, settled into seat number 7. Gleason and Sammy Davis, Jr., were nearby, and so were the mobsters from Las Vegas, Chicago, St. Louis, New York. A cloud of cigar smoke drifted through the ring lights. Cassius Clay threw punches into the gray floating haze and waited for the bell.

"See that? See me?"

More than thirty years later, Muhammad Ali sat in an overstuffed chair watching himself on the television screen. His voice came in a swallowed whisper and his finger waggled as it pointed toward his younger self, his self preserved on videotape: twenty-two years old, getting warm in his corner, his gloved hands dangling at his hips. Today, Ali lives in a farmhouse in Berrien Springs, a small town in southwestern Michigan. The rumor has always been that Al Capone owned the farm in the twenties. One of Ali's dearest friends, his late cornerman Drew "Bundini" Brown, once searched the property hoping to find Capone's buried treasure. He found beans.

Now Ali was whispering again, pointing: "See me? You see me?" And there he was, flanked by his trainer, Angelo Dundee, and Bundini, moonfaced and young and whispering hoodoo inspiration in Ali's ears: "All night! All night! Float like a butterfly, sting like a bee! Rumble, young man, rumble!"

"That's the only time I was ever scared in the ring," Ali said. "Sonny Liston. First time. First round. Said he was gonna kill me."

Ali was heavy now. He had the athlete's disdain for exercise, and he ate more than was good for him. His beard was gray, and his hair was going gray, too. Ali is a man who has all his life lived in the moment, thrilling to the moment, its comedy and battle, its sex and adulation, and it is only now, in late middle age, in the grip of illness, that he has had the time and the patience to make sense of what he was and what he has left behind, to think about how a gangly kid from segregated Louisville willed himself to become one of the great original improvisers in American history, a brother to

Davy Crockett, Walt Whitman, Duke Ellington. Even before he could vote, he consciously drew on influences as disparate as Sugar Ray Robinson and Gorgeous George, Marcus Garvey and Malcolm X, and yet he was utterly, and always, himself: "Who made me is me," he insisted. As Cassius Clay, he entered the world of professional boxing at a time when the expectation was that a black fighter would defer to white sensibilities, that he would accede to the same mobsters who ran Liston, that he would play the noble and grateful warrior in the world of southern Jim Crow and northern hypocrisy. As an athlete, he was supposed to remain aloof from the racial and political upheaval going on around him: the student sit-ins in Nashville, the Freedom Rides, the March on Washington, the student protests in Albany, Georgia, and at Ole Miss. Clay not only responded to the upheaval but responded in a way that outraged everyone, from the White Citizens Councils to the leaders of the National Association for the Advancement of Colored People. He changed his religion and his name; he declared himself free of every mold and expectation. He showed boundless courage; he made foolish mistakes. He was an enemy, a figure of scorn, long before he was a focus of admiration and love. He was himself. Cassius Clay became Muhammad Ali. *Who made me is me.*

As we watched the tapes that afternoon, Ali and I talked about the three leading heavyweights of the time — Floyd Patterson, Sonny Liston, and Clay himself — and the uncanny way they seemed to mark the political and racial changes going on just as they were fighting one another for the title. In the early sixties, Patterson cast himself as the Good Negro — an approachable yet strangely fearful man, a deferential champion of civil rights, integration, and Christian decency. The NAACP literally endorsed Patterson, as if he were running for Congress. Liston, a veteran of Missouri State Penitentiary before he came to the prize ring, accepted the role of the Bad Negro as his lot after he discovered that he would not be permitted any other. For most sports writers, Liston was monstrous, indomitable, inexplicable, a Bigger Thomas, a Caliban beyond their reckoning.

As Cassius Clay, Ali craved their champion's title but not their designated masks. "I had to prove you could be a new kind of black man," Ali told me. "I had to show that to the world."

As we watched and spoke, Ali was taken with the subject of himself, but sometimes his heavy lids would blink a few times and then stay shut and he would sleep, mid-conversation, for five minutes or so. He used to do that occasionally when he was young. Now he did it a lot more often. Sometimes the present world, the life going on all around — the awards dinners, the standing ovations, the visits to the king of Morocco or to the aldermen of Chicago — sometimes it just bored him. He thought about death all the time now, he said. "Do good deeds. Visit hospitals. Judgment Day coming. Wake up and it's Judgment Day." As a devout Muslim, Ali prayed five times a day, always with death in mind. "Thinking about after. Thinking about Paradise."

But now he focused on another sort of paradise. The Liston fight began. In black-and-white, Cassius Clay came bounding out of his corner and right away started circling the square, dancing, moving around and around the ring, moving in and out, his head twitching from side to side, as if freeing himself from a neck crick early in the morning, easy and fluid — and then Liston, a great bull whose shoulders seemed to cut off access to half the ring, lunged with a left jab. Liston missed by two feet. At that moment, Clay hinted not only at what was to come that night in Miami Beach but at what he was about to introduce to boxing and to sports in general — the marriage of mass and velocity. A big man no longer had to lumber along and slug: he could punch like a heavyweight and move like Ray Robinson.

"It's sweet, isn't it?" Ali smiled. With great effort, he smiled. Parkinson's is a disease of the nervous system that stiffens the muscles and freezes the face into a stolid mask. Motor control degenerates. Speech degenerates. Some people hallucinate or suffer nightmares. As the disease progresses, even swallowing can become a terrible trial. Parkinson's comes on the victim erratically. Ali still walked well. He was still powerful in the arms and across the chest; it was obvious, just from shaking his hand, that he still possessed a knockout punch. For him the special torture was speech and expression, as if the disease had intentionally struck first at what had once pleased him — and had pleased (or annoyed) the world — most. He hated the effort that speech now cost him. ("Sometimes you won't understand me," he said when we first met. "But that's okay. I'll say it again.")

Ali was smiling now as his younger self, Cassius Clay, flicked a
nasty left jab into Liston's brow.

"You watchin' this?" he said. "So-o-o fast! So-o-o pretty!"

No matter how ruinous boxing is to boxers, there's no doubt that
part of Ali's appeal derived from boxing, from going into a ring,
stripped to the waist, a beautiful man, alone, in combat. It is perfectly plausible that as a basketball player or even as a swaddled
halfback he would have been no less famous and quicksilver. But
the boxer represents a more immediate form of dynamism, even
supermasculinity, no matter how retrograde. For all his verbal gifts,
Ali was first a supreme physical performer and sexual presence.
"Ain't I pretty?" he would ask over and over again, and, of course,
he was. If he'd had the face of Sonny Liston, he would have lost
much of his appeal.

Even as a schoolkid, Clay had a sense of glamour and performance. At Central High School in Louisville, he paraded up and
down the hallways shadowboxing and crying out his candidacy for
the heavyweight crown — all in a style so over the top that he
undercut the arrogance with laughter. He was probably our first
rapper and our best. At the 1960 Summer Olympics, in Rome,
when he was just eighteen, he wandered through the Olympic
Village meeting people from all over the world and charming them
with predictions about his great future. Clay was so much at ease
that he became known as the Mayor of the Olympic Village. His
experience in the ring in Rome was no less blissful. As a light
heavyweight, he marched easily through his first three bouts, and
then, in the finals, against a stubby coffeehouse manager from
Poland named Zbigniew Pietrzykowski, he came back from a
clumsy first round to win a unanimous decision and the gold
medal. By the end of the bout, the Pole was bleeding all over Clay's
white satin shorts.

In Rome, Clay had fulfilled his mission, but he had done it in a
style that offended the sensibilities of some of the older writers.
Big men were supposed to fight like Joe Louis and Rocky Marciano: they were supposed to wade in and flatten their opponent.
A. J. Liebling wrote in *The New Yorker* that Clay, though amusing to
watch, lacked the requisite menace of a true big man. Liebling was
not offended by Clay's poetic pretensions: he was quick to remind

his readers of Bob Gregson, the Lancashire Giant, who used to write such fistic couplets as "The British lads that's here / Quite strangers are to fear." It was Clay's boxing manner that left Liebling in doubt. "I had watched Clay's performance in Rome and had considered it attractive but not probative," he wrote. "Clay had a skittering style, like a pebble scaled over water. He was good to watch, but he seemed to make only glancing contact. . . . A boxer who uses his legs as much as Clay used his in Rome risks deceleration in a longer bout."

Whatever Liebling's reservations, Clay was awarded his medal, with the word "PUGILATO" emblazoned across it. "I can still see him strutting around the Olympic Village with his gold medal on," the late Wilma Rudolph, a great Olympic sprinter, once said. "He slept with it. He went to the cafeteria with it. He never took it off. No one else cherished it the way he did."

After the awards ceremonies, a reporter from the Soviet Union asked Clay, in essence, how it felt to win glory for a country that did not give him the right to eat at Woolworth's in Louisville.

"Tell your readers we've got qualified people working on that problem, and I'm not worried about the outcome," Clay said. "To me, the USA is still the best country in the world, counting yours. It may be hard to get something to eat sometimes, but anyhow I ain't fighting alligators and living in a mud hut." That remark was printed in dozens of American papers as evidence of Clay's good citizenship, his allegiance to the model fighters (and black men) who had come before him. Clay, it appeared, was ready to submit.

Boxing has never been a sport of the middle class. It is a game for the poor, the lottery player, the all-or-nothing-at-all young men who risk their health for the infinitesimally small chance of riches and glory. All Clay's most prominent opponents — Liston, Patterson, Joe Frazier, George Foreman — were born poor, and more often than not into large families, often with fathers who were either out of work or out of sight. As boys, they were part of what sociologists and headline writers would later call the underclass. Cassius Clay, though, was a child of the black middle class — "but *black* middle class, black southern middle class, which is not white middle class at all," says Toni Morrison, who, as a young editor, worked on Ali's autobiography. True enough, but still Clay was born to better circumstances than his eventual rivals. One of the less entertaining components of the Ali act was the way he tried to "out-black" someone like Frazier, calling him an Uncle Tom, an "honorary white," when in fact Frazier had grown up dirt poor in South Carolina. If Ali was joking, Frazier never found it funny.

Clay's mother, Odessa, was a sweet, light-skinned woman who took her sons to church every Sunday and kept after them to keep clean, to work hard, to respect their elders. Cassius Clay, Sr., who earned his livelihood as a sign painter, was a braggart, a charmer, a performer, a man full of fantastic tales and hundred-proof blather. To all who would listen, including reporters who trooped off to Louisville in later years, the senior Clay talked of having been an Arabian sheikh and a Hindu noble. Like Ralph Kramden, Jackie Gleason's bus driver with dreams, the senior Clay talked up his schemes for the big hit, the marketing of this idea or that gadget which would vault the Clays, once and for all, out of Louisville and into some suburban nirvana. Cassius Sr. always worked, but he had a weakness for the bottle, and when he drank he often became violent. The Louisville police records show that he was arrested four times for reckless driving, twice for disorderly conduct, and twice for assault and battery, and that on three occasions Odessa called the police complaining that her husband was beating her. "I like a few drinks now and then," the senior Clay said. He often spent his nights moving from one bar to the next, picking up women whenever possible. (Many years later, Odessa finally grew so tired of her husband's womanizing that she insisted on a period of separation.) John (Junior Pal) Powell, who owned a liquor store in the West End, once told a reporter for *Sports Illustrated* about a night when the old man came stumbling into his apartment, his shirt covered with blood. Some woman had stabbed him in the chest. When Powell offered to take him to the hospital, Clay refused, saying, "Hey, Junior Pal, the best thing you can do for me is do what the cowboys do. You know, give me a little drink and pour a little bit on my chest, and I'll be all right."

At an early age, Cassius Clay appears to have learned how to block these chaotic incidents from his mind. He would joke about his father's having an eye for women — "My daddy is a playboy. He's always wearing white shoes and pink pants and blue shirts and he says he'll never get old" — but he would not let the discussion go much deeper. "It always seemed to me that Ali suffered a great psychological wound when he was a kid because of his father and that as a result he really shut down," one of Ali's closest friends said. "In many ways, as brilliant and charming as he is, Muhammad is an arrested adolescent. There is a lot of pain there. And though he's always tried to put it behind him, shove it out of his mind, a lot of that pain comes from his father — the drinking, the occasional violence, the harangues."

Cassius's father did work hard to earn a living for his family, and there was a time in Louisville when his signs were everywhere. But the senior Clay was a resentful artisan. His greatest frustration was that he could not earn his living painting murals and canvases. He was not exceptionally talented — his landscapes were garish, his religious paintings just a step above kitsch — but then he had not had any training. He had quit school in the ninth grade, a circumstance he blamed, with good reason, on the limited opportunities for blacks. He often told his children that the white man had kept him down, had prevented him from being a real artist, from expressing himself. He was never subtle about his distrust of whites. And, though he would one day accuse the Nation of Islam of "brainwashing" and fleecing his two sons, Cassius and Rudy, he often went on at the dinner table and in the bars about the need for black self-determination. He deeply admired Marcus Garvey, the leading black nationalist after the First World War and one of the ideological forebears of Elijah Muhammad. He was never a member of a Garvey organization, but like many blacks in the twenties, he admired Garvey's calls for racial pride and black self-sufficiency, if not, perhaps, the idea of a return to Africa.

Like any black child of his generation, Cassius Clay learned quickly that if he strayed outside his neighborhood — into the white neighborhood of Portland, say — he would hear the calls of "Nigger!" and "Nigger go home!" Downtown, blacks were limited to the stores on Walnut Street between Fifth and Tenth streets. Hotels were segregated. Schools were de-facto segregated, though there were slight signs of mixing even before *Brown v. Board of Education.* There were "white stores" and "Negro stores," "white parks" and "Negro parks." "That was just the way we lived," said Beverly Edwards, one of Cassius's schoolmates. "Kentucky is known as the Gateway to the South, but we weren't too much different than the

Deep South as far as race was concerned." When Clay's father told him all about the case of young Emmett Till, who had been beaten, mutilated, shot in the head, and thrown into the Tallahatchie River in the summer of 1955 by a pair of white men, Clay saw himself as Till, who was just a year older than he was. The killing helped reinforce in him the sense that he, a black boy from Louisville, was going out into a world that would inevitably deny him, rebuff him, even hate him. Cassius was no student — he graduated thanks only to the mercy of his high school principal, Atwood Wilson — and so he sought a means of escape in the ring. "I started boxing because I thought this was the fastest way for a black person to make it in this country," he would say years later.

Even before Clay went off to Rome, he had become fascinated by the Nation of Islam, better known as the Black Muslims. According to one biographer, Thomas Hauser, Cassius first heard about the group in 1959, when he traveled to Chicago for a Golden Gloves tournament. Chicago was the home base for the Nation and its leader, Elijah Muhammad, and Clay ran into Muslims on the South Side. His aunt remembers him coming home to Louisville with a record album of Muhammad's sermons. Then, the next spring, before leaving for the Olympics, Clay read a copy of the Nation's official newspaper, *Muhammad Speaks*. He was clearly taken with what he was reading and hearing in the Muslim rhetoric of pride and separatism. "The Muslims were practically unknown in Louisville in those days," Clay's high school classmate Lamont Johnson told me. "They had a little outfit, a temple, run by a black guy with white spots on his skin, but no one paid it any mind. No one had heard about their bean pies, the way they lived, what they thought. It wasn't even big enough to be scary in 1959."

Clay stunned his English teacher at Central High when he told her he wanted to write his term paper on the Black Muslims. She refused to let him do it. He never let on that his interest in the group was more than a schoolboy's passing curiosity, but something had resonated in his mind — something about the discipline and the bearing of the Muslims, their sense of hierarchy, manhood, and self-respect, the way they refused to smoke or drink or carouse, their racial pride.

After coming back from Rome, Clay attended meetings, in various cities, of the NAACP, of CORE — the Congress of Racial Equality — and of the Nation of Islam. Other athletes, like Curt Flood and Bill White, of the St. Louis Cardinals, had stopped in to hear Muslim preachers, too, but had left after listening for a few minutes to the rhetoric about "blue-eyed devils." Clay, however, was impressed by the Muslims in a way he was not by any other group or church. "The most concrete thing I found in churches was segregation," he said years later to the journalist Jack Olsen. "Well, now I have learned to accept my own and be myself. I know we are original man and that we are the greatest people on the planet Earth and our women the queens thereof."

Through 1961 and 1962, Clay kept his interest in the Nation of Islam quiet (he was well aware that to announce his new loyalty would put a title fight at risk), but he was quite publicly gaining strength both as a fighter and as a performer. He beat a succession of heavyweights — Alonzo Johnson, Alex Miteff, Willie Besmanoff, Sonny Banks, George Logan, Billy Daniels, Alejandro Lavorante — and even at the most perilous moment, when he got too careless in the first round, too glib, and Banks knocked him down, he showed a new ability to take a punch, and he recovered to win easily in four. Afterward, Harry Wiley, Banks's cornerman and a legendary New York boxing fixture, described the phenomenon of fighting Clay: "Things just went sour gradually all at once. He'll pick you and peck you, peck you and pick you, until you don't know where you are."

By then, Clay may have been the most self-aware twenty-year-old in the country. Like the most intelligent of comedians or actors or politicians, he was in complete command of even the most outrageous performances. "Where do you think I'd be next week if I didn't know how to shout and holler and make the public take notice?" he said. "I'd be poor and I'd probably be down in my hometown, washing windows or running an elevator and saying 'yassuh' and 'nawsuh' and knowing my place."

In his sixth fight as a professional, in April 1961, Clay took on Lamar Clark, a tough heavyweight with forty-five knockouts in a row. Clay made a prediction, the first of many: Clark would be gone in two. And so he was. Two rounds into the fight, Clay had broken Clark's nose and dropped him to the canvas twice, and the referee ended it there. "The more confident he became, the more

his natural ebullience took over," one of his cornermen, Ferdie
Pacheco, told me. "Everything was such fun to him. Maybe it
wouldn't have been so much fun if someone had knocked him
lopsided, but no one did. No one shut him up. And so he just kept
predicting and winning, predicting and winning. It was like *Candide*
— he didn't think anything bad could happen in this best of all
possible worlds."

Clay's next fight was in Las Vegas against a gigantic Hawaiian,
Duke Sabedong. One of Clay's prefight promotional duties was to
appear on a local radio show with Gorgeous George, the preeminent professional wrestler of the time. Gorgeous George (known to
his mother as George Raymond Wagner) was the first wrestler of
the television age to exploit the possibilities of theatrical narcissism
and a flexible sexual identity — Liberace in tights. His hair was
long and blond, and when he entered the ring he wore curlers. In
his corner, he would release the curlers and let one of his minions
brush out the golden hair to his shoulders. He wore a robe of silver
lamé, and his fingernails were trimmed and polished. One lackey
sprayed the ring mat with insecticide, another sprayed Gorgeous
George with eau de cologne.

At the radio interview, Clay was not exactly silent. He was already
known by various nicknames in the press (Gaseous Cassius, the
Louisville Lip, Cash the Brash, Mighty Mouth, Claptrap Clay, etc.),
and he was quick to predict an easy win over Duke Sabedong. But
compared with Gorgeous George he was tongue-tied. "I'll kill him!"
Gorgeous ranted. "I'll tear his arm off! If this bum beats me, I'll
crawl across the ring and cut my hair off, but it's not gonna happen,
because I'm the greatest wrestler in the world!"

Gorgeous George was already forty-six — he had been retailing
this shtick for years — but Clay was impressed, the more so when he
saw Gorgeous George perform. Every seat in the arena was filled
and nearly every fan was screaming for George's gilded scalp. But
the point was, the arena was filled. "A lot of people will pay to see
someone shut your mouth," George told Clay after that bout. "So
keep on bragging, keep on sassing, and always be outrageous."

In November of 1962, Clay fought Archie Moore, who was by then
forty-seven (more or less) and was the veteran of two hundred
fights. "I wasn't a fool. I knew how old I was, and I knew Clay from

training him for a while," Moore told me decades later. "But I felt pretty good about Clay, and I thought if I could bear down I could beat him. I had to outbox him or wait him out. He was so young, and you can never tell what a young man can do in boxing." The truth was, Moore badly needed the purse. His only chance was that Clay's inexperience would yield an opening for a right hand and a knockout. That was unlikely, according to the oddsmakers. Clay was a three-to-one favorite, and his prediction was for a quick night: "When you come to the fight, don't block the aisle and don't block the door. You will all go home after round four."

Clay and Moore sold out the arena in Los Angeles, not least because they kept up the verbal sparring at every venue possible, and especially on television. The two fighters even staged a half-hour mock debate.

"The only way I'll fall in four, Cassius, is by tripping over your prostrate form," Moore said.

"If I lose," said Clay, "I'm going to crawl across the ring and kiss your feet. Then I'll leave the country."

"Don't humiliate yourself," the old man replied. "Our country's depending on its youth. Really, I don't see how you can stand yourself. I am a speaker, not a rabble-rouser. I'm a conversationalist, you're a shouter."

Moore, a Liebling favorite, played the avuncular elder to the boorish wanna-be. With his Edwardian diction, Moore looked upon Clay as a duke would upon the unwashed. After their exchange, he reflected on the upstart with a certain professorial remove. "I view this young man with mixed emotions," he said. "Sometimes he sounds humorous, but sometimes he sounds like Ezra Pound's poetry. He's like a man who can write beautifully but doesn't know how to punctuate. He has this twentieth-century exuberance, but there's bitterness in him somewhere. . . . He is certainly coming along at a time when a new face is needed on the boxing scene, on the fistic horizon. But in his anxiousness to be this person he may be overplaying his hand by belittling people. . . . I don't care what Cassius says. He can't make me mad. All I want to do is knock him out."

Once the two fighters were in the arena, stripped of their robes and their promotional poses, it was impossible to ignore the physical difference. Clay was sleek as an otter, and not even at his peak of strength. He would fill out later. Moore was middle-aged. His hair was going gray. Fat jiggled on his arms. He kept his trunks pulled up around his nipples.

In the first round, Clay conducted a survey. Moore had a reputation for speed (now gone) and as a sneak, the master of the quick, unseen punch. He was known as the Mongoose. But Clay, as he flashed his jabs into Moore's face, seemed to convince himself that there would be no answer coming. Each jab that Clay bounced off Moore's scalp assured the younger man of the cruelty of age — a soothing discovery to him, if not to Moore.

In the second, Moore actually caught Clay with a right hand. It shot up out of a crowd of tangled arms and gave Clay a start, but there was nothing much to it. In the third, Moore was already so exhausted from trying to keep up that his arms began to sink. His inclination to send any damage Clay's way was down to nothing. Moore crouched, lower and lower, as if to meld with the canvas, but Clay's reach was long, and he leaned over to drill one left hook after another into Moore's bald spot. Years later, Moore would say that those punches, in their accumulation, made him dizzy: "They stirred the mind."

Clay was doing whatever he wanted. Every punch landed — the jabs, the hooks, the quick overhand rights — and Moore was barely hanging on, squatting lower and lower. Midway through the third, Clay hit Moore square on the chin. Moore wobbled. Then he took a few running steps backward to the rope, found it, and hung on. Clay refused to follow up, more for aesthetic reasons, it seemed, than for lack of intent. He had predicted a fourth-round knockout and wanted to maintain his pure vision of the fight.

Clay came out flat-footed in the fourth, the better to leverage his punches, and after a few preliminary jabs to warm up his shoulders, he started looking for the knockout. Moore bent at the waist again, as if in prayer, but he could not bow low enough. He took a few wild swings to preserve his name, and Clay jabbed back, scolding him for the delay. Clay circled and circled, then suddenly jumped in with an uppercut that straightened Moore out of his crouch, and then a few more punches, all sharp and straight, like clean hammer raps on a nail, put him down. Clay stood over the prostrate lump to take his bow, shuffled his feet in a flash, and then retreated, reluctantly, to the neutral corner. He disdained this obligatory retreat; it meant leaving center stage.

Moore, meanwhile, roused himself and rolled onto his left side, an old man waking from a fitful sleep. Then he pridefully lifted himself to his feet just before "ten." With a look of annoyance (he'd thought it was over), Clay met Moore again in the center of the ring and started punching. Moore took one wild swing, as if to acquit himself of any lingering charges of resignation, and then slowly melted back to the floor as Clay hit him on top of the head. The time had come, and Moore knew it. He stayed on his backside.

With the fight over, Clay hugged Moore sweetly, the way one would embrace a grandfather.

Later, Moore responded with an endorsement. "He's definitely ready for Liston," he told the reporters gathered around him. "Sonny would be difficult for him and I would hesitate to say he could beat the champ, but I'll guarantee he would furnish him with an exceedingly interesting evening."

In 1963, when Clay signed to fight Sonny Liston for the title the following February, print was still the supreme medium of communication and hype, and the most powerful men in sports were the columnists. To promote the fight, to create an image of himself in the public mind, Clay would have to work through them. As a filter, the press was monochromatic. Nearly all the columnists were white, middle-aged, and raised on Joe Louis as the beau ideal of proper black comportment. Despite Liston's multiple arrests, two-year prison term, and baleful disdain, they were inclined to like Clay even less than Liston. At least, they thought, Liston could fight. Clay was a talker, and they resented that. Language was *their* property, not the performer's. Jim Murray, of the *Los Angeles Times,* remarked of Clay that "his public utterances have all the modesty of a German ultimatum to Poland but his public performances run more to Mussolini's Navy." According to one poll, 93 percent of the writers accredited to cover the fight predicted that Liston would win. What the poll did not register was the firmness of the predictions. Arthur Daley, the *New York Times* columnist, seemed to object morally to the fight, as if the bout were a terrible crime against children and puppies: "The loud mouth from Louisville is likely to have a lot of vainglorious boasts jammed down his throat by a ham-like fist belonging to Sonny Liston."

Jimmy Cannon, late of the *Post* and with the *Journal-American* since 1959, was the king of the columnists. Cannon was the first thousand-dollar-a-week man, Hemingway's favorite, Joe DiMaggio's buddy, and Joe Louis's iconographer. Red Smith, who wrote for the *Herald Tribune,* employed an elegant restraint in his prose, which put him ahead of the game with more high-minded readers, but Cannon was the popular favorite: a world-weary voice of the city. Cannon was king, and Cannon had no truck with Cassius Clay.

One afternoon shortly before the fight, Cannon was sitting with George Plimpton at the Fifth Street Gym, in Miami Beach, watching Clay spar. Clay glided around the ring, a feather in the slipstream, and every so often he popped a jab into his sparring partner's face. As he recalled in his book *Shadow Box,* Plimpton was completely taken with Clay's movement, his ease, but Cannon couldn't bear to watch.

"Look at that!" Cannon said. "I mean, that's terrible. He can't get away with that. Not possibly." It was just unthinkable that Clay could beat Liston by running, keeping his hands at his hips, and defending himself simply by leaning away.

"Perhaps his speed will make up for it," Plimpton put in hopefully.

"He's the fifth Beatle," Cannon said. "Except that's not right. The Beatles have no hokum to them."

"It's a good name," Plimpton said. "The fifth Beatle."

"Not accurate," Cannon said. "He's all pretense and gas, that fellow. . . . No honesty."

Clay offended Cannon's sense of rightness the way flying machines offended his father's generation. It threw his universe out of kilter. "In a way, Clay is a freak," he wrote before the fight. "He is a bantamweight who weighs more than two hundred pounds."

Cannon's objections went beyond the ring. His hero was Joe Louis, and for Joe Louis he composed the immortal line that he was a "credit to his race — the human race." He admired Louis's "barbaric majesty," his quiet in suffering, his silent satisfaction in victory. And when Louis finally went on too long and, way past his peak, fought Rocky Marciano, he eulogized the broken-down old fighter as the metaphysical poets would a slain mistress: "The heart, beating inside the body like a fierce bird, blinded and caged, seemed incapable of moving the cold blood through the arteries of Joe Louis' rebellious body. His thirty-seven years were a disease which paralyzed him."

Cannon was born in 1910, in what he called "the unfreaky part of Greenwich Village." His father was a minor, if kindly, servant of Tammany Hall. Cannon dropped out of school after the ninth grade, caught on as a copyboy at the *News,* and never left the newspaper business. As a young reporter, he caught the eye of Damon Runyon when he wrote dispatches on the Lindbergh kidnapping trial for the International News Service.

"The best way to be a bum and make a living is to be a sportswriter," Runyon told Cannon, and he helped him get a job at a Hearst paper, the *New York American,* in 1936. Like his heroes Runyon and the Broadway columnist Mark Hellinger, Cannon gravitated to the world of the "delicatessen nobility," to the bookmakers and touts, the horseplayers and talent agents, who hung out at Toots Shor's and Lindy's, the Stork Club and El Morocco. When Cannon went off to Europe to write battle dispatches for *Stars & Stripes,* he developed what would become his signature style: florid, sentimental prose with an underpinning of hard-bitten wisdom, an urban style that he had picked up in candy stores and nightclubs and from Runyon, Ben Hecht, and Westbrook Pegler. Cannon would begin some columns by putting the reader inside the skull and uniform of a ballplayer ("You're Eddie Stanky. . . . You ran slower than the other guy"), and elsewhere, in that voice of Lindy's at three in the morning, he would dispense wisdom on the subject he seemed to know the least about — women: "Any man is in difficulty if he falls in love with a woman he can't knock down with the first punch," or, "You could tell when a broad starts in managing a fighter. What makes a dumb broad smart all of a sudden? They don't even let broads in a joint like Yale. But they're all wised up once a fighter starts making a few."

The wised-up one-liners and the world-weary sentiment belonged to a particular time and place, and as Cannon aged he gruffly resisted new trends in sports writing and athletic behavior. In the press box, he encountered a new generation of beat writers and columnists — men like Maury Allen and Leonard Shecter, of the *Post.* He didn't much like the sound of them. Cannon called the younger men Chipmunks, because they were always chattering away. He hated their impudence, their irreverence, their striving to get outside the game and into the heads of the people they covered. Cannon had always said that his intention as a sports writer was to bring the "world in over the bleacher wall," but he failed to see that this generation was trying to do much the same thing. He couldn't bear their lack of respect for the old verities. "They go up and challenge guys with rude questions," Cannon once said of the Chipmunks. "They think they're very big if they walk up to an athlete and insult him with a question. They regard this as a sort of bravery."

Part of Cannon's anxiety was sheer competitiveness. There were seven newspapers in New York in those days, and there was terrific competition to stay on top, to be original, to get a scoop, an extra detail. But the younger writers — and even some contemporaries, like Milton Gross, of the *Post* — knew they were in competition now not so much with one another as with the growing power of television. Unlike Cannon, who was almost entirely self-educated, the younger men (and they were still all men) had gone to college in the age of Freud. They became interested in the psychology of an athlete ("The Hidden Fears of Kenny Sears" was one of Milton Gross's longer pieces). In time, this, too, would no longer seem especially voguish — soon just about every schnook with a microphone would be asking the day's goat, "What were you thinking when you missed that ball?" — but for the moment the Chipmunks were the coming wave and Cannon's purple sentences, once so pleasurable, were beginning to feel less vibrant, a little antiquated.

The new generation — men like Pete Hamill and Jack Newfield, Jerry Izenberg and Gay Talese — all admired Cannon's immediacy, but Cannon begrudged them their new outlook, their educations, their youth. In the late fifties, Talese wrote many elegant features for the *Times* and then, in the sixties, even more impressively, a series of profiles for *Esquire,* on Patterson, Louis, DiMaggio, Frank Sinatra, and the theater director Joshua Logan. When Talese left the paper, in 1965, he had one heir in place, a reporter in his mid-twenties named Robert Lipsyte. It was left to Lipsyte to interpret this new phenomenon Cassius Clay to the elite, to the readers of the *Times*.

Like Cannon, Lipsyte grew up in New York, but he was a middle-class Jew from the Rego Park neighborhood of Queens, with a Columbia education. Lipsyte made the *Times* reporting staff at twenty-one with a display of hustle and ingenuity: one day the hunting-and-fishing columnist failed to send in a column from

Cuba, so Lipsyte sat down and, on deadline, knocked out a strange and funny column on how fish and birds were striking back at anglers and hunters. Lipsyte wrote about high school basketball players like Connie Hawkins and Roger Brown. He helped cover the 1962 Mets with Louis Effrat, a *Times* man who had lost the Dodgers beat when they moved out of Brooklyn. Effrat's admiration for his younger colleague was, to say the least, grudging: "Kid, they say in New York you can really write, but you don't know what the fuck you're writing about." If there was one subject that Lipsyte made it a point to learn about, it was race. In 1963, he met Dick Gregory, one of the best comics in the country and a constant presence in the civil rights movement. The two men became close friends, and eventually Lipsyte helped Gregory write *Nigger,* his autobiography. Even as a sports reporter, Lipsyte contrived ways to write about race. He wrote about Chicago's Blackstone Rangers gang, and he got to know Malcolm X and Elijah Muhammad. He covered rallies at which African Americans expressed their outrage against a country that would celebrate blacks only when they carried a football or boxed in a twenty-foot ring.

In the winter of 1963–64, the *Times's* regular boxing writer, Joe Nichols, declared that the Liston-Clay fight was a dog and that he was going off to spend the season covering racing at Hialeah. The assignment went to Lipsyte.

Unlike Cannon and the other village elders of the sports pages, Lipsyte found himself entranced with Clay. Here was this entertaining, beautiful, skilled young man who could fill your notebook in fifteen minutes. "Clay was unique, but it wasn't as if he were some sort of creature from outer space for me," Lipsyte said. "For Jimmy Cannon, he was, pardon the expression, an uppity nigger, and he could never handle that. The blacks he liked were the blacks of the thirties and the forties. They knew their place. Joe Louis called Jimmy Cannon 'Mr. Cannon' for a long time. He was a humble kid. Now here comes Cassius Clay popping off and abrasive and loud, and it was a jolt for a lot of sports writers, like Cannon. That was a transition period. What Clay did was make guys stand up and decide which side of the fence they were on. Clay upset the natural order of things at two levels. The idea was that he was a loud braggart and brought disrespect to this noble sport. Or so the Cannon people said. Never mind that Rocky Marciano was a slob who would show up at events in a T-shirt so that the locals would buy him good clothes. They said that Clay 'lacked dignity.' Clay combined Little Richard and Gorgeous George. He was not the sort of sweet dumb pet that writers were accustomed to. Clay also did not need the sports writers as a prism to find his way. He transcended the sports press. Jimmy Cannon, Red Smith — so many of them — were appalled. They didn't see the fun in it. And, above all, it was fun."

A week before the Liston fight, Clay stretched out on a rubbing table at the Fifth Street Gym and told Lipsyte and the rest of the assembled reporters, "I'm making money, the popcorn man making money, and the beer man, and you got something to write about."

Clay's uncanny sense of self-promotion didn't stop at his daily monologues. The next day, Lipsyte heard that the Beatles would be dropping by the Fifth Street Gym. The Beatles were in Miami to do *The Ed Sullivan Show*. Liston had actually gone to their studio performance and was not much impressed. As the Beatles ripped through their latest single, the champion turned sourly to the public-relations man Harold Conrad and said, "My dog plays drums better than that kid with the big nose." Conrad figured that Clay, and the younger reporters, would understand better.

Lipsyte was a card-carrying member of the rock-and-roll generation, and he saw that, for all its phoniness, a meeting between the Beatles and Clay was a meeting of the new, two acts that would surely mark the sixties. The older columnists passed, but Lipsyte saw a story.

The Beatles arrived. They were still in their mop-top phase, but they were already quite aware of their own pop status and appeal. Clay was not in evidence, and Ringo Starr was angry. "Where the fuck's Clay?" he said.

To kill a few minutes, Ringo began introducing the members of the band to Lipsyte and a few other reporters, though he introduced George Harrison as Paul and Lennon as Harrison, and finally Lennon lost patience.

"Let's get the fuck out of here," he said. But two Florida state troopers blocked the door and somehow kept them in the gym just long enough for Clay to show up.

"Hello, there, Beatles," Cassius Clay said. "We oughta do some road shows together. We'll get rich." The photographers lined up the Beatles in the ring, and Clay faked a punch to knock them all to the canvas: the domino punch.

Now the future of music and the future of sports began talking about the money they were making and the money they were going to make. "You're not as stupid as you look," Clay concluded.

"No," Lennon said, "but you are." Clay checked to make sure Lennon was smiling, and he was. The younger writers, like Lipsyte, really did see Clay as a fifth Beatle. This was just a few months after the Kennedy assassination, and the country was already in the midst of a social and political earthquake; the fighter from Louisville and this band from Liverpool were part of it, leading it, whether they knew it yet or not.

For most of the older columnists, however, this P.R.-inspired scene at the Fifth Street Gym was just more of all that was going wrong in the world — more noise, more disrespect, more impudence from young men they could not hope to comprehend. "Clay is part of the Beatle movement," Jimmy Cannon wrote a few years later. "He fits in with the famous singers no one can hear and the punks riding motorcycles with iron crosses pinned to their leather jackets and Batman and the boys with their long dirty hair and the girls with the unwashed look and the college kids dancing naked at secret proms held in apartments and the revolt of students who get a check from Dad every first of the month and the painters who copy the labels off soup cans and the surf bums who refuse to work and the whole pampered style-making cult of the bored young."

At the Fifth Street Gym, Clay was also setting a physical and psychological trap for the fighter he called "the big ugly bear." While Liston prepared for the fight by eating hot dogs and hanging out with a couple of prostitutes on Collins Avenue, Clay trained hard every day. Then, afterward, in his sessions with reporters, he described how he would spend the first five rounds circling Liston, tiring him out, and then tear him apart with hooks and uppercuts until finally the champion would drop to all fours in submission. "I'm gonna put that ugly bear on the floor, and after the fight I'm gonna build myself a pretty home and use him as a bearskin rug. Liston even smells like a bear. I'm gonna give him to the local zoo after I whup him. People think I'm joking. I'm not joking. I'm serious. This will be the easiest fight of my life." He told the visiting reporters that now was their chance to "jump on the bandwagon." He was taking names, he said, keeping track of all the naysayers, and when he won "I'm going to have a little ceremony and some eating is going on, eating of words."

In honor of the fight, Clay composed what was surely his best poem. Over the years, Clay would farm out some of his poetical work. "We all wrote lines here and there," Dundee, the trainer, said. But this one was all Clay. Ostensibly, it was a prophetic vision of the eighth round, and no poem, before or after, could beat it for narrative drive, scansion, and wit. It was his "Song of Myself":

> Clay comes out to meet Liston
> And Liston starts to retreat.
> If Liston goes back any further
> He'll end up in a ringside seat.
>
> Clay swings with a left,
> Clay swings with a right,
> Look at young Cassius
> Carry the fight.
>
> Liston keeps backing
> But there's not enough room.
> It's a matter of time.
> There Clay lowers the boom.
>
> Now Clay swings with a right,
> What a beautiful swing,
> And the punch raises the bear
> Clear out of the ring.
>
> Liston is still rising
> And the ref wears a frown,
> For he can't start counting
> Till Sonny comes down.
>
> Now Liston disappears from view.
> The crowd is getting frantic,
> But our radar stations have picked him up,
> He's somewhere over the Atlantic.

> Who would have thought
> When they came to the fight
> That they'd witness the launching
> Of a human satellite?
>
> Yes, the crowd did not dream
> When they laid down their money
> That they would see
> A total eclipse of the Sonny!

Nearly all the writers regarded Clay's bombast, in prose and verse, as the ravings of a lunatic. But not only did Clay have a sense of how to fill a reporter's notebook and, thus, a promoter's arena; he had a sense of self. The truth (and it was a truth he shared with almost no one) was that he knew that, for all his ability, for all his speed and cunning, he had never met a fighter like Sonny Liston. In Liston, Clay was up against a man who did not merely beat his opponents but hurt them, damaged them, shamed them in humiliatingly fast knockouts. Liston could put a man away with his jab; he was not much for dancing, but then neither was Joe Louis. When he hit a man in the solar plexus, the glove seemed lost up to the cuff; he was too powerful to grab and clinch; nothing hurt him. Clay was too smart, he had watched too many films, not to know that.

"That's why I always knew that all of Clay's bragging was a way to convince himself that he could do what he said he'd do," Floyd Patterson told me many years later. "I never liked all his bragging. It took me a long time to understand who Clay was talking to. Clay was talking to Clay."

Up in Michigan, more than thirty years later, Ali sat in his office on the farm. The office was on the second floor of a small house behind the main house, and it served as the headquarters of the company known as GOAT — the Greatest of All Time. Outside, geese glided along a pond. A few men were working in the fields. Someone was mowing the great lawn that rolled away from the house and up to the gates of the property. There were various fine cars around, including a Stutz Bearcat. There was a tennis court, a pool, and playground equipment sufficient for a small school in a well-taxed municipality. Ali is father to nine children: the oldest is Maryum, who is thirty, and the youngest is Asaad Ali, a seven-year-

old boy, whom Muhammad and his fourth wife, Lonnie, adopted.
"Muhammad finally found a playmate," Lonnie told me. "He wasn't
around much for his other children, but now he gets to play with
Asaad all the time." The Alis loved living on the farm, but lately they
had been looking for a buyer. When I was there, they talked to some
people who wanted to buy the place and convert it into a wellness
center. They had even tried to unload it on a television home-shop-
ping network. Eventually, Lonnie said, the family will move back to
Louisville, where they hope a Muhammad Ali center will be built.
Ali's parents have died, but his brother still works in Louisville.

Although Ali insists he spends most of his time these days "thinking about Paradise," it's not as if he's put his past behind him. He
earns his living making appearances and signing pictures, which
are then sold at auction and to dealerships. Sometimes, when he is
sleeping, Ali dreams about his old fights, especially the three wars
in the seventies with Joe Frazier. When the documentary film about
his triumph in Zaire, *When We Were Kings,* opened in 1996, Ali
watched the tape many times. In Los Angeles, when the film won an
Academy Award for best documentary feature, Ali was called onstage and wordlessly accepted a standing ovation.

His greatest triumph in retirement came on the summer night in
Atlanta when, to the surprise of nearly everyone watching, he sud-
denly appeared with a torch in his hands, ready to open the 1996
Summer Olympics. Ali stood with the heavy torch extended before
him, and three billion people could see him shaking, both from the
Parkinson's and from the moment itself. But Ali carried it off.
"Muhammad wouldn't go to bed for hours and hours that night,"
Lonnie said. "He was floating on air. He just sat in a chair back at
the hotel holding the torch in his hands. It was like he'd won the
heavyweight title back a fourth time."

Lonnie Ali is a handsome woman with a face full of freckles. She
is fifteen years younger than her husband and grew up near the
Clay family in Louisville's West End. When Ali's third marriage, to
Veronica Porsche, was on its way out, he called her to come be with
him. Eventually, Ali and Lonnie married. Lonnie is precisely what
Ali needs. She is smart — a Vanderbilt graduate — she is calm and
loving, and she does not treat Ali like her patient. Besides Ali's
closest friend, the photographer Howard Bingham, Lonnie is probably the one person in his life who has given more than she has

taken. In Michigan, Lonnie runs the household and the farm, and when they are on the road, which is more than half the time, she keeps watch over Ali, making sure he has rested enough and taken his medicine. She knows his moods and habits, what he can do and what he can't. She knows when he is suffering and when he is hiding behind his symptoms to zone out of another event that bores him.

When Lonnie came into the room where we were watching a tape of the Liston fight, Ali didn't look up from the television. He merely reached out and rested his hand on the small of her back.

"Muhammad, you've got to sign a couple of pictures, okay?" she said. She put a couple of eight-by-ten glossies in front of him. Cassius Clay was dancing around the ring, stopping only to needle a tattoo on the meat of Sonny Liston's face.

"Ali, can you make that 'To Mark'? M-A-R-K. And 'To Jim.' J-I-M. And later on you've got to sign some pictures and some boxing gloves."

Ali made plenty of money in boxing, but he didn't keep as much of it as he could have. There were alimonies, hangers-on, the IRS, good times, the Nation of Islam.

"I sign my name, we eat," he said sheepishly.

The tape kept rolling. By the third round, Cassius Clay was in complete control of Sonny Liston. There were welts under both of Liston's eyes. He had aged a decade in minutes. Ali loved it then, and he was loving it now. "People shouted every time Liston threw a punch," he whispered. "They was waitin'. But now they can't believe it. They thought Liston'd knock me into the crowd. Look at me!" Clay danced and jabbed. By the sixth round, Clay was a toreador filling a bull's back with blades.

Now it was over. Ali smiled as he watched his younger self dancing around the ring, shouting "I'm the king of the world! King of the world!" and climbing the ring ropes and pointing down at all the sports writers: "Eat your words! Eat your words!" The next day, Clay would announce that he was a member of the Nation of Islam. Within a few weeks, he would accept a new name. And within a couple of years he would become the most recognizable face on the planet.

A cleaning woman walked into the room, put aside her vacuum cleaner, and sat down to watch the tape with us. Cassius Clay was still shouting "King of the world!"

"Ain't I pretty?" Ali asked her.

"Oh, Ali," she said. "You had a big mouth then."

"I know," he said, smiling. "But wasn't I pretty? I was twenty . . . twenty what? Twenty-two. Now I'm fifty-four. Fifty-four." He said nothing for a minute or so. Then he said, "Time flies. Flies. Flies. It flies away."

Then, very slowly, Ali lifted his hand and fluttered his fingers like the wings of a bird. "It just flies away," he said.

J. D. DOLAN

Pool: A Love Story

FROM ESQUIRE

MAYBE IT ALL STARTED when I got kicked out of the women's powder room at the Masonic Lodge. I was, I don't know, four or six — old enough to be lovestruck over my oldest sister's friends and young enough to be more or less invisible to them. I'd play quietly in the corner and sneak looks as these young women applied fresh lipstick, as they adjusted their bras just so and rolled pale stockings into the dark region between their pale legs. Sometimes, I wouldn't even have to look — I'd just close my eyes and breathe in their perfume, a scent as beautiful as their orchid corsages.

"Hey — what's *he* doing in here?" one woman I was in love with said, whereupon I was scooted out of the women's powder room forever.

The door shut behind me with a little whoosh of perfumed air, and I slowly scuffed my way downstairs to the poolroom, which right then happened to be empty. I was just above eye level with the huge mahogany pool table, and I rolled a few balls around the green baize — angrily at first and then with building interest. The solid weight of the table, the sea of green cloth, the click of the brightly colored balls, the soft thunk of the rails, the surprising angles — all of it was mesmerizing. This was, I realized, a beautiful game.

Or maybe it started about thirty years later, in Syracuse, New York. I moved there to go to graduate school, and I met a smart, beautiful woman, also in graduate school, and we fell in love fast. We were both passionate about our work, and that passion seemed to carry

over into the time we spent together. She'd stop by my office between classes, and we'd lock the door and turn out the lights and
kiss for a while in the dark. And we'd go cross-country skiing out at
Green Lakes, then come back to my apartment and make love, and
afterward we'd have cozy dinners and Belgian beers in front of
my fireplace, right beside my pool table — my first — a beautiful
1920s model made of solid birch, with walnut rails and mother-of-
pearl points.

And in Syracuse, I became friends with one of the great legends
of pool, Arthur "Babe" Cranfield, the 1964 World Professional
Pocket Billiard Champion, who was seventy-nine when I met him at
Cap's Cue Club for my first lesson.

Babe Cranfield is frail and slight, and in his checked polyester
slacks and yellow polo shirt he looks like an old duffer from a
country club, except that the cuffs of his polyester slacks are rolled
and his yellow shirt is faded. His right eye tears from a childhood
baseball injury; his father had thought he was spending too much
time in the poolroom, so Babe took up baseball and was nearly
blinded by a line drive. He soon went back to pool, at which he was
a prodigy.

Before we started the lesson, we both watched a shooter doing a
tricky shot at a nearby table. The shooter did the same shot over
and over, and he didn't miss.

"Wow!" I said.

Babe said, loud enough for the shooter to hear, "He's not shit."

The shooter ignored Babe, and Babe turned his back on the
shooter.

"Look at him," Babe commanded.

I looked.

"What's he doing?"

"A hard shot?" I said, knowing already that my answer would be
wrong.

"No, no, no!" Babe said. "He's just showing off. He's just practicing what he *knows*. Let me ask you something. You want to be a
champion?"

My stomach clenched at this question. To answer it honestly —
Yes, *of course* I want to be a champion — seemed, given my current
abilities, absurd.

I said, hesitantly, yes.

There were tears coming from Babe's right eye, as if whatever he was about to say had come at great cost. Then he leaned close and whispered, "If you want to be a champion, practice your *weaknesses*."

A lot of guys seem to think that the ability to shoot pool is not something you learn but something you're born with. You simply are or are not a good pool player, and to not be a good pool player is to have been born deficient. And since most guys don't want to be deficient, they will play a game of pool — shooting too hard, missing horribly — and when they get lucky and pocket a ball, they'll think, Hmm, pretty good.

I was one of those guys. I actually fancied myself something of a pool shark when I first got to Syracuse. I could win beers in bars, relieve drunks of their money, hold court on a seven-foot coin-op.

All of which was not shit at Cap's Cue Club, a dingy poolroom filled with great players. I soon learned that I was no pool shark — I was no *player.* This knowledge came to me not through getting hustled or getting in any way beaten. It was worse than that. The players at Cap's Cue Club weren't just unimpressed with my game, they were *bored* with my game. For these players — skulking at the front counter, drinking coffee and smoking cigarettes, their hands blue with chalk dust — the prospect of playing me was more boring than, say, staring at Formica. I couldn't run a rack of balls, which, to a player, is the equivalent of crawling. I couldn't do a stop shot, a follow shot, a draw shot — or not with any consistency, and players are nothing if not consistent. I had no stroke, which meant that the cue ball would sometimes do as it was intended and sometimes, usually when a player was glancing my way, it would not.

In the Sunday night handicapped tournaments at Cap's Cue Club, the ratings go from double-A all the way down to D. I was rated a D. There is nothing lower than a D, and several of the other D's could beat me.

Not long after we got together, my girlfriend told me she still had a lingering relationship with a man in Los Angeles, but it was a relationship mainly of inertia, she said. In truth, she made this man she once loved sound like an old dog she couldn't quite bring herself to shoot. But she didn't mention him often, and when she did, her voice took on a tone of bitterness at worst and pity at best.

One night, my girlfriend and I were snuggled in bed and talking about our future together, and we got onto the subject of names we might choose for a baby. We snuggled a little closer and talked some more, and as I was drifting off to sleep, she started crying into my shoulder. "*He* never even *talked* to me about our relationship," she said.

I was suddenly awake, but I didn't know how to react. How are you supposed to react when a woman sees you not for what you are but for what another man isn't? At that moment, though, it seemed convenient, and even noble, to be what he was not. Still, I didn't know what to tell her, so I told her the truth. "I love you," I said.

She held me tightly and said, "I love you, too." Then she said, "You're different."

The next morning, after she'd left, I found on my bathroom mirror a fresh, red lipstick kiss.

Every day at noon, I'd watch Babe shoot straight pool, and what I learned from watching him was cue-ball control. His days of three- and four-hundred-ball runs were long gone, but it wasn't unusual for him to run a hundred balls, shooting difficult shots when he had to — kisses, combinations, massés, banks — but usually positioning the cue ball so that his next shot was easy. His game had the logic and beauty and complexity of a chess match, and if you closed your eyes and just listened, it *sounded* like a chess match: *click, click, click* . . . In practice, Babe once had a high run of 768. My high run stood at 16.

But my pool game was improving, and I got it into my head that I'd be an A-rated player by the time I left Syracuse. I was beginning to pocket balls consistently, and every now and then I'd even manage to run out in nine ball and shoot eighteen or twenty balls in straight pool. I wasn't a very good player yet, but I was less of a bad player.

My game improved dramatically, though, when I broke up with my girlfriend. She hadn't been able to end that other relationship, so eventually I had to end ours. Which, of course, left me wishing I'd ended it sooner, wishing I'd never gotten involved with her in the first place, and wishing more than anything that we could get back together. But our lives had become so intermingled that everything in my life reminded me of her, so I'd go down to Cap's Cue Club in an effort to get away from both of us.

And it worked. I developed a seriousness — a sudden dark concentration. Pool was still a beautiful, mysterious game, and I still loved to play it, but the beauty now was in understanding the mystery instead of just being amazed by it. The world was reduced to four and a half by nine feet. There were fifteen balls. Everything you needed was right there on the table. The rest was up to you.

By the time my girlfriend and I got back together, I was rated a C.

She'd ended that other relationship, she said, and we were for a while very happy, and I happily spent more time with her than I did at Cap's Cue Club. But even though I spent less time at it, my game continued to improve. My dark concentration had been replaced by a calm focus. And by the time we broke up again, when she told me she'd only *conditionally* ended that other relationship and I boxed up her nightgown, her toothbrush, her CDs, and all the rest of her stuff from my apartment and handed them to her with the sincere wish that she stay the fuck out of my life, I was rated a C-plus.

And this was when I got *very* serious about my game. Even the players at Cap's Cue Club noticed, and a few of them would play me once in a while. Sometimes, I'd come home from the poolroom and find pleading notes that my girlfriend — my ex-girlfriend — had left on my doorstep. One time, I found flowers. Another time, I found her. She assured me that the other relationship was over, it was done, it was dead. Common sense told me to run from her, but I couldn't shake the notion that the only roadblock in our relationship had come down — the road was open. I was rated a B.

My high run was now forty, which was respectable, if not stellar, pool. But my learning curve had gone flat. I'd become a B, and I stayed a B.

One day while I was watching him shoot, Babe started ranting to me about Minnesota Fats — one of Babe's favorite rants. "That bum couldn't run fifty balls," Babe said, and fired off a perfect wing shot. All serious pool players know that Minnesota Fats was little more than a middling player who happened to be a spectacular self-promoter. But if running fewer than fifty balls constituted a bum . . .

I was nearly done with graduate school. I had a teaching job lined up in the fall, and my girlfriend would be gone for a good part of the summer, finishing up her fieldwork. I knew that if there was ever a time to get my game up to A level, this was it.

Babe had just been inducted into the Billiard Congress of America Hall of Fame, and I thought about asking him to train me. I knew he'd probably agree to do it, but in pool, as in golf and tennis, the best players are not always the best teachers. Babe's stroke was unorthodox, and his teaching methods included whanging his ancient Herman Rambow cue against the rail and saying, "No, no, no!"

So I called a man whom many consider to be the best pool instructor in the country, former pro Jerry Briesath, a BCA Master Instructor who's trained hundreds of players, from beginners all the way up to top pros such as Danny Harriman and Jeff Carter. When five-time world champion Nick Varner wanted to give his father some pool lessons, he sent him to Jerry Briesath in Madison, Wisconsin.

Jerry said, "You say you're about a B-level player right now, huh? Well, what is it you want to do with your game?"

"Oh, not much," I said. "I'd just like to be able to beat Efren Reyes, Mike Sigel, and Earl Strickland."

Jerry got a good laugh at the idea of a B player suddenly able to beat three of the greatest pool players alive.

I was laughing, too, but secretly I was dead serious.

Jerry said, "Some people come for a day, some people come for as long as a week . . ."

I thought about my upcoming summer alone and said, "A month. How good do you think I can get in a month?"

"Well," he said, still laughing a little, "you should definitely get better."

On the flight to Madison, I got myself worked up into something of a panic. Here I was with my thousand-dollar cue, a Mike Bender five-point made of ebony and bird's-eye maple with sterling-silver rings — a cue worthy of the player I wanted to become. But what if my best efforts were an utter flop? I was going to Madison with the assumption that I could get my game up to A level (which is, by the way, nowhere near good enough to beat a professional player, only good enough to *play* one). What if I practiced pool all day every day for a month with the best pool instructor in the country and I was *still* a B player, a B person — a man consigned to a B life?

Jerry didn't say I *would* definitely get better; he said I *should* definitely get better. And he was laughing when he said it.

I leaned back in my seat and thought about my girlfriend. Her flight had left a few hours before mine, and our goodbye at the airport — one of those clenched hugs and a swift, deep kiss — had been sad but also something of a relief. When I held her like that, I could smell her shampoo — a faint scent of clove and, I don't know, maybe cherry. I could almost smell it still, but not enough. This time apart, I figured, would be good for us. We'd gotten up that morning at 4 A.M. and made love like two people who have forever and who'll see each other in a month anyway.

A big sign at the airport read, WELCOME TO MADISON, WISCONSIN, THE NO. 1 CITY IN AMERICA. All airports everywhere have signs like this, but as I rode in a taxi from the airport to the hotel, it seemed as if the sign had been right. Every yard seemed to be weedless; every flower seemed to be in perfect bloom. Everybody looked happy and healthy and well fed.

It was sort of creepy. "Is there a *bad* part of town?" I said to the cabdriver, and she looked at me in the rearview mirror and said, "Well, there are parts that aren't as *good*."

I kept seeing signs that read, MADISON, WISCONSIN, THE NO. 1 CITY IN AMERICA, and when I asked the driver about it, she said, "*Money* magazine. *Last* year, they rated us number one."

"Oh, that's terrific," I said. I looked at the rearview mirror and noticed her eyes glaring at me.

Jerry Briesath has a camera pointed at me — a video camera — and he positions a few balls on the pool table and says, "Just shoot this shot the way you normally would." He says this the way a doctor might say, "Just breathe naturally" while checking you with a stethoscope for lung cancer.

But it's a simple shot, and I make it and most of the other shots that Jerry sets up — stop shots, draw shots, follow shots — and so I'm feeling pretty confident until we sit down to look at the video.

The Green Room is sort of a pool player's version of heaven.

There are huge skylights overhead; there are twenty gorgeous new Brunswick Gold Crowns; there are two Verhoeven billiard tables with heated slates; and overlooking all of this is a big bar with lots of dark wood and polished brass and a good-looking waitress named Natalie.

None of which shows up on the video. What Jerry has chosen is a tight focus — not on the pool table or the pockets or the balls but on my arm. And what the video shows, again and again, is an impatient, spasmodic jab — the motion of a timid kid poking a frog with a stick.

The video seems endless, but Jerry finally stops the tape and says, "Do you *know* what a good stroke is?"

I've been shooting pool long enough to know that I'm supposed to know the answer to this. "Follow-through?" I say.

"Well, that's part of it," Jerry says, "but not all of it." He is sixty but looks ten years younger; he's tall and dark-haired, and with his thin, old-fashioned mustache, he reminds me of William Powell. It seems obvious that he likes the line he's about to deliver. "A good stroke," Jerry says, "is a beautiful throwing motion." He does a graceful golf swing with an imaginary club. "A beautiful throwing motion," he says. He winds up and pitches an imaginary baseball. "A beautiful throwing motion." Jerry pitches another imaginary baseball, but this time with the jerky urgency that's clearly an analogue to my pool stroke. "*Not* a beautiful throwing motion," he says, and lets out a high, cartoonish laugh. "Pool is one of those games where if you don't *look* good while you're doing it, you're *not* good."

This whole first week, I'm working on my system — that's what Jerry calls it, my *system* — which is everything I do from the time I look at the ball until it stops rolling, and it should CHIN LOCK be easy, learning what is, in essence, a simple swinging of the arm, but is ADDRESS THE BALL also a matter of *unlearning* something, unlearning SIGHT IN *everything*, and the mechanics have become complex, and in the complexity, I keep SLOW BACKSTROKE losing track of what I'm used to doing, namely pocketing balls, and so while STROKE TWICE I'm supposed to be here to improve my pool game, my pool game at present is worse than ever, it is, in fact, DON'T DROP THE ELBOW wretched, and my stroke does not resemble a beautiful PAUSE throwing motion, it is awkward and stiff and forced SIGHT IN and resembles the spasm of a broken robot, and what would have been a simple shot a week SMOOTH RHYTHM ago now seems impossible if I do everything else right, and there is a lot SLOW BACKSTROKE to do right, and I find myself mumbling Jerry's system like a mantra — his twangy, midwestern STROKE TWICE voice stuck in my head — and my first week of serious pool instruction has PAUSE my arm aching and my back aching, not from any difficulty SIGHT IN AGAIN of movement but from focusing so fucking LOOK AT THE OBJECT BALL much, and in the evenings, I walk away from the poolroom feeling SLOW BACKSTROKE regressive and whipped, sometimes skipping dinner SHOOT and sometimes going FOLLOW THROUGH for a sullen walk along beautiful Lake Mendota, and back at DON'T DROP THE ELBOW the hotel, I call my girlfriend to hear how she's doing and to take in the pure comfort KEEP THE TIP ON THE CLOTH of her voice, but we keep trading telephone messages, and we just can't seem to STAY DOWN connect.

By the second week, I've worked my way up to stop shots. Stop shots. I'd thought that by now I'd be working on three-rail kicks, pattern play, strategies for breaking up clusters. But no, I'm working on stop shots, and every now and then, I'll still hear Jerry's voice, sometimes real and sometimes imagined, telling me to slow down my backstroke and pause before I shoot — bad habits I can't seem to shake.

There are other people here like me, usually two or three every day, people who love pool and who've come here to have Jerry Briesath change their pool games and their lives, although almost nobody will admit it.

One young man from Michigan tells me he's come here to get better but not *too* much better — it would screw up his rating in the bar league back home. But later, he admits that he hasn't told anybody about coming here — not even his girlfriend. He doesn't want to look foolish if his game, as he puts it, "still sucks." An old guy on vacation stops in for a lesson. His Winnebago's out in the parking lot. He says he plays pool at about seventy senior centers around the country every year and wants to improve his game, but not *too* much, or else nobody at the senior centers will play him.

It makes me want to laugh — in fact, after I hear about the eighth guy say, "I don't want to get *too* much better," I do laugh. But it's safer, I guess, to believe that you actually *could* get too much better, that your capacity for transformation is boundless, and that your mediocre pool game is really the result of a shrewd and well-reasoned decision.

Jerry comes over to my table and studies me as I shoot a stop shot.

I shoot, the object ball drops in the pocket, and the cue ball stops as if it had hit glue. Perfect!

Jerry shakes his head gravely and says, "Pause! Pause before you shoot!" He's said this to me about a million times so far. It seems as if what he's really getting at is some kind of monstrous character flaw.

Maybe it's the payoff of endless repetition, or maybe it's the notion of enjoyment as a component of perfection. Whatever. By the end of the second week, my game, my *system,* is beginning to take shape.

My focus has shifted from what's happening out there on the table to what's happening right here with my arm, my stroke. Whether I'm shooting a draw shot or a shot with lots of English (and English, by the way, is sidespin), I take slow backstrokes, I pause, I follow through after I shoot, and I make sure that the tip of the cue is touching the cloth when I'm finished. Now when I do a follow shot, the cue ball hits the object ball, then rushes forward. When I do a draw shot, the cue ball hits the object ball, pauses for a second, then comes racing backward like a yo-yo on a string. What Jerry has been hammering into my head is beginning to make sense, and I'm beginning to feel it. My stroke is becoming a beautiful throwing motion.

I leave the poolroom feeling dizzy with accomplishment and walk along the State Street Mall — the number-one street in the number-one city in America. There are no cars allowed, only pedestrians and bicyclists and clean white buses that run on time. The bicyclists actually signal when they turn. The pedestrians stop at red lights. There are students and panhandlers and folk musicians and kids with blue hair and tattoos — and they all look so well scrubbed and cute! The State Street Mall, in its trendiness and diversity, reminds me of New York City's East Village, if the East Village had been built in Switzerland and run by Disney.

Madison seems to exude number-oneness, and I feel, with my new pool game, that I'm a part of it.

The next week, Jerry works with me on bank shots, rail-first shots, frozen-to-rail shots, pattern play, safeties, two- and three-rail kicks, and by the end of the week, he says, "You should get into a low-stakes money game with somebody better than you and plan on losing twenty or thirty dollars. You need to practice under pressure."

So, as soon as I can, I get into a nine-ball game, with a guy named Gary, a fine player with a beautiful stroke. As he's putting together the flashy McDermott cue he won in a state tournament, he says, "What are you rated?"

I tell him I'm rated a B, and he offers to give me the eight ball, ten bucks a set, race to seven. I figure he'll make short work of my thirty dollars.

I'm a little nervous at first, but then I settle into my system — *sight in, slow backstrokes, pause before I shoot* — and soon I'm up a few games, and then I end up winning the set. This has to be some sort of fluke, I think, but we play another set, and I win that one, too.

"I'll play you the next set even," Gary says. "Otherwise, I'm done."

I feel this giddiness as I step up to the table — and miss my first shot, a simple one I should have made. So I concentrate on my system when I get to the table again — *sight in, slow backstrokes, pause before I shoot* — and I win the set, seven games to four.

Gary says, "That's all for me." And as he's unscrewing his flashy McDermott cue, he says, curtly, "You are *not* a B."

When I call my girlfriend that night, the first thing I tell her is "I'm not a B anymore!"

"What?" she says.

I start to tell her about the match, and about Gary, and about how we played the last set even, and she interrupts me and says, without enthusiasm, "That's great."

I ask her how things are going, and she says, "Fine."

I ask her how she's feeling, and she says, "Tired."

I ask her from what, and for a long time she doesn't say anything.

Then she says, "I've just been feeling different lately." And when I ask her specifically *how* she feels different, she says, "Just different."

A few days later, I play in the weekly tournament at the Green Room. My first match is against a loudmouth from Kentucky who keeps snapping at Natalie the waitress and under his breath calls her a bitch. I have this urge to hit him upside the head with my pool cue, but my pool cue is too good for that. So I take extra-special pleasure when I win the match — easily. I win my next one easily, too, and the next, and the next, and it's not so much that the matches are easy as that I'm not making things difficult for myself.

My system, it seems, is working, because I end up winning the tournament. It's only forty dollars, but I'm still excited about it, and the first thing I do when I get back to the hotel is call my girlfriend and say, "What do you *mean*, 'different'?"

She seems moody and says she's tired and would rather not talk about it right now, and I say, "Talk about *what?*"

"I just feel different about *things*," she says.

"Things," I say, and wait.

"Different about *us*," she says. There is pity in her voice, a pity edged with bitterness, and I get this sickening feeling not just that our relationship is ending but that it's already ended, and that she's ended it without bothering to include me in the process. And it's clear — I can hear it in her voice; it's a voice I know well — she's included someone else.

"No, sir," the desk clerk at the hotel says, "there *still* aren't any messages for you."

I hang up the pay phone and stalk back to my pool table, where I shoot another rack of balls too hard and too fast, and I really don't give a shit. In the last week, my game has abandoned me completely. Utterly. There is not a letter of the alphabet to categorize me now. It's my last day in town, thank God, since the Green Room and all of Madison have become sort of hellish. Even *Money* magazine seems to agree: its new list has come out, and Madison has been demoted to the seventh-best city in America. I keep ordering coffees from Natalie just to catch the scent of her perfume. I've got so much caffeine in me, I'm vibrating. And I keep thinking, *differ-*

ent, and shoot, *different,* and shoot — hard enough to send the balls to the moon.

At a nearby pool table, two hackers are narrating every shot they make, and the whole thing sounds disturbingly like a porno flick.

"Ooo, baby!"

"Stroke it!"

"Come, come, come!"

"Closer!"

"Oh, yeah! Oh, yeah!"

I try a long, difficult cut shot, and the ball is rolling toward the pocket, rolling *almost* in a perfect line, and I find myself standing up and leaning in the direction I want the ball to go. But the ball jaws in the pocket and doesn't drop.

Jerry materializes beside my table. "No," he says. "Do a mature miss." Jerry pronounces it "ma-toor."

"What's a *mature* miss?" I ask.

"A mature miss," he says, "is when you stay down and figure out what you did wrong. As long as you keep jumping up like that, you're just going to keep making the same mistake over and over." Jerry is just standing there, but he seems to be looming over me.

"Missing is part of the game," he says. "Learn from your misses."

ALLEN ABEL

When Hell Froze Over

FROM SPORTS ILLUSTRATED

"The WHA was like buying a motor home. There are only two great days — the day you buy it and the day you sell it."
— Derek Sanderson

"We are without merit. We are in free fall. We are a generation of guys with no statistics — only stories. We are WHA guys living in a WHA world."
— Al Smith

THIS IS THE HOUR to celebrate hockey's great pretender: a league where Bobby Hull soared, Gordie Howe scored, and Maurice Richard coached (for a week). Where Wayne Gretzky arrived, Frank Mahovlich thrived, and Derek Sanderson — when his team's first home game was canceled because the Zamboni crashed through the ice — was pelted with pucks by irate fans.

Mark Messier played here, and scored one goal all season. Harry Neale coached a team, but it folded. Twice. (Another team went under five times.) The league's championship trophy was sponsored by a finance company. The Dayton and Miami franchises never played a game. The Ottawa team, in its second incarnation, lasted only two nights. The league's most memorable moment came when a brawler yanked the toupee off the number-one star. Yet the league endured — and, in places, flourished — for seven unforgettable years.

This was the World Hockey Association, created in the Watergate autumn of 1972 by a marriage of California confidence men and giddy millionaires with major league dreams. The new league didn't just change the face of hockey; it drew a mustache and beard on the portrait of a fossilized sport. The WHA terrorized the NHL's fraternity of plantation slaveholders, blithely kidnapped teenage prospects, crusaded bravely into the Sun Belt, enriched a few headliners and an underclass of ordinary puck chasers beyond their wildest nightmares, and went head-to-head with the NHL in every major North American city — and lost every time.

In its brief and addled existence, the WHA spanned the continent from Boston to Vancouver, from St. Paul to Birmingham. Its rosters included many of the icons of the sport: Howe, Hull, Mahovlich, Gerry Cheevers, Paul Henderson, Dave Keon, Bernie Parent, and Jacques Plante. The league sent its All-Stars to Moscow as the proxies of Canada's national pride — and won one game out of eight. It enlisted some of the fiercest goons in hockey history, yet it embraced Europe's daintiest pros and welcomed the American collegians and Russian militiamen whose kind would rise to rule the game today.

Twenty-five years after the first blue WHA pucks were dropped, the Chicago Cougars and Minnesota Fighting Saints, the Michigan Stags and New York Golden Blades are ancient history. (Only the Edmonton Oilers endure, by a thread. The fact that the NHL has planted teams in every U.S. city larger than Hope, Arkansas, keeps the Oilers in Canada.) But the legacy of the WHA — from Gretzky and Messier to the explosion of American and European players — remains vibrant even as the defunct circuit's bankers search for dozens of former players who are entitled to small pensions but have disappeared.

To WHA veterans, the league's bequest varies from riches to rags. Some of its former stars remain prominent in pro hockey as players, executives, scouts, commentators, and coaches. The luckiest of them glide through middle age in an Elysium of golf and beer. Most, however, have returned to a less celestial existence in the mortal grip of families and work. Several are dead. Some live in poverty. One is in prison. Another, a sportscaster, was murdered outside an Ottawa television studio by a madman with a hatred of reporters.

As a charter member of the WHA press corps, I was assigned to track down a few of the survivors. My search stretched across the continent, around the clock, and far beyond the arenas where, for an instant, they found their fame.

Outside the Cheshire Inn, St. Louis

At 2:45 A.M. on the silver anniversary of the day he signed the contract that ignited hockey's most hilarious revolution, Bobby Hull is roaring merrily in the parking lot of a mock-Tudor tavern while a friend of one of his innumerable sons drives golf balls into the heavily populated night. Dimpled spheres fly past a distant Amoco sign toward the cars on Clayton Road as the rest of Hull's entourage — a young handler from a hockey-card company and I — gloomily prophesy the headline in the morning *Post-Dispatch:* KILLER SOUGHT IN GOLF BALL DEATHS.

Meanwhile, the Cheshire Inn, at closing time, is extruding dozens of tipsy twenty-something couples, and as they pause to kiss under the street lamps right in the flight path of the golf balls, they are counseled by an incorrigible frat boy of a Hall of Famer. "Hey!" Hull calls out to them. "Get a room!"

It is June 27, 1997. Exactly a quarter century earlier, amid a delirious throng in downtown Winnipeg, Manitoba, Hull endorsed his $1 million bonus check. That was the ante collectively coughed up by all the franchise holders of an upstart association whose every hope was riding on the mile-wide shoulders of hockey's Golden Jet.

After a decade as the NHL's most flamboyant, virile, and marketable superhero, Hull had first broached jumping from the Chicago Blackhawks to the Winnipeg Jets as a canard, a gibe at the Blackhawks' owners. After all, what lunatic would pay him ten times what he was earning? But the WHA's offer proved valid, and with sons Brett (the future NHL goal-scoring champion), Blake, Bobby, and Bart looking on, the man put pen to paper on that warm June day. The prairie crowd went loco. Hull committed himself to the Jets even though on another occasion his spouse, Joanne, not knowing that she could be heard by Ben Hatskin, the three-hundred-pound jukebox magnate who owned the new team, had angrily demanded of her mate, "Why would you ever want to live in Winnipeg and play for that fat Jew?"

Twenty-five years later, Joanne is another man's missus in Vancouver, Hull's pockets are bulging with fistfuls of twenty-dollar bills from a couple of autograph sessions, and his prodigious appetite has been slaked by chicken wings and cabernet. He has finished reciting, from memory, "The Cremation of Sam McGee" by Robert

W. Service. Dawn is fast approaching, and Hull recalls his tenure as player-coach in Winnipeg with the following judgment: "I couldn't coach a dog out of a doghouse with a T-bone steak."

He is wearing a rainbow seersucker shirt that barely contains his Java man arms, blue trousers stretched over his lumberjack thighs, a tousled blond rug glued above his gray temples, and a ring fitted with a gold coin that depicts the late shah of Iran — a gift from some Persian-American fans of the Blackhawks, who haven't won the Stanley Cup in the quarter century since Hull departed. He has spent the evening signing his name in gold ink for a generation of white boys who never saw him explode across the blue line, grinning, head up, legs churning — and for their fathers who did and will never forget it.

"Going to the WHA was not one bit about money," Hull says as we sit quietly for a moment on the patio of another bar, toasting the anniversary. "I had been at war with the Blackhawks' management for years. We hated each other. I had held out for eighteen games and called them everything but white men. Then Ben Hatskin drew my name out of a hat when they were dividing up the players the new league would go after.

"I met him in Vancouver, in secret. He offered me $250,000 a year, plus $100,000 more as coach and general manager, plus $1 million to sign. I thought it was a joke. I pretended to go along with it, just to scare Chicago. Then my agent, Harvey Weinberg, said, 'Bobby, these guys are serious.' I told Harvey, 'I don't want to go to some frozen place I've never been in my life in the middle of nowhere with an extravagant wife and five kids.' Had I known they were serious, I'd have asked for $20 million."

But one thing led to another, and by the fall of 1972 the Blackhawks had called Hull's bluff, he had signed the million-dollar contract, other NHL stars were jumping to the new league for hallucinogenic amounts of money, and the Jets were in training camp in the resort town of Kenora, Ontario. Meanwhile, thanks to a niggling injunction by the NHL, Hull could neither suit up for nor even coach his embryonic team.

Apollo astronauts were riding buggies on the moon, and George McGovern was winning Massachusetts. Hull convened a clandestine meeting of his former Blackhawks comrades and begged them to join him in the outlaw league. Only a few dared to. In Winnipeg the Golden Jet made numerous public appearances on behalf of the corpulent Hatskin and his bare-bones enterprise. "I had some great experiences," Hull says. "Not that I needed to build character."

The Jets would endure for all seven WHA seasons — six of them with Hull aboard — and would be one of four franchises in the association (out of the thirty-two that existed at one time or another) to be accepted into the NHL in 1979, after everyone on both sides had been bled as dry as a kosher chicken. In the interim, the Jets would win the AVCO World Trophy three times, would import several of the most creative and fluid Swedish and Finnish athletes ever to play the sport, and would turn barren Winnipeg, with its eleven-month winters, into a major league city (for a time). Hull would score seventy-seven goals in one memorable season, 1974–75; one of his sons would marry his linemate's daughter; the Jets would be the only WHA team to defeat the Soviet nationals; Hull's rug would be ripped off in a fracas during a game against the Birmingham Bulls in 1978; and his marriage would end in one of the most raucous and profane dissolutions in the annals of Canadian law. Joanne Hull would take the children with her. Bobby wouldn't be close to Brett for more than seven years.

"Do you ever regret going to the WHA?" the eternal youth is asked at 3 A.M. in St. Louis, after the golf balls finally come down to earth.

"My only regret is that I lost my family," he says. "Of course, I should have lost my wife a long time before."

Audrey's Restaurant, Seekonk, Massachusetts

White-haired, limping on artificial hips, desperate for a cigarette in a nonsmoking universe, Derek Sanderson, once hockey's Hugh Hefner, yawns as he enters the breakfast room at 7:15 A.M. on June 29, 1997. He is embraced by John (Pie) McKenzie, another original WHA jumper. McKenzie, a Bruins hero from Boston's Stanley Cup years of the early seventies, is smaller and less ornery than memory held him: beaming and wrinkled, a BMW salesman from the suburbs south of the Hub. "Look at us," Sanderson says proudly. "Both sober!"

They are on the outskirts of Providence for a charity tournament in a dotage of endless golf. McKenzie played seven seasons for five WHA teams, or maybe six; they folded so fast, he can't remember. Sanderson, signed by the Philadelphia Blazers (formerly the Miami Screaming Eagles, though they never touched the ice in Florida), lasted seven games (he says) or eight (quoth the WHA record book) before a more divine Providence brought him back, begging, to the Bruins.

"We were in Sherbrooke, Quebec, for an exhibition," Sanderson recalls of his ephemeral career as a Blazer. "There were fifty-eight people in the stands, and forty-five of them were on free tickets from one of our players, Claude St. Sauveur, who came from there. Bernie Parent, our goalie, looks around and says, 'What are they? Politely late?' Then he disappears back into the dressing room.

"Pie's the coach," Sanderson continues. "I'm the captain. Pie calls me over and says, 'Go in the dressing room and get Bernie! The game's gonna start!' So I go in there, and Bernie is taking his equipment off. He says, 'I don't risk my life for no people.' He talked me out of it, too! I didn't play either."

Blazers management couldn't demote Sanderson for being AWOL — his contract gave him the right to veto any Philadelphia player's relegation to the minors (including his own). It also permitted him to skip all road games that he couldn't get to by train (he was a nervous flier), to be team captain forever, to be on the ice for all Blazers power plays, and to earn $2.65 million, which was exactly and deliberately $50,000 more than the soccer god Pelé was pulling down from Santos of Brazil.

That made Sanderson, a talented but unexceptional playmaker from Niagara Falls, Ontario, the highest-paid athlete in the world. Not long before, the Bruins, having paid him $10,000 for an entire season as the 1967–68 NHL Rookie of the Year, had offered him a $1,000 raise. That's how the old league operated, until the new one came along. "My first thought when the Blazers offered me the contract," Sanderson says, "was, How do I turn this down without them putting me in the Bridgewater state mental institution?"

He didn't want to jump to the WHA — nobody did, really. He just wanted to wake up the Boston management and to be a Bruin forever; the penthouse playboy of mod-squad New England; Joe Namath's partner in a chain of saloons; drunk and oversexed and a walking Walgreen's, addicted to a variety of prescription drugs. He would gladly have stayed in Boston had the Bruins offered him a piddling eighty grand. But they didn't. They concentrated on keeping Bobby Orr from leaping to the Fighting Saints. The Bruins, like the Blackhawks, haven't won the Stanley Cup since.

"I had always worked very hard," Sanderson says. "I was aggressive. I was chippy. I loved to play. I loved to win. Then, suddenly, all that money has an effect on you. You don't want to suffer. You don't want to put up with the sweat, the bleeding, the pain it takes to win. There's no reason to try harder. There's no incentive to get better. All I could think was, They're paying me $2 million, and I'm just a penalty killer. I can't score seven goals a game. I can't carry the parade."

The Blazers' season was to open on an October evening at the dilapidated Philadelphia Civic Center. The arena's elevator could take only four players at a time down from the clubhouse, leaving the others to clomp down three flights of stairs with their skates on. The refrigeration piping stopped well short of the boards, producing a ribbon of soggy black slush around the edge of the rink. Captain Sanderson — "dressed in the most hideous orange-and-black uniform in the world," he says — went to the referee, Bill Friday, and begged him to call off the game.

"We can't cancel," Friday said. "It's opening night."

Then the Zamboni broke through a crack in the playing surface, carving up great blocks of ice. Sanderson went back to Friday and said, "I presume this is sufficient?"

It was. But thousands had come to witness this historic game and had been given souvenir red Blazers pucks as they entered the Civic Center. Sanderson felt it was his rightful duty to apologize to the faithful. He headed for center ice, where a red carpet and a microphone had been set up for the ceremonial first face-off.

"Frank Rizzo, the mayor, was there," Sanderson recalls. "He warned me, 'Derek, I'll teach you something about politics in this town. Don't touch that microphone. Nobody can calm those people down. Just get down that corridor and get out of the building.' I didn't listen to him. I took the microphone and began, 'I'd like to apologize on behalf of the team . . .' when *ping* came the first puck, right at my head. Then, *ping, ping*. Two more! *Ping, ping, ping*.

"I said, 'Ladies and gentlemen, remember that there was only one entrance to the parking lot when you came in? Well, there's only one exit going out. Good luck!' It was a complete debacle. There were fights everywhere. We hid in our dressing room until one A.M."

Having survived that fiasco, the Blazers took to the road. Playing the Crusaders in Cleveland, Sanderson scored two goals against his old Boston net minder, Cheevers — another astonished new millionaire — before suffering the injury that would, much to his delight, end his WHA career. "I was in the penalty box, and the fans were throwing stuff at me," Sanderson says. "I said, 'I don't need this s—,' and I jumped out. I landed on a piece of garbage and slipped a disk in my back."

"There was a crucial face-off in our end of the rink," McKenzie says, continuing the tale, "and I wanted Derek to take it. I went to him on our bench and said, 'Get out there for that face-off!' But instead of going out, he starts barfing."

A week or so later, it was over. Sanderson went to the owners of the Blazers, pleaded to be allowed to return to the Bruins, and made a settlement that, he says, is still tied up in legal wrangling somewhere. The buyout might have been $1 million, or half that; he isn't sure. What Sanderson is sure of is that he eventually wound up broke and broken, once sleeping on a park bench, and existing on the charity of friends, insensate, nearly dead from the bottle and the pills. "I stopped drinking in 1980," he says, "but I didn't get sober until 1985." Now married and the father of two children, he is a senior vice president at an investment firm that caters primarily to athletes.

"It worked out well for both of us," McKenzie says. "I got him into the WHA. He got me into Alcoholics Anonymous."

In Beck's Taxi No. 364, Toronto

At 5:15 A.M., emerging from the early twilight in a garish green-and-orange cab, the former All-Star goalie hauls up in front of my apartment building and opens the car door. We ride off together. Allan Robert Smith — an original New England Whaler; an original, period — has spent the past fourteen years at the wheel of a Toronto hack and, in the off hours, at a keyboard, hacking out the

first novel that, like the WHA, will leave him neither rich nor understood.

Smith went end to end (except for a brief return to the NHL) in
the revolting league — from the first whispers in Detroit, when
rumors of a challenge to the NHL began to swirl, all the way to the
WHA's termination in the "merger" of 1979. He was, at the start, a
brash, long-haired net minder who had played a little with the
Pittsburgh Penguins, the Detroit Red Wings, and the Toronto Maple Leafs before leaping to the Whalers. He is, at the end (for he
sees this as his end), a portly, bald, mad, funny, jittery, divorced,
streetwise cabbie, working dawn to dusk to support his writing
habit, having blown his WHA signing bonus on a newsletter for
lacrosse enthusiasts.

He turns off his dispatch radio, cruises north on Spadina, east on
Bloor, south on Yonge, west on Front, around and around and
around. Fourteen years. "Nothing I ever did in the WHA put me in
the cab," he says. "Trying to be a writer put me in the cab."

He calls the league "the Waaah," sounding like a *Peanuts* charac-
ter bawling. He talks of "being a Waaah guy in a Waaah world." He
says, "Every Waaah player understands it. We're in this free fall. Ken
Dryden has merit — he won the Stanley Cup all those times in
Montreal. We are without merit. I'm not a writer — I'm just an old
Waaah player."

"Did you ever think you were as good as a Dryden or a Plante or a
Terry Sawchuk?" I ask him.

"I was always gonna be," he replies, "but I never was."

The Waaah, he says, was Valhalla for the superstars and the burial
ground of the ordinary pro. "It left a lost generation who'll never
know how good they really were," Smith says. "We had a guy named
Terry Caffery who was the best passer I ever saw. He came to me
once and said, 'Al, if it wasn't for the WHA, I'd be nothing.' And I
told him, 'No — if it wasn't for the WHA, you might be in the Hall
of Fame. You'd be in the NHL; you'd have to push yourself; you'd
have to try.'"

The novel that took Smith twenty years to write is called *The
Parade Has Passed*. A star forward in the Waaah — Lonnie "Lahdee
Dahdee" Daniels — hitchhikes north from Toronto to attend the
funeral of his former coach, Red Eastman, who has been murdered
by a pick-swinging man:

Sylvester Collins was out of breath and trembling from the amount of violence needed to cause this much devastation. He looked down at Red slumped on the ground below, but Sylvester wavered on the second floor because he was being blinded by a resplendent deflection of light that was propensitizing off the hallowed remains of Red's body. The light was blinding him and he tried to shield his eyes from it. He tried to see what was causing this blinding light and, sure enough, that's what it was. Red had put the Stanley Cup ring on to show him. . . .

Fifty copies of *The Parade Has Passed* have been printed; two, including mine, have been sold. The back cover defines the work as "picaresque" and proclaims, "Faulkner faces off with Howe." Smith wrote those blurbs himself.

There was a time when Smith considered himself a rebel, a power-play flower child, the Jerry Rubin of a hidebound sport controlled by half a dozen old, old men. But now, Rubensesque and defeated, he says, "It wasn't us, it was the owners; rich young men with money who wanted to buy things. The Baldwins, the Pocklingtons — the capitalists shook up the system." And again, disbelievingly: "It was the capitalists who made the revolution."

Lewis & Wood Law Offices, Trenton, N.J.

The capitalist who took the Waaah into the capital of the world sits under a portrait of Napoleon Bonaparte and ponders what might have been. Richard I. "Dick" Wood, owner of the New York Raiders in the first year of the WHA, wasn't the only wealthy young man to take a flier on the new league, but he might have been the only one who made a profit. The Raiders, a dreadful hockey team, went on to become the New York Golden Blades, the Jersey Knights, and the San Diego Mariners before being euthanized, but by that time Wood was long gone.

In 1972 the thirty-two-year-old Wood was commuting from Sea Girt, on the Jersey shore, to his office in Trenton when he read that another man had sagely let his option on the WHA rights to the New York metropolitan area expire. "It was a long trip every day," Wood recalls. "I had time to think it over and over. I was never a hockey player, just a fan — a Rangers fan. But the more I thought about it, the more I told myself, 'I could do that.'"

He could, and he couldn't. For $50,000, the young lawyer bought the franchise rights and signed a lease with the vultures who ran Madison Square Garden. He hired a baseball man, Marvin Milkes, to run the operation, and the two geniuses brought in a group of fringe NHL players without a Hull or even an Al Smith in the bunch. Wood says he thought about trying to lure forty-three-year-old Gordie Howe out of retirement — the old man, of course, would return to play with his sons Mark and Marty in 1973, for the WHA's Houston Aeros — but the Red Wings, who controlled Howe's rights, never returned his phone calls. Hull, whose presence in New York might have changed everything, was the property of Hatskin, and no one had the nerve to ask Hatskin to relinquish his prize for the good of the league. "I wasn't going to poach," Wood says. "Even though having Bobby in New York would have been more synergistic, everybody wanted to win for himself."

The Raiders did sign the hairy Cowboy Bill Flett and the horrific Dave "the Hammer" Schultz from the Philadelphia Flyers, but the two men immediately came to their senses and jumped back to the NHL before ever wearing a Raiders uniform, a blue-and-orange creation that featured a left-handed player in a twin-horned Viking helmet skating between skyscrapers.

Wood knew after only a handful of home games that the Raiders were doomed. The cost of the unionized Garden ushers and concessionaires was murdering him. The Raiders' coach, Camille Henry, was a former Rangers star embittered by the wealth and nonchalance of his athletes. The faceless players — Ron Ward, Norm Ferguson, Bobby Sheehan, some Minnesota collegians, even a black man named Alton White — were out of their depth against Hull and Cheevers and the tight, well-coached Whalers and Quebec Nordiques.

Wood went to the Garden and asked the unions to give him a break. They said, "We have to have a full staff every night in case the game is a sellout." (The Raiders were averaging 5,868 customers in an 18,000-seat building.) Wood sold the Raiders to an investment group for a good profit. He bought a restaurant and a Texas oil well and went back to lawyering.

While we are admiring the Napoleon, a man named Barry Rednor comes into Wood's office with a carton of junk. Rednor, an old friend of Wood's and a former member of the Raiders' board of directors, unloads Raiders pucks, Golden Blades pennants and posters, and a giant frosted brandy snifter autographed by several members of the long-dead team.

"They only made ten of these," Rednor announces, holding up the vessel. "I've got a basement full of this stuff — and a lot of autographed sticks."

"They must be worth a lot of money," I venture.

"Not around here," Rednor replies.

Room B3–542, Hôpital de Saint-François d'Assise, Quebec City

In maroon pajamas and hand-knit slippers, sallow, shrunken, defeated: Camille Henry. In the 1950s and early 1960s, Henry was a darting, darling Rangers forward. He scored nearly three hundred goals when goals were hard to come by. In '57–'58 he won the Lady Byng Trophy as the most gentlemanly barracuda in the NHL. His wife, in those golden years, was Dominique Michel, then (and still) the most popular comedienne in French Canada, the Carol Burnett of Quebec.

In '72, retired from playing right wing and hired by the Raiders as a drawing card in a bow to Rangers glory, Henry coached Wood's team into last place. I walked in on him in his semiprivate hospital room in la Belle Province last summer, and he barely looked up. He was sitting in a chair, having his blood drawn. "I would like to talk about your WHA memories," I say.

"I have only bad ones," he replied.

In the 1972–1973 New York Raiders Inaugural Edition Souvenir Book, an advertisement for a hair-replacement system called Henry "a young man of action." But that day, at sixty-four, after decades of diabetic crises, odd jobs as a watchman and janitor, two divorces, and estrangement from his nation's game, his melancholy hung in the air as heavily as disinfectant. He would be dead within three months.

"I was disgusted with the whole WHA," he said in a low voice. "The players I had made it even worse. Some of them were making four and five times what I was making as coach, and they didn't try, they didn't care. That's all they cared about, the money. I can't blame them. The owners offered them the big money — they

didn't ask for it. I had one player, he was drunk after every game.
He was an alcoholic."

He lowered his voice even further. "And I was an alcoholic, too."

Henry had been sober since 1985 — and in and out of diabetic
comas for almost as long. He had been in the hospital this time, he
said, for eight months, although the exact dates escaped him, as did
so many of his memories. He said, "I'm not crazy yet, but I'm almost
there." He tried to smile.

I told him that I had been in St. Louis with Bobby Hull and in
Providence with Derek Sanderson and John McKenzie, and that
these men were earning good money for doing nothing more than
playing golf, shaking hands, and signing their names. This as-
tounded him. For the previous few years he had received a few
autograph requests every day in the mail — "I've moved five times,
I don't know how they find me," he said — but he had always
signed for free, "not to disappoint the kids."

We proceeded to the past. He told me how, when it became clear
early in the second WHA season that the Golden Blades, né Raiders, were doomed, he and the Blades' trainer hurriedly piled all the
team's equipment into a truck and drove it through the Lincoln
Tunnel to New Jersey, where New York authorities couldn't im-
pound it. That was his swan song in hockey.

"Nobody wants to make contact with me," Henry said. "It's not
my choice, it's their choice. I don't get no offers. I believe it is
because I went to the WHA. I wanted to believe that. I needed to
believe that, so I'd have no more excuses why people didn't ask
for me."

"Bobby Hull went to the WHA, and they still call him," I said.

"Bobby Hull was a good hockey player," Henry responded.

Devous Banquet Center, Maryland Heights, Missouri

A woman pays her five dollars and comes up to Bobby Hull with a
color photograph of the Golden Jet in a Blackhawks sweater and
asks not only for his autograph but also for his thumbprint on the
picture. "The last time I did that, it had ink on it," her hero says.
"You know, those guys who make you go like this" — he holds his
tree-trunk wrists together and laughs.

"You still look tough," another woman tells him.

"Tougher than a night in jail," Hull says, chortling.

"I wouldn't know about a night in jail," the fan shrugs.

"Believe me," Hull says.

Twenty-five years after he overturned his sport, dragged it to corners of an uninterested continent, made many ordinary men rich and a few rich men much poorer, only Hull remains unchanged. And this is a man who, as he says, "was only smart enough to talk back to my wife."

"There are still things I want to do," Hull says. "I want to go to Italy and help my nephew crush grapes and drink some Chianti. I want to go to places where they don't know where Chicago is. I want to see Brett in the Hockey Hall of Fame, and I want to see one of my grandsons follow suit."

Now we are in a quiet bar called Massa's, reflecting. "I came from an old-fashioned home," says Hull, one of eleven children and the father of eight, five by Joanne, who was his second wife. They were married in 1960 and divorced in 1980. Hull says he has regrets, not about Joanne but about what they destroyed. Suddenly, at fifty-eight, it is family that matters to him.

"I never dreamed that a man could live with a woman for so many years and raise a family with her and then break up," he says. "The two older boys understood, but Brett was right on the cusp when we split. . . ."

"What was the legacy of the WHA?" I ask, trying to brighten the mood.

"I think we gave entertainment to a lot of people," Hull says. "And the year after the leagues merged, ten of the top twenty scorers in the NHL had come from the WHA."

On the silver anniversary, there have been no parades. Dennis Murphy, the Orange County entrepreneur who helped to create the WHA — and who more recently turned a $1 million profit on Roller Hockey International — hopes to stage a gala reunion in September to honor Hull, Howe, Gretzky, and Messier. "We've got the champagne on ice," Murphy says on the phone.

A few men cherish the memory of what happened to their lives when the hockey world split in two. Joe Daley, the maskless Winnipeg goalie from the league's start to its finish, tells of a "true brotherhood" of teammates who cared for each other and their city, and still do. Sitting in a doughnut shop in Kenora, Ontario, the town where those infant Jets once trained, we scroll down the roster of the '72 team and see Danny Johnson, dead of Lou Gehrig's disease; Bob Woytowich, dead of a heart attack at the wheel of his car; Norm Beaudin, struggling in Florida to meet the medical bills for his bedridden daughter, Carrie, who was once married to Hull's son Blake.

It was long ago, in a fairy tale. The WHA's pioneers, opportunists, puck chasers, and playboys opened the portal to everything that has come to characterize hockey: the international cavalcade of stars, the carpetbagging franchises, the power of the players' union, the ascent of U.S. hockey.

One man's signature, a quarter of a century ago, made it happen. "Only one guy ever thanked me," the pathfinder says, shaking his phony hair. "In 1972 I was out in Vancouver to do a department store commercial with Arte Johnson from *Laugh In*. The Bruins were in town. Wayne Cashman came up, all misty-eyed, and he started going, 'Thank you! Thank you! Thank you! I got my salary tripled thanks to you.'

"He was the only one who ever thanked me," says the Golden Jet. "The only one."

DAN WETZEL

Not Your Ordinary Bear

FROM BASKETBALL TIMES

THE OLD COWBOY who coaches here, basketball's John Wayne, is getting run from his own gym because the refs blew a call and he blew up at them. Isn't that a fitting ending to a University of Texas at El Paso basketball game — the Miners lose, Don Haskins is tossed from the Don Haskins Center, and no one has an answer as to how to prevent either situation from occurring again.

Is this what legends are worth nowadays?

Tonight Bear Haskins won't get career win number 704, a good night's sleep, or a celebratory whiskey, since this loss and that referee will gnaw at his triple-bypassed heart with frightening intensity. Haskins may be getting up in years, sixty-six, but he hasn't lost an iota of the competitiveness that has driven him to a Hall of Fame career in his thirty-seven years at UTEP.

Doesn't Don Haskins deserve better than this? Isn't this the Don Haskins who accelerated the integration of college basketball when he took unheralded Texas Western College (now UTEP) to the 1966 national championship game, started five black players, and beat Adolph Rupp and his all-white Kentucky Runts in one of the significant games in college basketball history?

"The next year black kids throughout the South got calls from schools saying they were now open," says Nolan Richardson, who played for Haskins from 1961 to 1963 and now coaches the University of Arkansas. "He literally got thousands and thousands of black kids scholarships to college."

"Even Adolph Rupp himself finally recruited one," notes Haskins.

What Haskins got for his effort was one national championship watch, about a dozen death threats, and forty-thousand pieces of hate mail sent to him back in El Paso.

"Most of them started the same way," Haskins recalls. "'Dear Niggerlover.'"

Isn't this the Don Haskins whom his peers consider to be the best coach still pacing a sideline? Not the one who coached the most All-Americans or made the most money or has television announcers offer paeans to him night after night, but the one who is the best *coach*? The one who outcoaches everyone? The one whose defensive system is still analyzed and studied by his peers? The one who has had only four losing seasons in nearly four decades at a remote school with no recruiting base, no media market, and virtually no blue-chip talent? The one who gets the most out of every player who slips on a uniform, regardless of ability? The one who turns projects into players and players into pros?

"He'll beat you with his'n, then he'll beat you with your'n," Haskins's old trainer, Ross Moore, used to say, claiming it didn't matter which team in a game Haskins coached, he'd win with either of them.

"The people that understand what coaching is, the people who really know what great coaching is, are all going to talk about Don Haskins," says Indiana coach Bob Knight. "Haskins, certainly in my era, is one of the truly outstanding coaches."

"You listen to the announcers and they don't talk about Don Haskins, but you listen to the great coaches and they'll talk about Don Haskins," says Gene Iba, a former Haskins assistant and now coach of Pittsburg (Kansas) State. "The problem is, the announcers haven't been there. But you won't find a coach who coached against him or has been around him that won't list him as either the best coach or among the best coaches ever."

Isn't this the Don Haskins who still teaches defense and discipline the way he learned it from Mr. Henry Iba himself back at Oklahoma A&M in the 1940s? The one who hasn't let up on his teams since he ran high school boys and girls to exhaustion in tiny Texas towns, where he drove a school bus to pay the bills? The one who commands the ultimate respect from his players? The guy who runs the hardest practice and demands the most effort? The guy who accepts no excuse now, because he never has?

"People talk about Bob Knight, but he makes Bob Knight look like Cinderella," says Richardson.

"He's one of the finest defensive minds to ever coach," says Utah coach Rick Majerus. "When I got the job at Utah, I pulled out films of his teams and patterned a lot of my defense after him."

"He's probably the most direct descendant of Henry Iba there is," says Knight. "His system of defensive play is as good as I've seen coached. He also has a great way of getting the most out of kids."

"I remember back in the 1960s when I was an assistant at Lamar, Coca-Cola sent out these coaching tapes," says Texas Christian coach Billy Tubbs. "One of them was Don Haskins's defense and the drills he used. We still use them. We play a totally different style of defense" — full-court pressure — "than Haskins, but that system is a great system. It still translates."

But tonight this is the Don Haskins who has been tossed from the game, just like the time, as a young coach in Hedley, Texas, he set an unofficial record for the most technicals in a game, sixteen, one for each step he took out onto the court. Want to know how intense he was then? That was in a girls' game.

And this is the Don Haskins who sits in the coaches' room, postgame, in a plaid flannel shirt staring silently at a stat sheet. He actually looks like he's staring through the paper. He is so distraught he can't stand to read anything. He takes this defeat as bitterly as most coaches take a season-ending NCAA tournament loss. Just minutes earlier he told the media just what he thought of Western Athletic Conference officiating, comments that would earn him a one-game suspension from the league office.

Is this what legends are worth nowadays?

One thing about Haskins, he's easy to read. He wears his emotions on his sleeve for all to see, and tonight the emotions are deep hurt and bitter disappointment. Too bitter, you think. No one takes losses this hard. No one can be this competitive.

This loss, any loss this season, shouldn't be too big a surprise, because his team isn't very good and its best players are young ones. To put it simply, the Miners can't shoot. Oh, they play defense like hell, just like Haskins's teams always do, but in terms of perimeter shooting, they don't have much. The fact that they are 12–9 is a testament to Haskins's getting every last drop from them. You'd think he'd be willing to accept limitations and move on. Instead, he sits in a chair, elbows on knees, hunched over staring at the paper, brooding about his team's fate.

He thinks of how he might have let them down. He thinks of the refs' terrible performance and the technicals that followed when he informed them of his opinion. He thinks about how the NCAA conducted some bogus investigation a half-dozen years ago, found some minor violations, and still hammered his program with major scholarship limitations. UTEP did a fraction of what Kentucky did in the 1980s. It received ten times the penalty. Some of those scholarships would be seniors right now. Some of them might be able to shoot. And then Haskins wouldn't be staring through a piece of paper, but instead looking forward to slipping into some dive bar for a quiet postgame Dewar's.

"I sure as hell didn't goddam cheat," Haskins will tell you.

And worse, when the NCAA said his assistants gave players rides around town — the most damning charge and now NCAA legal — he had to call up Mr. Iba, his former coach, his best friend, his conscience, the one person in the world he cared the opinion of, and explain.

"He was getting up there in years and it is difficult to explain what happened. I don't know if Mr. Iba understood. I tried to explain it to him. But it's hard to explain that someone is getting you and you didn't do a damn thing. When I took this job he told me, 'You do it straight, son,' and I did."

Think that can make you bitter? Don't legends deserve better than that?

Out here in the Southwest they produce remarkable sunsets, big mahogany, red, and orange numbers that light up the desert sky bigger than Texas itself. And here in El Paso at dusk you can drive along Rim Road, which curves along a mesa overlooking the city, pull into a park, and take in a show of nature second to none.

Not that Haskins would know. He has no time for sunsets. He never drives along Rim Road. In the sunset of his career he is focused on the present. Winning every game like it was his last. Winning every game like he was still that young coach, five years removed from the Texas prep ranks, facing Adolph Rupp. He has no shooters. He has average talent. He expects to win, same as ever. John Wayne doesn't lose, does he?

"Goddam, I hope we play tonight," he says pregame tonight, any night, every night.

He's getting dressed. Buttoning up a white shirt over a chest with a heart-surgery scar on it. Grabbing an old blue tie he wears as he enters the arena, only to remove it and stuff it into his coat pocket before the opening tip. The tie is a clip-on. The old cowboy who coaches here, basketball's John Wayne, doesn't have time to bother with tying ties.

And you think he's got time for sunsets? Or holding his tongue about bad officiating? Or NCAA investigators?

"Goddam, I hope we play."

Don Haskins learned to shoot a basketball in the back yard of his family's home in Enid, Oklahoma. His dad, Paul Haskins, custom made a hoop that was smaller than regulation, sort of like those hoops they have at the carnival games so no one can win.

Haskins learned how to win, how to put a ball through a hoop that was just a fraction bigger than the ball. "By the time I got to the high school, the hoop was like a big tub," Haskins says.

As a prep player he was a star. He was an athletic 6'1" guard who could dunk but also drain shots from all over the court. As a senior he was named All-State, received loads of adulation, and held a dirty little secret: while everyone said he was the best player in all of Oklahoma, he knew he wasn't even the best player in Enid. Herman Carr was. But Herman Carr was black.

"It used to bother me as a kid," Haskins said. "I was supposed to be the best player in the state, but I wasn't the best player in town."

Carr and Haskins were close friends and used to play together in the summer at a park in the center of Enid. Carr, being black, lived on the other side of the tracks from Haskins and attended Carver High, while Haskins went to Enid High. That's just the way things were back then. But it stuck with Haskins that maybe that's not how it should be.

Not that he had much time to think of social issues. He was too busy playing basketball and baseball. Paul Haskins worked at a local supply company driving a truck and the Haskinses were "neither poor nor rich."

By the time he was a senior in high school, it became apparent that Don Haskins would become a college man. More than one

hundred schools offered him a scholarship, including North Carolina and other faraway operations. Kentucky, and Adolph Rupp,
were not one of the suitors.

"But I could have played for him, because I could shoot and you
had to do that to play for him."

Even though Haskins, as a shooter, would have benefited from a
more open offensive system than the defense-first one that Iba ran
at Oklahoma A&M, the pull of the Cowboys and the legendary Iba
was too much. Enid is less than an hour from campus, and Haskins
grew up listening to A&M games on the radio. By the time Iba came
to town for a home visit, Haskins was as good as signed.

What Haskins found in Stillwater was a coach who was even
tougher than his reputation. Iba was the original disciplinarian,
ruling with an iron fist and accepting no quit nor comment from
his charges.

"It was four years of hell," Haskins said. "But I wouldn't trade it
for the world. Knowing what I know now, I'd do it again. I remember I talked to this guy who I played with who joined the Marines
right out of college. I said, 'Bob, what was the Marines like?' And he
said, 'It was a piece of cake after Mr. Iba.'

"I said two words in four years," Haskins said, laughing. "One
day I said, 'I thought . . .' and the tirade began: 'You never had a
thought in your life,' and all this stuff."

Haskins wanted out of Stillwater, desperately — "I quit every
night for four years." He despised the system, the drills, the demanding workouts, and the heavy-handed ways of Iba. After games
in which he performed particularly well, Haskins would write the
opposing coaches and ask if they would accept him as a transfer.
The coaches, fearful of Iba in their own right, never responded.

To understand Iba, you have to understand the culture. Neither
the term "old-time coach" nor "player's coach" existed. All coaches
were the former; there was no such beast as the latter. There was
also no such thing as tough love, either. Just tough coaches. Players
had few options, and the NCAA had fewer rules. At the time, there
was no October 15 starting date for practice — meaning Iba could
drill his troops year-round for as many hours a day as he wanted.

"We'd go for nine hours a day in the summer and during Christmas holiday," Haskins recalls. "It would get so hot in the summer
I'd go from 180 pounds to 160. We'd practice nine A.M. to noon,

two P.M. to five, and finally seven until ten. Going to play a game was a goddam joke.

"One day I'll never forget. I was there during the Christmas holiday and I was a sophomore. And he started in on me at nine in the morning. Every so often he'd get on a guy and ride him all day, and God, you'd feel sorry for him. This was my day to be in the barrel. And I never, ever left the floor that day. Everyone else would rotate in, but I had to stay out there.

"The seven-to-ten session was a three-hour scrimmage. The clock don't stop. You don't stop and rest or any of that. See, we used to have huge blisters back then, and before the seven o'clock scrimmage the balls of my feet were moving. That night I scrimmaged the first hour and thought, It's over — he'll take me out. Nope. I got the second hour, and the third.

"After practice, I was walking off the floor on the sides of my feet and the president of the school, Dr. Bennett, was there. He was Mr. Iba's friend. And he said, 'Son, is your feet sore?' And I said, 'No, sir.' And he said, 'Good, they shouldn't be, because you haven't done a goddam thing all day!'

"I got into the training room, took off my sock, and the ball of my foot came off. The fat part, just came off. I taped it on the next day and went back to practice."

In 1952, after four years of hating Iba, Haskins left Stillwater and saw his old coach in a new light.

"Mr. Iba, he was my best friend after I got out of college. He would do anything for you."

It was a friendship that would grow by the day. Iba helped Haskins get jobs, helped him discuss strategy, and was with him when he won the national championship. In return, Haskins looked to his mentor for advice at every turn; hired his son, Moe, and nephew Gene as assistants; and served as an assistant to Iba when he coached the 1972 U.S. Olympic team in Munich. That team would go on to lose the gold medal to the Soviet Union in one of the most controversial games ever played. In protest, Haskins, like the rest of the team, has never accepted his silver medal.

"It was the worst night of my life," said Haskins. "It was horrible to see that happen to him. It was a travesty."

Immediately after college, Haskins went to play basketball for a team in the old National Industrial League, in Artesia, New Mexico.

He was married then to his college sweetheart, Mary, and they had a young son, Mark. The money was good and, post-Iba, life was easy until Haskins realized he couldn't play forever. Mary suggested he become a coach. He hadn't given it much thought, but he decided to listen to his wife.

"I think I started [coaching] because I didn't know anything else."

In 1955, Iba and his friends helped him land a job coaching in tiny Benjamin, Texas, a 230-person town 130 miles southeast of Lubbock.

He had a problem, though — he found out he had to coach six-man football, a wide-open game still played in some rural Texas schools without enough students to field regular teams. "I had never even seen a game."

Benjamin went on to win the district championship.

"We played in the bi-district game and we lost the son of a bitch, and I thought I was going to die," Haskins said. "People don't understand, whatever level you are competing at, you can only hurt so much. I mean, that was as deep a hurt as I have ever had. After losing that bi-district game I wanted to commit hara-kiri."

But basketball season was next, and Haskins coached both the boys and the girls with Iba-like seriousness.

"I coached the boys and the girls exactly the same. And I'll tell you this, I've had boys quit on me, but I never had a girl quit. Not one."

The new coach in town put blisters on the kids' feet and discipline in their minds, but his driven nature worried some parents.

"One day I almost got fired. We were on the road and my boys got beat by Noodle, Texas, by one point, 31–30. And Paint Creek beat the girls in a one-pointer. I was upset. And I'm driving the bus home, and we got the girls on one side and the boys on the other. And there's no talking. I didn't let them talk on my time.

"So we got home and we practiced until three in the morning. I got the girls on one end and the boys on the other and I am giving them hell. God, I was hard on those kids. The next day they had a school board meeting, and they were going to reprimand me and give me hell, but all the players came. Every damn one of them came to support me, and the school board decided not to do anything."

Haskins went on to coach in Hedley and Dumas, both small towns in north Texas, where he continued to experience success running his program the way Iba ran his. All the while he kept in contact with George McCarty, a friend of Iba's who worked as dean of men and athletic director at Texas Western. It was McCarty who was determined to bring Haskins, a man he called Hoss, to El Paso.

Basketball at Texas Western wasn't much in the late 1950s and when the head coaching position opened in 1961, no one at the school thought twice about hiring an unknown prep coach from an unknown town. In fact, the number-one requirement of the job was to live in the athletic dorm and keep the rowdy football players under control.

"I met with the school president, Dr. Joseph Ray, and he never asked me if I could coach. He just said, 'That athletic dorm is driving me crazy. You are a big man — can you run that dorm?' And I said, 'Yes, sir.' And that was it. George McCarty vouched for me. If it wasn't for him, I might still be in high school."

So Haskins packed up Mary and their now four boys and drove to El Paso. Haskins was thirty years old, and there waiting for him on the front steps of the athletic dorm, there to help him move in, was a junior named Nolan Richardson. He was one of the first black players Haskins ever coached.

By the time Texas Western's chartered flight to the 1966 Final Four lifted off from El Paso International Airport, Haskins's team had more than a couple of black players — it had seven, including five talented enough to start. Those two facts — that the players were talented and they were black — made the Miners two things: a 26–1 national championship contender and very controversial.

Texas Western wasn't the first team in the country to play and start blacks — at this point, all-white teams were generally found only in the Southeastern, Atlantic Coast, and Southwestern conferences. Most schools in the West and Midwest had already integrated, and Cincinnati won back-to-back national championships, in 1961 and 1962, with as many as four black starters. But five? Five was pushing it in the face of not only Dixie but much of white America. Teams often started a token white even though a second stringer who was black might be better.

"That was the thing," says Richardson, who graduated from

Texas Western in 1963, and as a sophomore, the year before Haskins arrived, was barred from three games because Centenary College, in Shreveport, Louisiana, prohibited blacks from playing on its home court. "Five starters were too much for people to handle."

"A lot of coaches would act like it never existed," says Andy Stoglin, who played at Texas Western from 1963 to 1965 and is now the head coach at Jackson State. "A white player would start in front of a black player who was better and the coach would never say anything about it. But everybody knew, everybody knew."

While Haskins says he never thought twice about whom he played — "Out on the floor, they are just players" — both Stoglin and Richardson recall similar experiences in 1963 that suggest the decision and its backlash weighed heavily on Haskins.

"He called me into his office because I was not starting," said Stoglin. "He said to me, 'I know you should start, but I can't start five black players.'

"He pulled out his drawer and dumped these letters out and said, 'Read these and tell me what you think.' He left me in the office for thirty minutes and I read some of them. The mail said, 'You're playing too many niggers.' All sorts of awful things like that. They said they were going to fire Coach Haskins.

"He told me not to tell the other players about it. I could tell the pain it was causing him."

Richardson had a similar experience that same year.

"I was a senior and he called me into his office one day," said Richardson. "His five best players were black, but he was not going to start all five of us. He called me in and said, 'Nolan, I need you to do me a favor. I'm probably not going to start you tonight. I don't want to get into a situation where I am starting all black kids. I don't want to deal with what everyone is going to say. I'm asking you to sit because you're a senior and you're from El Paso and I think you can handle it. But you are going to play, don't worry.'

"And I said, 'Okay, coach.'"

Neither player was bitter at their coach. In fact both consider it the most upstanding thing Haskins has ever done. While it takes a strong man to ignore his fears and start five blacks, they reason, it takes an even stronger man to admit he is too weak to do it and calmly explain why.

"That's the kind of man he was," said Richardson. "Straight up.

He wasn't making any excuses why he wasn't going to start me. He wasn't going to lie. He wasn't going to ignore it. I wasn't mad at him because I was young, but I wasn't no dummy. I knew exactly where he was coming from."

Said Stoglin, "The way it was hurting him showed me the type of person Coach Haskins was. After that we bonded, because he trusted me enough to talk to me about it."

The day he spoke with Richardson was the day Haskins may have decided to ignore his fear.

"Right before the game that night, he yells, 'Richardson!' And I run over and say, 'Yes, Coach?' And he says, 'Piss on them, you're starting. Piss on what they'll say.' And that was it.

"He'll probably want to deny that story because he doesn't want to get into it. He doesn't want the controversy. He's too humble," Richardson said.

Indeed, Haskins seems baffled by those recollections, almost surprised. Haskins is as self-effacing and kind off the court as he is intense on it. He has always shrugged off his decision to start five black players, saying simply, "I just played the best players."

"I don't even remember," Haskins said when told of his players' recollections. "Nolan and Andy? I think they are dreaming. No, I never worried about it. I don't remember getting the hate mail back then. I don't know, I don't remember."

Regardless, by 1966 Haskins was starting five blacks and using two as key subs. And his unknown commuter school from dusty west Texas was crashing a Final Four party that also included all-white Duke, Utah, and, of course, Kentucky.

As he took stock of his team during the flight to Maryland, he talked briefly with each of his players.

There was the formidable 6'7", 240-pound center, David Lattin from Houston, who was not only bull-strong but, like modern players today, capable of putting it on the floor and dunking with reckless authority. One time in a scrimmage the year before, Lattin took the ball at the top of the key, drove the lane, and went up for a vicious dunk. In the process he kicked Stoglin in the head, knocking him out cold, tore the rim off the backboard, and slashed his own arm wide open.

"Damndest thing I ever seen," says Haskins, who had to load up his truck and drive everyone to the hospital.

At one forward spot Haskins played the thin, 6'8" Nevil Shed, a free-spirited but hard-nosed defender from New York City they called the Shadow. At the other he relied on 6'5" David Flourney, whose high school career in Gary, Indiana, consisted of spending his sophomore and junior years in the school band before averaging three points a game as a senior. "I knew a guy up in Gary named Jack Hobbs who told me he'd be a hell of a rebounder." He was averaging more than ten a game during the championship seasons.

In the backcourt Haskins relied on 6'1" Orson Artis, a defensive specialist and shooter who came with Flourney from Gary. "He was our secret weapon," said Shed.

And at the point was one of Haskins's all-time favorites, the 5'10" left-hander Bobby Joe Hill of Detroit. Haskins says Hill was every bit as good as future Miners guards such as Nate "Tiny" Archibald and Tim Hardaway, but he wound up getting bored with basketball and after the season quit the game and got married. "There's no telling how much money he could have made," says Haskins. Hill is now a businessman in El Paso.

Off the bench Haskins relied on 6'5" Willie Cager, a legendary swing man from the New York City playgrounds nicknamed Scoops, and 5'6" point guard Willie Worsley, a very steady ball handler also from New York.

The fact that three top players from New York City were willing to head all the way to El Paso is telling of recruiting at the time. Texas Western was hardly a cool place for a Brooklyn or Harlem kid to play.

"We'd go back to New York with our TWC stuff," says Shed, "and the boys in Harlem would be like, 'Here comes Shed out of Teeny Weeny College.' Or 'Here's Scoops from Texas Women's College.'"

Trendy or not, Haskins had a team on his hands that was rough, tough, and confident. Smart, too.

"I had a bunch of smart guys," Haskins said. "They're not supposed to be, because they're black — you've heard all that stuff. Don't buy that. That goddam Bobby Joe Hill is smart."

Arriving in College Park, they were the team no one knew about. During an open practice the day before the semifinal game against Utah, Haskins shocked fellow coaches and the media by running a typically brutal and vocal practice, putting his troops through the ringer — even throwing Hill out of practice for lack of concentration.

After the session, a coach came up to Haskins and asked, "How can you talk to these black players that way?"

"Same way I do white guys," the Bear responded.

In the semifinals, Texas Western beat Utah 85–78 and Kentucky edged Duke 83–79, setting up a matchup between the all-white Wildcats — a traditional power team led by Larry Conley, Pat Riley, and Louis Dampier — and the majority-black Texas Western Miners, true interlopers at the Final Four. Not that many people were aware of the social implications at the time.

"The press built the game up as the whiteys versus the blacks, but we went into the game thinking about playing the University of Kentucky and Mr. Adolph Rupp," said Shed, now the director of intramurals at the University of Texas at San Antonio. "We knew if we went in with the racial attitude of 'Hey, let's beat these whiteys,' then we may not have been successful. If we played the way we had to get there, we could win it."

Kentucky entered the game ranked number one, with a 27–1 record. The Wildcats boasted no player over 6'5" — leading to their nickname, Rupp's Runts — but they could run and shoot and score. With both Riley (now the head coach of the Miami Heat) and Dampier averaging more than twenty points a game, UK broke the century mark six times that season.

Although Haskins recalls having deep headaches throughout the weekend, he says he was never nervous going into the game.

"It's real funny about how a lot of things bother you, but when I came here as a high school coach, if there was one thing that I never sweated, it was the coaching," Haskins said. "No sweat. Now I sweat going to a Kiwanis Club and speaking, but not coaching."

As for being intimidated by the legendary Rupp, Haskins said, "I played for the best coach that ever lived. I wasn't intimidated by anyone."

In the finals, he would prove why his peers consider him on par with Iba. First Haskins took Shed out of the starting lineup and inserted Worsley, who had never started before but gave him a third capable ball handler, along with Hill and Artis. Haskins knew he needed to control the tempo of the game. Ironically, although Texas Western was black and Kentucky was white, it was Rupp's team that was more explosive offensively.

"The reason for starting Worsley was we could walk it up," Haskins explained. "When the ball went on the board, we rebounded with two and put three back to defend and made them walk it up the floor. They broke us a few times, but we controlled the tempo. Once we got the tempo where we wanted it, then I slipped another big guy back in there."

At the beginning of the game Haskins also instructed Lattin, his physical center, to take it to the hole at his first chance and dunk one like only he could.

"I told Lattin, 'I want you to dunk one on them like they ain't never seen. Like they ain't seen on TV, like they ain't seen anywhere. I don't care if you get called for a foul.' We needed to scare them a little. And you know what the guy [covering Lattin] did? He ran out of the way. He got the hell out of there."

The last great hurdle was dealing with the Kentucky defense. There was no scouting back then and no videotapes to watch. Texas Western went into the finals virtually blind, Haskins having seen Kentucky play only once, in the semis against Duke the day before. Against the Blue Devils, UK played man-to-man. Against the Miners, they came out in the traditional Kentucky 1-3-1 zone, a defense Texas Western hadn't seen all season.

"So we took a time-out and I told them, 'Let's practice against the damn thing.' There was no shot clock, so we needed to practice against it and figure out how they matched up with it. And this is the good thing about having a great guard like Bobby Joe Hill. A hell of a head on him. A real leader. He could control everything."

So when the Miners retook the floor, they passed the ball around the court, allowing the UK zone to expose its tendencies. The Miners tried different ways of getting the ball in to Lattin in the post, saw how the zone moved on cross-court passes, how it recovered on the perimeter. They never took a shot. Haskins stood, hands on his hips, in front of his bench and watched the passing display intently for a couple of minutes.

"Then I called time-out," he said. "I took out a piece of paper and said, 'It's a one-three-one trap. This is what they are doing. This is how we beat it.' It was the basic Kentucky defense, but I didn't know anything about it."

That was the end of the Kentucky defense and, effectively, the game. Texas Western won, 72–65. Hill had a game-high 20, Lattin added 16, and Artis 15. Dampier and Riley led UK with 19 apiece.

"When we won it was fantastic," said Shed. "I realized that my team and I were NCAA National Champions."

Not that the victors got all the spoils.

"Our big thing was during those days the national championship team got to appear on *The Ed Sullivan Show*," Shed said. "So afterwards Cager and I, we're like, 'Hot damn, free trip to New York.' But do you think we got to go on *The Ed Sullivan Show?* Heck, no. And we didn't get a phone call from the President, either."

It would be the last time Haskins made it to the Final Four, a fact he isn't pleased about. Following the championship, his program had momentum — a difficult thing to gain if you are in El Paso. Around the country black kids had watched the flickering images of the game on television, seen Texas Western beat the hated Adolph Rupp, and quickly developed a place in their hearts for the team.

And around the South, everything changed for black players.

"What he did, without him knowing, back in 1966, is amazing," said Richardson. "For him to carry Texas Western, with five black starters, to the national championship against a person who, in my mind, is literally a bad person in terms of discrimination on race, is amazing.

"That's why I say I don't know why the good Lord gives gifts to certain people, but He does. And He gave Don Haskins a gift. Why would Don Haskins direct a school in a little old community like El Paso to the national title with everyone watching on television? The good Lord works in mysterious ways."

Stoglin said, "I talk in black coaching circles that Don Haskins has as much to do with integrating college basketball as anyone, because he had the guts to start five black players when no one else did."

Unfortunately for Haskins, this didn't pay off on the recruiting trail. The opening to black players by so many schools, while a positive for the kids, also increased the recruiting competition, a negative for Haskins. Where the coach could once walk into New York City and recruit three players with no other scholarship offers, he now bumped into college coaches everywhere he went.

"Back in '66, the Southwest Conference was all-white," said Haskins. "A few years later I pick up a newspaper and they've got the pictures of the All–Southwest Conference first team in it. They're all black."

The competition for blacks exposed UTEP's (the school changed its name in 1967) constant problem — location, location, location. "This is a remote town," said Haskins. "It's always been difficult to recruit to."

El Paso, which now boasts of some 700,000 residents, sits along the Rio Grande in distant west Texas near the Mexican border. It has more in common with Juarez, Mexico, the million-person city across the river, than any town north of the border. The nearest major city is Phoenix, some seven hours away. San Diego is actually closer than Houston. And it almost never produces players.

"I was there nine years," said Tim Floyd, Haskins's assistant from 1977 to 1986 and now head coach of Iowa State, "and there wasn't a prospect in town the entire time."

Compounding UTEP's disadvantages were a number of media reports casting Haskins in a negative light. *Sports Illustrated* came to town following the championship season and labeled Haskins as a coach who exploited black athletes and El Paso as an unfriendly community for minorities.

Then James Michener released his book *Sports in America* and declared Texas Western's championship "one of the most wretched episodes in the history of American sport." He promoted the notion that the Miners were criminals and nonstudents. Haskins filed a lawsuit against Michener but eventually dropped it, something he deeply regrets to this day.

Meanwhile, Rupp lambasted the Miners in newspaper interviews, calling them a "bunch of crooks" and claiming Haskins played a number of ineligible players. Both were unfounded accusations. He even told the *Louisville Courier-Journal* that Haskins had recruited Lattin out of Tennessee State Prison, when in fact Lattin had spent his freshman year at Tennessee State *University*.

The negative publicity was crippling. Haskins began receiving hate mail from not only whites but blacks.

"He said to me, 'Nolan, can you believe that?'" Richardson said. "I told him, 'Coach, we've got them on both sides. It's unfortunate the ones who think they are real smart don't know what you have done and what you are all about.' I look back now on those letters and it shows there are a lot of ignorant people in this world."

But Haskins quickly became a pariah and recruiting grew difficult.

"That killed us," Haskins said. "Lou Henson was up the road at

New Mexico State and he carried that *Sports Illustrated* around with
him everywhere he went."

And there were other negatives. The year after the championship, the Miners were set to play at Southern Methodist when the
team received a series of death threats.

"Nevil Shed calls me and says, 'Coach, some cat just called me
and said if I take the floor he's going to shoot my black ass.' Well,
pretty soon my phone rings and here's this redneck and he said,
'You mother so-and-so, if you play all those niggers you're going to
get your ass shot.'

"I never reported it to the papers but I called the police. There
were so many FBI people there that we could hardly get out of the
locker room. Then we are in the pregame huddle and Shed, he was
crazy, he's running around the huddle. And I said, 'Shed, what the
hell are you doing?' And he said, 'If someone is going to take a shot
at me, I'm going to be a moving target!'

"It was a tough time. I've said it before — sometimes I wish we
had never won the national championship."

While UTEP was never again a serious threat to win another national championship, Haskins kept on coaching like a title was
possible. Year after year he would run his players into the ground,
pound home discipline and defense, and teach them what basketball was about. And UTEP was nearly always a winner, if not a
champion.

Twenty times, a Miners team coached by Haskins won at least
nineteen games. They made fourteen NCAA tournament appearances, and there were seven more trips to the NIT. UTEP has won
seven WAC regular-season titles under Haskins and captured four
WAC tournament titles. Haskins won his 700th career game —
joining Henry Iba (767 wins) as one of only nine Division I coaches
ever to accomplish that feat — on January 3, with a 66–64 victory
over Southern Methodist.

He has coached some great players, too. He recruited Tiny
Archibald out of New York City in 1967, when the point guard
weighed only 125 pounds. "I said to myself, how can I recruit a
goddam 125-pound player?"

Also during the 1960s there was Jim "Bad News" Barnes, a highly
sought player from Cameron A&M, a junior college in Lawton,

Oklahoma. Haskins spent his entire $5,000 recruiting budget traveling to and from Lawton, and on his final trip he figured he'd better return with a signature, because he couldn't afford to come back. So he challenged Barnes to a free-throw shooting contest. If Barnes won, Haskins promised to go back to El Paso and leave him alone. If Haskins won, however, Barnes would sign on the spot. Barnes went first and hit nineteen of twenty-five free throws.

"I made the first twenty and said, 'Sign,'" Haskins said. "And boy, he did. He got right on his hands and knees, with all his teammates giving him hell, and signed."

And in the 1980s there were recruiting gems like guard Tim Hardaway and forwards Antonio Davis and Greg Foster.

And even when he didn't have Hardaways or Archibalds, he would win. Haskins is regarded as the best at making something out of nothing. He is adept at adapting his game plan to meet his team's strengths while teaching the game so his personnel improve.

"He is simply able to get more out of people than any other coach in the country," said Gene Iba, a former assistant.

"A lot of guys are interested in recruiting a guy who is a better fit into a system," said Floyd. "He says, 'Let's make this guy better. Let's work with him individually until he's better.' He has the best understanding of people of anyone I have ever been around."

Says Utah's Majerus, "He takes a player and looks at what he can do and then changes his offense to suit that. He maximizes a player's ability probably better than any coach in the college game."

Haskins's demanding style has changed little. He also commands unparalleled respect from his players. The stories Haskins tells of Iba, his players tell of him.

"People used to ask us what was the toughest game we played," said Shed. "And we'd say, 'Practice.' Games were a pleasure after what he put us through. We used to get blisters — oh man, were they bad. He'd come by and say, 'Shed, are your feet burning?' And I'd say, 'No, sir,' even though I was playing on my ankles.

"I hated him when I was there. God knows I hated the man. But for what he's done for me since I graduated, I wouldn't trade it for anything. He is a great, great man. He is the best thing to ever happen to me."

The best run of Haskins's career was from 1983 to 1992, when UTEP averaged a 24–8 record, won five consecutive WAC championships, and made eight NCAA tournament appearances in nine years.

Floyd was an assistant coach during some of that era, and he, more than anyone, moved UTEP into the modern age. A dynamic recruiter with an eye for hidden talent, he scoured the country in search of players for Haskins to coach. "Tim was the best recruiter we ever had," said Haskins, who has a close, father-son relationship with Floyd to this day.

It was a match made in heaven. Floyd was a tireless worker, an avid writer of recruiting letters, and a stubborn assistant who would make Haskins go out and recruit players the coach didn't think they had a chance to land. And he helped the old cowboy learn about the modern player.

"We went to recruit a guy, Jerry Jones, in Chicago," said Floyd. "It was before tattoos were a big thing, and he had one and Coach didn't know he had one. We pulled up to the gym — Country Club Hills High School — and I say, 'Hey, Coach, there are a couple of things I have to tell you about this guy.'

"He said, 'Oh hell, here we go again. Why didn't you tell me about this in El Paso? I would not have gotten on the plane.'

"I said, 'Coach, he's a good kid but he's got a tattoo on his arm with the initials *J.J.* in the middle of a basketball.'

"He said, 'Well, let's just turn around and go back to the airport. We don't need a guy like him on our team.'

"I said, 'Coach, it's barely recognizable. We're here, we might as well go in, and maybe we'll see someone else we like.'

"So we go in, and they are just playing a pickup game, but our guy comes down the court and dunks one and the backboard is shaking. Then, down the other end, he blocks a shot and then runs up the court and dunks another one. He's 6'7", 240 pounds, and I can tell Coach is getting excited about his ability.

"Afterwards we drive back to O'Hare, and I said, 'Coach, what did you think of that tattoo on Jerry's arm?'

"And he said, 'Hell, I never even noticed it.'"

And the cowboy, in turn, taught Floyd about the old school.

"We go on a recruiting trip to some little town in Louisiana," Floyd said. "We're going to fly out of Shreveport the next morning, and we are staying in a hotel with a bar next to it with one of those neon cowboy boots kicking. Coach says, 'Tim, let's go get a beer.'

"It's pretty empty but there are a couple of guys playing pool in back. Coach goes up to the table and puts a quarter down. One of the guys says, 'Hey, buddy, let me tell you something. This is a money table. If you want to play, you're going to have to bet.'

"Coach says, 'I guess that'll be all right.'

"So they play for ten bucks a game and Coach goes on to reel off eighteen straight — and I mean games. And many of those games he just runs the table. They never got to shoot. He'd just alternate beating each guy.

"Finally he decides it's time to leave. Now, you could tell these two guys didn't have much. So Coach walks over to them and gives them back their money and says, 'You best be careful who you gamble with in the future.'

"Then he just walks out and never says another word about it."

UTEP had some great teams during that era but, despite Floyd's recruiting skill, wasn't landing McDonald's All-Americans. It was signing projects. For Tim Hardaway — whom Haskins describes as "a fat kid who couldn't shoot" when they signed him out of Chicago — the Miners beat Northeastern Illinois. For Antonio Davis, it was UTEP and Portland State.

"Coach Haskins made me look like a recruiter," Floyd said. "My last year there we went 27–4 and everyone said I was a great recruiter, but three of our players were from New Orleans and didn't have any other offers. He makes players."

The culmination of the run came in 1992 when UTEP, starring forwards Marlon Maxey and Johnny Melvin, entered the NCAA tournament 25–7 and beat Evansville to set up a meeting with the number-one-seeded Kansas Jayhawks, featuring the explosive back-court of Rex Walters and Adonis Jordan. Haskins turned back the clock and went to a four-corners offense that slowed the game down and gave UTEP a number of easy lay-ups. The Miners won, 66–60, in a shocker to advance to the Sweet Sixteen.

"That was a Don Haskins team," says Gene Iba. "When he beat Kansas he had a good basketball team, but it wasn't in that league. I think coaches everywhere believe that if you give him equal talent, the other team will be at a disadvantage."

Haskins looks at it another way. "We were better than people thought we were. We should have beaten Cincinnati" — a 69–67 loss — "in the next round."

Momentum was again on UTEP's side. With Hardaway and Daniels blossoming into NBA stars and the high-profile win over Kansas, the Miners seemed prepared to keep their run of good fortune rolling. But in 1989 *New York Newsday*, citing a few former players, all of whom transferred from the program, described a system of "sugar daddies" in El Paso who provided cars and other benefits for players. Although dozens of former Miners, including Tim Hardaway, disputed those claims and Haskins called the story "the most fictitious thing you've ever read," the fallout was considerable.

The NCAA arrived on campus in 1991 and began its own investigation of the program. Not helping things was Haskins's decision three years earlier to call his old friend Norm Ellenberger to work as a volunteer assistant. Ellenberger had left New Mexico during the late 1980s under a mountain of NCAA violations and was clearly persona non grata with the governing body. (Ellenberger is now a volunteer assistant coach at Indiana.)

The NCAA, Haskins is convinced, was angry that Ellenberger had any involvement in the program — in 1989 when Haskins missed several games due to an acute case of laryngitis, Ellenberger became the bench coach.

There was also UTEP's place in the world of college basketball. The Miners are neither a major revenue-producing nor a politically powerful program. Their national appeal and ability to attract television viewers are minimal. The NCAA has a history of making an example out of the weakest of its flock. As former Texas coach Abe Lemons quipped in the 1980s, "The NCAA was so mad at Kentucky, it gave Cleveland State an extra two years of probation."

The NCAA found no sugar daddies — the most heinous crime was that "on several occasions" assistant coaches provided players with rides around town — but there were a half-dozen minor violations uncovered.

Although NCAA investigators concluded that there was "limited recruiting and competitive advantages gained by these violations," the infractions committee hammered the program anyway, reducing to two the number of scholarships it could offer during the years 1992–93 and 1993–94, as well as applying other recruiting restrictions.

"That's when my program began to go downhill," said Haskins.

Worse for Haskins, the school fired his two full-time assistants, Rus Bradburg and Greg Lakey.

"It was unbelievable. It was a nightmare," said Haskins, still emotionally bitter about the process. "All the NCAA wants you to do is lie. Ellenberger is giving me all this advice, he had been through this, and he said don't talk to them. I said, 'I'm not afraid of them because I have nothing to hide.' But they ask you, 'Have you ever given a kid a ride?' Well, in all those years of coaching I am supposed to say I've never given a kid a ride? It's ridiculous.

"To me, cheating is giving guys cars and apartments. Now, I can't control a fan somewhere who gives a player fifty dollars. And I am sure over the years that has happened. But I didn't know about it.

"With the NCAA, it's about power. I think it's funny that a guy who is not eligible [Kenny Thomas] is currently playing his third year at New Mexico because the NCAA can't handle a federal judge. I think that is funny. I think that is ironic. [Jerry] Tarkanian coached [thirteen] years after they said he couldn't, because they couldn't handle a federal judge in Nevada. And I know when you write your article, because I just said that, they'll come and get me. They can come and do their looking and they can probably find something similar to a car ride, but that's it.

"I think the frustrating part is trying to do your job right for all those years and you still get your ass beat. You know, I can get some money together and buy a player, but I wouldn't want to have some guy have me by the balls. And I played for a man who would roll over in his grave.

"During those two years I lost thirteen of my fifteen scholarship players and I replaced them with four. Two worked out, two didn't. It is killing us right now."

The post-probation days have not been good ones at UTEP. The record has slumped, attendance has dwindled, and there have been no NCAA appearances.

In January 1996, with the Miners holding a 10–4 record, Haskins had a heart attack in the locker room during halftime of a game against New Mexico. So tough was the Bear that he refused to be carried out on a stretcher and instead got to his feet and walked to the ambulance. He underwent successful triple-bypass surgery, but UTEP, without Haskins, dropped ten of thirteen the rest of the way, posting its first losing season (12–16) since 1979. Last season ended at 13–13.

When Eddie Mullens, who retired in 1996 after a long stint as UTEP's sports information director, received word of the 1996 inductees into the Basketball Hall of Fame, in Springfield, Massachusetts, "it was just like someone hit me in the face." The list had some good players, it had some good coaches, but it didn't have Don Haskins. Again. For Mullens, who had spearheaded the Haskins campaign a half-dozen years before, over his friend's vehement objections, that was a travesty.

"I was terribly upset," Mullens said. "I don't normally get worked up like that, but I couldn't help it. This was the most frustrating project I ever worked on. I immediately got the nomination form out, filled it out, and faxed it to the Hall of Fame. And then I overnighted the original copy."

Getting inducted into the Hall of Fame has always been a political process, and critics can list dozens of coaches who have made it whose credentials can't match Haskins's but who coached college or pro basketball in the East, particularly in New York or Boston. Haskins, who was denied year after year, became their rallying cry.

"There are guys in there that couldn't hold a candle next to Don Haskins," said Richardson.

Most everyone blamed the East Coast media for ignoring the man and the eastern-based Hall of Fame for not caring.

"You're dealing with a guy who if he coached in New York would have a better reputation than Pat Riley or any of those guys," said Gene Iba. "We felt the media had passed him by because of his location. The media covers what is in front of them, and El Paso is hard to get to, it's in the Mountain zone. Even though he's done great things, the media has ignored him."

Haskins never engaged in the campaign, just as he has never promoted himself in thirty-seven years at UTEP. He forbids the school's sports information department from putting him on the cover of the media guide — he prefers the seniors and a team photo. He never courts the media or joins coaching associations and eschews any kind of attention.

And in El Paso, he can find that. And even here he lies low. When he goes out for meals or a drink, he often patronizes local dives or even hotel bars because they are generally empty and the only customers are out-of-towners who won't recognize him.

"There isn't anybody in there," Haskins says. "People ask for my autograph around here like I'm some big hero."

He is never seen at the hotter spots in town, places where bankers and lawyers hang out, like the grill room at the El Paso Country Club or Jackson's over on Mesa Boulevard. That makes him even more beloved to the working people of El Paso. Haskins is more at home in their shot-and-a-beer joints than anywhere else. He is not so much one of them as they are one of him. They idolize him.

Haskins could have left El Paso but never did. He accepted the head coaching job at the University of Detroit for one day in 1969, but quit because he didn't see eye to eye with the school's administration. And Oklahoma State — his alma mater — contacted him a few times, but he always said no. "I never wanted to follow Mr. Iba," he says.

He's stayed in El Paso because he's comfortable here. If that hurt his national reputation or delayed his entry into the Hall of Fame, he was finally enshrined in 1997, so be it.

"I don't think I deserve to be in the Hall of Fame," Haskins says. "I've only been to the Final Four once."

His followers disagree.

"It was long overdue," says Knight. "When you take what he has accomplished, where he has accomplished it, and, generally, the talent he's accomplished it with, then his being elected to the Hall of Fame becomes a very belated thing."

"You put any major coach in his setting and it would be the same thing," says Gene Iba. "If you take Dean Smith or Bobby Knight or Rick Pitino and put them in El Paso, they'd still be great coaches. That isn't going to change. But they wouldn't be as well known."

"If Don Haskins had ever gone to a school that could recruit itself, like a Kentucky or a Syracuse, he'd probably have six national championships," says Stoglin. "He's a hell of a coach."

"It's easy to forget about him unless you have to play against him," says Floyd. "He's not interested in being the center of attention or pointing out his accomplishments, but I don't think there is a better coach in the country. I couldn't imagine anyone putting up the numbers he did in El Paso. He's a man's man and a coach's coach."

Haskins doesn't know what to say about all that. Nor does he know what to say when guys like Richardson say, "If I hadn't have gotten to meet him, I wouldn't know what I know today."

Or when middle-aged black men he doesn't know stop him in airports and tell him they received athletic scholarships because of what he did in 1966.

Or when everyone compares him to Mr. Iba.

Or when Majerus says, "I idolize him. He's a hero to me."

Or when Knight says, "I am honored when he calls me a friend."

Or when Stoglin says, "I love Coach. I really love that man."

He doesn't like to hear it. With the exception of visiting Iba's plaque, he didn't enjoy the Hall of Fame induction weekend because he had to give a speech — about himself, no less — and he got so nervous he couldn't stand it.

He knows he's in the sunset of his career. A career worthy of a Rim Road–caliber sunset. "A year or two more," he says. His health isn't great and there are all these doctors who don't like the stress, the travel, or the whiskey. But can you imagine John Wayne in a retirement home, eating egg whites and drinking grapefruit juice?

"It's been a lot of fun over the years," he says. "I've had some great players."

He smiles while folding and unfolding his hands. He is wearing a ring commemorating his induction into the Hall of Fame. Haskins didn't wear jewelry until he was given this ring. His friends say he wears it every day, although he denies it. He also wears a custom-made Rolex with the Hall of Fame emblem on it. They say it shows how proud he is, although he denies that too. He's too humble to admit being proud.

He changes the subject. That last loss is still eating at him, so he'd rather talk about an upcoming game. The old cowboy's next battle.

"I'm telling you, we're going to get out there and play some goddam defense."

SIMON WINCHESTER

Sheep of Fools

FROM GQ

CASMER "BUTCH" KUFLAK was halfway up a low mountain range in the far south of Mexico's Baja California peninsula. It was blisteringly hot, and the terrain was pitiless. He had been wandering there for the previous eight days and nights, searching — ceaselessly, it had seemed, during the bone-wearying lows of the adventure — for what he now, at long last, had fixed firmly in the crosshairs of his shooting scope. He was revived. Indeed, he was frantic, jittery. He battled to stay calm. He focused the centerpiece of his scope on that flat area between the shoulders and the head of the enormous white animal that stood before him, two hundred yards away. He inhaled as he had been taught, slowly let the breath out, and, as he did so, carefully squeezed his weapon's tiny steel trigger. Kuflak saw the head go down and then the body suddenly collapse, deflating heavily, like a punctured water balloon. He stood up, waved exultantly to his Mexican guides, and began to run forward.

Within seconds, after stumbling wildly over boulders and fissures and tangles of sagebrush, he reached the animal. Blood was oozing from a wound under its neck — oozing, not frothing, an indication that the wound was small and clean, that the animal's heart had stopped beating, that it was dead. It was a prime specimen of *Ovis canadensis*, better known as a bighorn sheep, that he'd killed — though he prefers to use the word "harvested." He turned to see his guides rushing toward him, smiling. It was at that moment that Casmer Kuflak, named after a famous Polish warrior, lost it.

"I suddenly started to cry so hard, I plain near dropped my rifle.

I bawled and I bawled," he says. In describing the final moments of the Baja triumph in eloquent, highly emotional terms, and in talking generally of the almost mystical climax of a sport he regards with a pure passion, Kuflak still finds one word difficult to apply to the hunt, and that word is "challenging." A sheep hunt, he admits, may well be arduous, uncomfortable, draining, and fit for only the strong of mind as well as body, but it is rarely challenging.

The varieties of the genus *Ovis* that are hunted are not the everyday, wool-covered bundles of timidity from which we get mutton and sweaters. No, the sheep that sheep hunters like to take, harvest, cull, dispatch, what have you, are the big, horned wild sheep of the mountains. And yet, despite their horns and their formidable size — formidable for sheep, that is — these animals are not particularly fierce, not even for sheep. Indeed, the sheep the hunters tend to hunt are invariably elderly sheep. And these senior sheep are often "taken" while they are resting, best taken, in fact, when they are lying on the ground. And, as technically sound sheep hunters know, these sheep are most properly taken when they are sleeping.

This, then, is no bullfight, no struggle with the mighty tarpon, no contest to quicken the pulse of a Hemingway or a José Ortega. Rather, it is a duel between man and powerful firearms on the one hand, and wool, old age, and the beguiling clutches of Morpheus on the other. There is seldom any doubt who will win.

Kuflak's prey wasn't sleeping, he recalls, but "grazing, walking slowly, hanging out chatting to the girl sheep." Nonetheless, it was a good, clean kill. (The less active the prey, the slower the heartbeat and thus the less blood on the coat.) Moreover, what made this particular shot so significant was that it gave him his first Grand Slam of North American wild sheep. That virile, girl-crazy desert bighorn was the fourth wild sheep he'd nailed in three years' time. Kuflak had already killed, like the 775 others who have achieved the distinction Grand Slammer, a Rocky Mountain bighorn in Montana, a Dall sheep in the Northwest Territories, and a beautiful stone sheep in British Columbia. (For the record: of the four sheep Kuflak shot during his long and costly quest for a Grand Slam — all of them stuffed and mounted in his rather cramped den in Hermosa Beach, California, as an ever-present reminder of his hunting prowess — all were quite, quite still at the moment he pulled the trigger.)

"An ordinary guy from Los Angeles, a contractor, someone new to the game — and now," says Kuflak, "I was one of only some seven hundred people in the entire world who had managed to get a Grand Slam. It was awesome. It brings tears to my eyes to think of it even now."

And yet, as impressive as the Grand Slam is, it is still very much in the cadet branch of the sheep-hunting honors system. The true corps d'élite is made up of no more than thirty people — all men, it is believed — and these top guns of sheepdom have achieved the World Slam.

Bagging the four North American sheep is a standard for the World Slam, which demands the taking of twelve animals (only rams — male sheep, that is — are shot) from a list that includes no fewer than twenty-eight officially recognized and warranted wild sheep. The list is dominated by members of the argali family. There's the mighty Transcaspian, the splendid Gobi, the lesser mouflon, and the pretty dwarf blue. And there is the Altay, the Eastern tur, the Kamchatka, the Himalayan blue, the Red, and the Karaganda, and then there is the greatest sheep of all, the huge and fantastic confection of wool, hoof, and horn known as the Marco Polo.

Most World Slam targets — and these sheep are finer than any of the fine specimens of North American sheephood — are found in distant locales, many of them lands once ruled from Moscow: Chukhotka in eastern Siberia, Tajikistan, Turkmenistan, Uzbekistan, Kazakhstan, Kyrgyzstan, Afghanistan, and the vast volcano-covered peninsula of Kamchatka; others can be found in Pakistan, Mongolia, Nepal, Tibet, Iran, Anatolia, and the less accessible parts of far western and northern China. It is an arduous affair, this sheep hunting, and costly. Those who think they are rich hunt Africa, as sheep hunters are wont to say; those who *are* rich hunt sheep. Before a man can even begin to try himself against the harsh climatic conditions in the upper reaches of, say, the Caucasus Mountains and climb fifteen, twenty thousand feet through the thick snow and thin air in pursuit of the great game, he (sheep hunting is an almost exclusively male entertainment) must first arrange to get to the particular faraway region that is home to his prey. There's the transatlantic flight to a strange Third World destination, then private transport in a dubiously constructed foreign

(sometimes Soviet-vintage) automobile, and at the journey's termi-
nus the local accommodations bargained for in a strange tongue
with strange peoples (this latter communication, however, generally facilitated with refreshingly familiar U.S. dollars). Sheep hunting, then, is not only man against nature in all its riotous glory, man
against the elemental extreme; sheep hunting also entails the battle
between man and the eternal vagaries, the brutally indifferent vicis-
situdes of modern tourism. This is man against travel agency at its
rawest.

Dennis Campbell is here to help. The owner and editor of *Ovis*
and *Grand Slam,* magazines devoted to the sport of sheep hunting,
and executive director of the Grand Slam Club, Campbell also
organizes trips for hunters. For the Grand Slam tour, Campbell can
more or less assure each participant the opportunity to kill the
requisite sheep. Twenty thousand dollars covers food and shelter
and guides skilled in locating and identifying the choicest, oldest,
most exhausted sheep. Airfare, guns, and ammo are not included.

"I charge these fellows $36,000 to go to Mongolia," says Camp-
bell, a man in his late middle age. "They pay because they can be
pretty sure they'll get a sheep. They'll be pretty sure they'll come
back with a trophy. At the end of the day, it's an easy shot. But it's a
good shot, too, for the sheep. We're doing good stuff for them."

It is part of the sheep hunter's credo that his indulgence benefits
even its victims. In spite of Campbell's best-of-all-possible-worlds
defense, a growing number of ecologists and environmentalists
are becoming concerned. The great argali, in particular, is under
threat, and the world's environmental organizations regard the
newly emergent international business of sheep shooting as abhor-
rent. But since the collapse of the Soviet Union, woefully underde-
veloped countries such as Tajikistan and Uzbekistan have had little
trade to offer beyond a few rare minerals and a supply of magnificent and, in some cases, endangered sheep.

"Everyone's happy," says Campbell. "My company makes money.
The guides get big tips. The hunter gets his trophy to take back
home. We select the biggest sheep — of course that's what our
people want for their trophy rooms. The biggest ones are always the
old ones, the sheep that would anyway be dying of old age in a year
or so. When you get up to a flock lying in the sun, you are going to
look for the biggest one, the oldest one, the one that's being lazy,
that's sleeping in the warmth. Sure, it makes it a bit easier to hunt if

he's not barreling along some mountain ridge. He's an easy target. It will have taken you days to get to him. But when you do find him, it's a sure shot. Bingo! You kill the guy with one clean shot in the neck, and what have you got? You've got out of the way a sheep that's of no use anymore. You've got out of the way a sheep that can't try to mate anymore in the rutting season, which means the younger guys, the stronger ones with better genes, get to cover the females."

Bingo!

Butch Kuflak agrees. Sheep hunting is good for the environment and for Third World economies. "The locals know that we Americans come in to shoot their sheep — so the sheep suddenly have a value to them, and they don't slaughter them in the way they used to, wholesale. What we do places a premium on their survival, and the only ones we take are the elderly males that would have died anyway. The anti-hunting people don't understand. What we do is actually good for the sheep, not bad."

The U.S. Fish and Wildlife Service is extra careful and demands permits and inspections for anyone coming back from a sheep-hunting trip. It has mounted raids on the trophy rooms of some of the better-known hunters, which is supposed to discourage men such as Campbell from excess.

"We know that with the loosening up of the old Soviet states and their need for cash, there is a huge temptation to allow the hunting of endangered sheep, but the officials at the airports here don't have any mercy," Campbell says. "If one of our people shoots something he shouldn't, he doesn't bring it home. It's as simple as that."

Appendix I of the multilateral Convention on International Trade in Endangered Species (CITES) treaty was written to protect endangered animals, including sheep. The CITES Appendix II lists those not-quite-so-endangered animals that may be hunted in limited numbers and with official permission.

Are there hunters who ignore the regulations?

"Stuff on Appendix I does get shot," Campbell admits. "Very occasionally. It can't be helped. But none of it comes into the States. The law is very tough. They go for you big time if you take stuff from Appendix I. That's for sure."

Campbell has been hunting since he was seventeen. His first kill was a white-tailed deer that he took close to the hardscrabble farm where he grew up. He discovered the peculiar joys of sheep hunting almost twenty years ago. Nowadays he is above all else a sheep hunter. "Once you've taken a wild sheep," he says, "there's no going back. The places that you go, the magnificence of the animals you then bring home — it's awesome."

And Campbell has brought many home to the midsize drugstore he owns and operates in Adamsville, Alabama, a mile or so outside Birmingham. Ranged high in serried ranks above the bottles of Pepto-Bismol and the curling tongs are dozens upon dozens of animal heads. A moose from British Columbia smiles amiably down at customers selecting their razor blades, an antelope strikes a disdainful pose above the tampons, and the pharmacy counter is festooned with horns and tusks and multipointed antler racks. (With this imposing menagerie as witness, what sort of courage would an Adamsville youth have to muster to buy a condom from Campbell's pharmacy?) Campbell's collection, if not the most extensive, is certainly one of the more unusually curated. He is one of the godfathers of the sport, having risen through the ranks to wield considerable authority, and yet he knows he and his brethren walk in the shadow of a legend.

Preeminent among the World Slammers rises one figure who has slaughtered sheep in every corner of the globe, a man so distinguished he has acquired not one but two World Slams. He is treated with utter reverence by all in the fraternity who know him or who are aware of his repute. His name is Hossein Golabchi, and he goes by the sobriquet Soudy.

"In this business, Soudy is a god," says Campbell. "To get the real flavor of this world, Soudy's the man to see. It'll be pretty difficult. He's always off hunting. Eight, nine months of the year. But if you can pin him down, he's the one. Of the guys who go out the farthest, who go to the wildest places and get the best, he's absolutely the number one. Like I say, he's a god."

He is also a property developer in Augusta, Georgia. He is wealthy, though a little less so than he was a few years ago, on account of a local plutonium plant's closing, which Soudy thought would discourage potential investors. (It is one of the happily plangent ironies of this sport that while the Cold War helped make Soudy a wealthy man, its conclusion opened up so much of the former Soviet states to primo sheep hunting.) He has, it is said, the biggest and best trophy room in the world.

A telephone call to Augusta is met with the somewhat predictable news that, yes, Soudy is away hunting sheep, in Tajikistan, and will go from there to his native Iran (the Dushanbe–Tehran shuttle being one of the new trails that the sheep-hunting fraternity is blazing) to see family members who remain there. He will return the following week and is scheduled to rest in Augusta for a day. He is then to go off to Moscow to hunt on one of the government's private estates for a rare type of Persian red deer, the maral.

Soudy is said to be a private man, one who never gives interviews and never sees outsiders. But his secretary thinks he might agree to talk to *GQ*, a magazine for men. So, after faxes are exchanged between Augusta and some faraway corner of the globe, Soudy suggests he could see me on that single free day a week hence.

He is in very good spirits when he arrives in Augusta. He has just come from Tehran and is full of the news that he has shot a world-record Marco Polo sheep. It is, he declares, absolutely the best sheep of his life. He explains how one could discern it is a world-record sheep. The method of measurement is cabalistic in its numerological complexity: start with the precise length of each horn, divide this number by four, and then add to this result the sum of four separate measurements of the horn's circumference at four different places along its length. The horn-measuring committees who award the records (there are similar bodies who deal with lesser animals, such as deer and elk) have just been given his data, he says, and will pronounce their verdict in due course. In the meantime, a photograph. He pulls it from his case. A picture of this sort fills the pages of popular reads such as *Ovis* and *Grand Slam*. In it are many mountains, much snow, one exceedingly happy man, and one very dead sheep. Soudy's Marco Polo does indeed possess a set of horns that, to this untrained eye, appear colossal.

We have breakfast in an enormous gift shop. He has the Egg Beaters. To explain why he is watching his cholesterol, he pulls open his shirt to show the long scars from two recent open-heart surgeries. His knees are shot as well. "Too many hours spent kneeling in snow," he says. But generally he is quite fit. In fact, he is wired — like a coiled spring. I tell him I wouldn't fancy meeting him in a dark alley. He laughs good-naturedly. "Nor on a mountaintop in Tajikistan," he says. I consider reminding him I am not a sheep.

He tells me the story of his recent triumph, a story he will submit, he says, to one of Dennis Campbell's magazines (for he is a keen writer as well). He pursued this particular Marco Polo for months. He had first seen it — huge, monumental, a vision of ovine splendor — back in midsummer, but decided not to shoot it because its skin was in poor condition, as happens in the summer.

"I thought I'd wait awhile, until the snows came and his fleece became thicker, so he would look better in the trophy room.

"I had the guides stay behind and keep an eye on him, and this time I came back and took him. In two months, he hadn't moved more than a couple of miles. They don't move much, these old sheep.

"The hunt was pretty good. I was up in the hills for a week before I met him. I had to make sure I was upwind of him, that he didn't hear me. Then it was just a question of getting close enough to shoot. He was an easy target. Sitting there, snoozing as usual. Big, big target. I got him in the neck. Perfect shot. Nothing for the taxidermist to repair. Took his picture. Skinned him. Packed him away. He's on his way back to America now. I ought to get him in a couple of months. Best ever. He'll go to the top of the mountain."

The mountain? I'm not entirely sure what that means until later in the morning, when we drive to his small estate outside of town and open the white warehouse where he keeps his trophies. I had expected something like a diorama in a small zoo. What opens before me, as the lights flicker on inside this vast hangar of a space, almost beggars belief.

A huge Styrofoam mountain, with rocks and trees and snow and running streams and waterfalls, looms at one end of the building. On it, in a kind of animal abundance not known since Noah landed his ark atop Mount Ararat, are dozens upon dozens of sheep and goats and urials and antelope, all in lifelike poses, all collected together at the altitude where they had lived and died. Down low, partridge and deer and small goats; up higher, bearded urials and small bears; and up among the snow and ice fields, gigantic argalis, bigger and bigger as the mountain narrows to its summit, with the blue-washed-sky wall behind serving as backdrop. Hossein Golabchi points to a space at the very top. "That is where he'll go. He'll look good up there, don't you think?" Yes, Noah. God will be pleased.

The mountain is not all. Behind me, standing on the acres of warehouse floor, are a huge rhinoceros, scores of bears and wildcats and hyenas and warthogs and four-footed beasts of all species and shapes and sizes. An African-elephant head looms over the rhino, its tusks six feet long and thick as a man's thigh. "Got him with a fifty-caliber," Soudy says proudly. "Good taxidermy, though. Impossible to see the wound."

A year ago, the Fish and Wildlife men paid an unannounced visit to Soudy Golabchi's warehouse, hoping to find something illegal in what all say is the biggest and best of American trophy rooms. But everything was in order. "There is stuff I can't bring in, though," he says. "There are animals that I've shot and which the Americans won't allow. These I keep in Mexico. Or back in Russia.

"Look at this snow leopard, for example." He brings out photographs of himself with a rare and well-protected leopard curled around his neck like a scarf, quite dead. "I shot him. But I bring that in and they find me, I go to prison. So it stays in Mexico.

"The Fish and Wildlife are so annoying. They keep shifting permission. One day I can get a polar bear; the next day I can't. These people blow in the wind. They come under pressure from these anti-hunting people, the Humane Society, the Sierra Club, people like that. We lobby for them to allow us to get the good stuff; the other side lobbies for them to ban hunting. We argue that what we do makes the stock better. They say shooting is bad.

"It's war out there. And people like me get caught in the middle. I want to hunt. I'm not just a collector, you know. I don't hunt just to tick off one of everything. I go out carefully, to get the best trophies."

I'm standing beside one splendid argali, perhaps the best of the collection, an animal whose magnificence might yield only to Soudy's Marco Polo in transit from Dushanbe. The pathos is palpable: the animal stuffed, glassy-eyed, and doomed to stand eternally in an air-conditioned warehouse. This was once a wild sheep, an Ur-sheep, a beast with a name suggestive of the Mongols, the Great Khan, the Golden Horde, of steppes, villages with yurts, small wild horses, and endless windswept grassy plains. Shouldn't this odd fellow have died there instead and taken his part in the natural economy of his surroundings, as much of that nature in death as he had been in life? At the very least, it's fair to wonder what this animal did to deserve the fate of ending up in the alien and synthetic meadows of a warehouse in Augusta, Georgia.

Soudy pats the rump of a huge urial. "You wouldn't want this old fellow to die unseen high up on some mountain, would you? Wouldn't you rather he was taken and brought back to stand here and be seen, yes? Isn't that a better fate for him? A better end? The anti-hunting people don't see it that way. They say all shooting is bad. They have no imagination."

What is it that makes men like Hossein Golabchi hunt?

"How else do you think I'm going to spend my life? You think I'll sit on my backside and just die?

"What else am I going to do? Is there anything more noble than going off to get these creatures? They are magnificent, don't you think? I think they deserve to be up here, set up so beautifully.

"I come in here on my own some days," Soudy continues, his hand on the rhino's gray haunch, his gaze on the plaster-board sky. "I gaze up at these animals I have taken and brought back, and I look in awe, real awe, at the wonder of the world I have created. It is quite beautiful. I have made something wonderful here. Not many people can say they have made something so beautiful in their life. What I have done is true creation."

DAVID MAMET

The Deer Hunter

FROM SPORTS AFIELD

NEW YORK WAS, of course, intolerable.

I found that I was organizing my day around those times when it was possible — just possible — to get a cup of gourmet coffee without standing in line a half hour.

But whose fault was it if not my own, who'd chosen luxury and fashion (at least for the fall) over a healthy life in the outdoors? I wasn't writing a word of any worth, either; and to complete the indictment, I was frittering away yet another deer season. Up in Vermont, archery season was over, as was centerfire rifle, and Morris, my neighbor down the road, had gotten a 175-pound buck in the orchard just across from my house.

And I had just turned fifty.

My friend and hunting companion Bob turned fifty some five or six years ago. An outdoorsman — a hunter, trapper, and forester — he had, his wife reported, spent his forty-ninth year complaining and full of crotchets about encroaching Old Age. But when the clock ticked over onto fifty, he was cured, and went back to an uncomplaining, aggressively active life. I had spent my forty-ninth year emulating his. But now I had turned fifty, and found myself still the slave of habit, sloth, and urban depravity; deer season was waning, and I had to get out of town.

I thought I'd look for an adventure somewhat greater than tripping around the back yard, but not quite as Herculean as going all the way to Maine. So I contacted Uncle Jammers (Jim Ehlers) out of Sugarbush, Vermont, who said he'd put me on some tracks up in the Northeast Kingdom, for the last days of blackpowder muzzle-loading season.

I flew to Burlington, Vermont, and drove to Plainfield, for lunch at the River Run Restaurant. Jimmy Kennedy was in the kitchen. He made me bacon and eggs and reminded me to take along a safety pin on the hunting trip. What for? To use as a touchhole pick for the muzzleloader.

Friend of his, he said, had a safety pin, and it saved the day on a blackpowder shoot when the touchhole clogged. Great idea. I remember old Pennsylvania guns, with a hole bored in the forestock, right below that for the ramrod, and in the hole was carried a long quill to clean out the touchhole.

I remembered hunting with blackpowder shooters in east Texas, sitting around in the evening at Bill Bagwell's forge, discussing the contributions blackpowder shooting had made to the language: hang fire; flash in the pan; lock, stock, and barrel; skinflint; keep your powder dry; shot his rod (corrupted into "wad"); chew the rag; spruce up (sprues up, i.e., with the sprue — the nonspherical portion of the cast ball, that portion left when the molten lead overflows the mold — up, that is, pointed toward the muzzle); and (which prompted this reflection) ramrod, used as a verb. So much of the appeal of field sports, at least to me, who practices them infrequently, is the gear and the language pertinent to the thing. I get out there only several days a year, but I, along with the legion of my sedentary coeval enthusiasts, am always up for an outdoorsy book or catalogue (anything's better than playing golf).

Here, blackpowder shooting was reminding me that the simplest gear — in this case, a safety pin — is the best.

Jimmy and I spoke about ice fishing for a while. I paid my check and headed out to my house. My first stop was up at my cabin to get my gear. I took down my .58-caliber Hawken and cleaned it. I blew through the barrel, but I found it clogged. I pulled the nipple and saw the lube had set up in the touchhole, and that, happy day, I could clean it out using a safety pin. I cleaned the nipple, cleaned the bore, polished the thimbles, got the whole thing shining, and went outside and set up a target at fifty yards. It's a pretty good range, as (a) it's going to be about the limit of any shot in the woods, and (b) it's a range I can actually hit from.

I put a couple of half-inch red Targ-Dots on the cardboard, and put my first shot two inches left and on for elevation. With a second shot I obliterated the Targ-Dot, and felt about as good as I'd felt since I first went down to the City.

The rifle exhibited a degree of forgiveness positively feminine. I was standing out there, waxing rhapsodic about the blackpowder rifle, its excellencies, its forgiving nature, its lack of recoil and general friendliness, when the sun went down. I cleaned my gun by the oil lamp, hurried back to the house, threw much too much gear into a pack, and got into the pickup for the drive to Sugarbush.

I remembered a cold and hungry Vermont holiday season, thirty-plus years before. I was out of work, and heard of an opening for an experienced bartender at the Sugarbush Inn. I called and made an appointment for an interview. I went to the Montpelier Library and found the *Old Mister Boston's Official Bartender's Guide,* and studied it night and day until the date of my interview, when that person upon whom I had counted for a lift to Sugarbush disappointed me. I sat out the remainder of the holiday season hungry, cold, and grumbling.

The awful thing about not winning an Academy Award is this: you don't get to give your speech. It just rather sits there and festers. *Yes,* you think, *it's all right that I lost, that's only fair, and that's the game. But there* must *be some way that,* having *lost, I can still mount the podium and give my most excellent and philosophical speech.*

But no. And neither did I ever get to display my (granted, theoretical) excellence as a bartender. And never before had I gotten to Sugarbush, that momentary Oz of my youth.

I arrived at the Snow Ridge Inn. A young woman told me that everyone was out snowmobiling, but that I could fling my stuff into one of the cabins, and work out the details of my stay later on.

I think snowmobiling, at least in Vermont, contains the story of a particularly American triumph. In my youth, up there, in the turbulent sixties, snowmobilers had the reputation of being rowdies — outlaw bikers on ice, bent on inebriation, vandalism, and whatever mischief one could get into whilst wrapped like a puff pastry at 40 below. But their image was changed, and by the most unusual of tactics — by changing their actions. Makes one think.

So I drove the pickup over to my cabin, where there would be no phone. No television. Privacy. I could enter and spread out and check and moon over my gear, I could sleep till dawn the next morning, I could open the windows, accountable to no one, I could live, for the moment, a free man.

I lugged my gear up on the porch and opened the door. I looked down, and at my feet was a note: "Call Norman Lear immediately."

Well, then, I was strong enough to get myself out of New York, but I was not strong enough not to call Norman Lear immediately. He told me he was working on a project and I was the only one to write it, and other irresistible flattery, and I made an appointment to meet him the next week, back in New York.

For, yes, *of course,* I was a fraud. Whom was I attempting to kid? As there was no one there but myself, I sussed that answer out fairly quickly. But was I not, on the other hand, nevertheless entitled to Go Hunting? Yes. I put away my gear and went out to meet Uncle Jammer's guides, Jim and Nathan, for dinner, and we made a plan: we'd meet at the Snow Ridge at 5:30 A.M. and drive up to Wenlock, the preserve by Island Pond. Fine.

I went shopping down in the town: tea, butter, eggs, bread, cheese, and ham. I went back to my cabin and fell asleep. The radio woke me at 5:00 with some symphonic music. I took a quick shower, dashed into the kitchen to make breakfast and a perfect sandwich: eggs, butter, cheese, bread, ham, put it inside several wax paper bags, closed it with a rubber band, and Jim and Nathan arrived.

I had, of course, high hopes for that rubber band. It was to fix my filled-out deer tag to my fallen buck. It, like the safety pin, was to be the talisman signifying foresight, and would therefore ensure an increased chance of success. It was not to be.

I am a bad rifle shot, and an inexperienced, inept (but happy) hunter. Larry Benoit, the king of hunters (*How to Bag the Biggest Buck of Your Life*), writes, and experience proves, you've got to get out there *every day* — you have to know what the woods look like before you start recognizing the unusual: the magnificently cam-ouflaged animal standing there. It seems to me a lot like writing — one may write only an hour a day, but that hour can't be scheduled in advance — it may come as part of a day devoted to reading or napping or skiving off, but the writer has to spend a lot of time alone and quiet before he's capable of recognizing the difference between an idea and a good idea.

Larry Benoit also wrote that the way to get a monster buck is to

follow a merely large buck, and when you get your shot, don't take
it — let the buck go. This seems to me to equal Hemingway's advice, to write the best story you can and then throw out all the good
lines. Best lesson I ever read about writing.

So there we were, up where the big bucks were. Nathan and James
and I were crammed into the front seat of an old pickup, drinking
vast travel mugs of coffee, driving two hours up to the Wenlock
Preserve and talking about fishing. Jim said the thing about fishing
is that you learn something new all the time, how there's always
something new to be learned. They composed a paean to ice fishing and I wanted nothing more than to go. We drove past Orleans
and they talked about the spawning trout jumping the dam there.

Nathan began talking about his Uncle Dwane, who was meeting
us in Island Pond, about how he was *always* learning from the deer,
about how Dwane had passed that, or was passing that, down to
him, Nathan, and about how much there was to learn. This is a
constant, and to me, invigorating, instructive, and grateful aspect
of outdoors people — their reverence for knowledge and their understanding that knowledge lies not in the self but in the world
around them (and if I get philosophic I had better take myself ice
fishing and let it burn off).

We rendezvoused with Dwane in Island Pond. Another coffee.
We began talking, for some reason, about traveling. Dwane had
been on the road. "With what?" I asked. It turned out he is in
antiques. Not only is he in antiques, he and Nathan are relatives
of the late Albert May, the great, lamented auctioneer of Molly's
Pond, Vermont.

I used to go to Albert's auctions Saturday nights, back in the
mid-sixties. He was the quintessential entertainer; he knew his material, he knew his audience, and he loved being up there, and they
loved him for it. He would auction off a bag of clothespins and then
say he had "just one more," and sell *that,* and be surprised that it
seemed there was just one more. And he'd sell clothespins for half
an hour.

Dwane said one time there was some hippie from the college
down the road came to the auction; and the hippie, not finding a
chair, had perched himself in the tree outside the auction shed.
Well, fine, but he was dressed in the tatters of that clan and that day.

His clothes were rags, and his genitals hung down through a rent in his jeans. Albert espied him and remarked to the crowd that it beat all of his knowledge of nature, how early the squirrels were putting nuts in the trees.

It was still early, not quite light. We ordered more coffee and talked about the estate auctions, the old farms broken up, the antiques business. I once found a 32 Winchester Low Wall, first year of manufacture (1885), for $25, covered in rust. They cleaned it up for me at Orvis, brought back the exterior metal (the bore was fine), and polished the wood. Lovely little rifle. Into the buttstock some early owner had carved his initials, *C.K.* It hung for a short time right above my desk, until my good friend and hunting companion Chris Kaldor stopped by one day and took the gun down to examine it. He and I registered the initials at the same time. Chris, gentleman that he is, handed the rifle back and mentioned something about the weather. The next week, after much soul searching on my part, the Low Wall went where it (obviously) was destined.

We'd had enough coffee, and it was up the mountain. We found the logging road Dwane and Jim had scouted, and we cut the track of a buck. I was given the lead, and started packing all of my useless gear onto my belt and back. Dwane suggested that the deer weren't going to wait while I festooned myself, and I acknowledged the logic of his position by watching my rifle fall apart.

"Works all year, but Not Up Here," the old phrase has it.

The wedge, which keeps the barrel in the stock and which had never in a decade budged without my deliberate intervention, dropped straight out of my rifle and into the snow.

Well, we found it, and pounded it back in with the hilt of a knife, and I was ready to set out when the rawhide holding my "possibles" bag onto the cunning period strap shredded, and my bag fell in the snow.

The bag was a loss, so I decanted powder-patch and ball into two plastic speedloaders, stuffed them, a full capper, my third spare compass, and a candy bar into the various pockets of my old red Johnson coat, and nodded to my similarly ready fellow hunters.

"Meet back here in four hours," Jim said. "Road runs north and south, you're going up the mountain west. To come back to the road, all you got to do is walk east."

Excellent. Up the mountain I went, tracking the buck in the snow. He went here, he went there, he eventually cut back east, onto the road, walked the road for a while, and jumped down into the lowland down below. He played me like a violin. He found some old tracks and walked in them, he jumped from one old set onto another, he'd spring down a little hill, and he was *never* walking fast — he had a city boy behind him, and his flight was a necessary but nontaxing academic exercise.

My morning was a bit more strenuous. The buck ran me down and up, across the road, and up the mountain. By noon I'd been tracking him over four hours, and I was drenched to the skin, and cold. My legs were shaking as I came down the mountain.

I met Nathan and we split my sandwich, which he pronounced excellent. We went back for lunch to Island Pond.

I changed into the spare silk underwear I had brought along (about my only display of hunting savvy, along with the safety pin and the rubber band). My shirt and coat were soaked through. I went next door to the gun store and bought a new green-and-black Johnson (short) jacket and one of their shirts, glad to be warm. I love that long red coat. I've hunted and worked and walked and slept under it the statutory twenty years, and it always proves to be too heavy for hunting. It's fine for sitting on a cold stand, but when you start moving it's too warm, too long, and has too many pockets into which I've put too much useless stuff. Well, I suppose I have not quite mastered that lesson yet.

James suggested a change of scene. (I think he took his cue from my physical state.) He said he knew a good spot to wait out a buck at sundown. Back in the pickup I slept the deepest sleep of my life on the two-hour ride to Sugarbush.

The sun was just going down, we had that extra half hour of legal hunting. We walked through a field of thigh-high snow. The moon started to rise.

Jim put me in the corner of a field. I sat the last half hour still as a log, and saw nothing. We walked back in the dark to the pickup truck. We had a bourbon at the Sugarbush Inn. I went back to the cabin and slept fourteen hours.

We spent the next day hunting around Johnson. It had turned cold and was blowing sleet. We were in fairly flat country and Jim said that they most probably bedded down around a given-up orchard he knew. He and Nathan walked in to start them, and put me on the inside, and back from them; that is, they planned to drive the deer across my path. To hunt deer in thick woods in a snowstorm is one of the most beautiful, the happiest, things that I know. I was enjoying it so much that I missed the deer. They'd passed right before me, twenty yards out.

We got on their trail and kept on it several hours, and then I was played out. There was a half hour left to the season. We went back into the woods, I stopped on the edge of a small clearing, the sun came out. I just sat there, delighted.

What a successful hunt.

I kept up for a couple of days, and told myself it was not a bad performance for a dissipated city fellow with a desk job. I drank some good bourbon in Sugarbush, and remembered that cold winter thirty years ago. I fell asleep three nights in a row at 8 P.M. and remembered what it is like to sleep well. I'd had a moment by myself. A very good way to celebrate the transition of my fiftieth birthday.

Back at the inn, James, Nathan, and I shot at a stump some thirty yards off to clear the guns. I drove home, cleaned the Hawken, hung it in the cabin, and flew back to New York.

As a hunter, of course, I am a fraud. But it was a hell of a good vacation.

Biographical Notes

Notable Sports Writing of 1998

Biographical Notes

After ten years as a sports columnist with newspapers in Albany, New York, and Toronto, ALLEN ABEL left full-time sports writing in 1983 to begin a career as a newspaper and television foreign correspondent. He has served as the Beijing bureau chief of the *Toronto Globe and Mail* and has presented television documentaries on subjects as diverse as the Romanian revolution, the burning of the Amazon rain forest, and the end of South African apartheid. He now is a freelance television and print journalist based in Toronto, contributing to a wide variety of publications, including *Sports Illustrated*. His most recent book is *Flatbush Odyssey: A Journey Through the Heart of Brooklyn*.

THOMAS BOSWELL has covered baseball and other sports for the *Washington Post* since graduating from Amherst College in 1969. He served as guest editor for *The Best American Sports Writing 1994* and had two stories selected to appear in *The Best American Sports Writing of the Century*. His books include *How Life Imitates the World Series: An Inquiry into the Game* (1982) and *Why Time Begins on Opening Day* (1984).

J. D. DOLAN teaches creative writing at Western Washington University.

STEVE FRIEDMAN writes for *Esquire, ESPN: The Magazine,* and other publications. A graduate of Stanford University, Friedman was formerly editor in chief of *St. Louis Magazine* and senior editor at *GQ*. He is the author of *The Gentleman's Guide to Life* (1997).

ADAM GOPNIK is a staff writer for *The New Yorker*. In 1997 he won a National Magazine Award and in 1998 received the George Polk Award for reporting.

DAVID HALBERSTAM served as guest editor of the inaugural edition of *The Best American Sports Writing* and as editor of *The Best American Sports*

Writing of the Century (1999). His most recent book is *Playing for Keeps: Michael Jordan and the World He Made.*

JOHN HILDEBRAND teaches English at the University of Wisconsin in Eau Claire. He is the author of *Mapping the Farm: The Chronicle of a Family* (1996) and *Reading the River: A Voyage Down the Yukon* (1997).

MELISSA KING is a freelance writer and an avid basketball player. Originally from Arkansas, she now lives in Chicago.

GUY LAWSON is a frequent contributor to *Harper's Magazine, GQ, Saturday Night, Maclean's, Toronto Life,* and other publications.

The author of *American Buffalo, Glengarry Glen Ross,* and *Sexual Perversity in Chicago,* Pulitzer Prize–winning playwright DAVID MAMET has also published a number of novels and screenplays and several collections of nonfiction. He lives in Vermont.

JOHN MCPHEE has been a staff writer for *The New Yorker* since 1965 and the Ferris Professor of Journalism at Princeton University since 1975. He is the author of more than twenty books, including *A Sense of Where You Are* (1965), about the basketball star Bill Bradley, and *Levels of the Game* (1970), about Arthur Ashe. His shorter work has been collected in several volumes, including *The John McPhee Reader* (1977) and *Table of Contents* (1985). He received the Award in Literature in 1977 from the American Academy of Arts and Letters, the John Burroughs Medal in 1990, and the 1999 Pulitzer Prize for his book *Annals of the Former World.*

JONATHAN MILES attended the University of Mississippi in Oxford, where he now lives. His work has appeared in the *Oxford American* and *Sports Afield.* He is an avid fisherman and an accomplished blues guitarist and pianist.

RANDALL PATTERSON is a staff writer for the *Houston Press.* His work has appeared in many publications, including *Sports Illustrated,* and has won numerous awards.

SHIRLEY POVICH (1905–1998) was a native of Bar Harbor, Maine, and a graduate of Georgetown University. He joined the *Washington Post* as a copyboy in 1923, and in 1926, at age twenty-one, was named sports editor. He later served the *Post* as war correspondent, columnist, and occasional contributor. In a distinguished career, he won virtually every award available to an American sports writer, including the Red Smith Award, the Grantland Rice Award, and the J. G. Taylor Spink Award in 1976, the same year he was inducted into the writers' wing of the National Baseball Hall of Fame. His autobiography, *All These Mornings,* appeared in 1969. His column in this collection was his last to appear in the *Post*.

DAVID REMNICK is a 1981 graduate of Princeton. In 1982 he joined the *Washington Post*, where he covered sports from 1984 to 1985. He later spent four years in Moscow as one of the *Post*'s foreign correspondents, where he witnessed the fall of the Soviet Union. This resulted in his book *Lenin's Tomb: The Last Days of the Soviet Empire*, which won a Pulitzer Prize in 1993. A staff writer for *The New Yorker* since 1992, he became its editor in 1998. His features have been collected in *The Devil Problem and Other True Stories*. His profile of Reggie Jackson was selected for *The Best American Sports Writing of the Century*.

DAN WETZEL, a graduate of the University of Massachusetts, is the managing editor of *Basketball Times*. His work has appeared in a variety of publications, including *Sport* and *Slam*. He is coauthor, with Don Yeager, of *Sole Influence*, a book about the impact of the footwear industry on basketball.

SIMON WINCHESTER served for many years as a correspondent in Hong Kong for the *Manchester Guardian*. He is currently the Asia-Pacific editor for *Condé Nast Traveler*. He is the author of *The River at the Center of the World* (1996) and *The Professor and the Madman* (1998).

Notable Sports Writing of 1998

SELECTED BY GLENN STOUT